MAXIMUM
ACHIEVEMENT

The Proven System
of Strategies and Skills
That Will Unlock Your
Hidden Powers to
Succeed

·

BRIAN TRACY

SIMON & SCHUSTER

New York · London · Toronto · Sydney · Tokyo · Singapore

SIMON & SCHUSTER
Simon & Schuster Building
Rockefeller Center
1230 Avenue of the Americas
New York, New York 10020

SIMON & SCHUSTER and colophon are
registered trademarks of Simon & Schuster Inc.

Designed by Liney Li
Manufactured in the United States of America

1   3   5   7   9   10   8   6   4   2

Library of Congress Cataloging-in-Publication Data
Tracy, Brian.
Maximum achievement : the proven system of
strategies and skills that will unlock
your hidden powers to succeed / Brian Tracy.
p.   cm.
1. Achievement motivation.   2. Success.
3. Self-actualization (Psychology)   4. Motivation (Psychology)
I. Title.
BF503.T73   1993
158′.1—dc20   93-4534   CIP
ISBN 0-671-86518-8

ACKNOWLEDGMENTS

•

Writing a book is an incredible undertaking, especially if you've never done it before. It takes years of research and experience, then months, if not years, of writing and rewriting. This book has emerged from the thousands of hours of seminars I've given, and the countless suggestions and observations from the thousands of men and women I've had the privilege of working with over the years.

My life has been one long, continuous process of personal and professional development, including reading thousands of books and articles, listening to thousands of hours of audiocassette recordings and attending innumerable courses and seminars. As Tennyson says in "Ulysses," "I am a part of all that I have met." I have been influenced by more people than I can even count but I want to thank some of them for making this book possible.

First, let me thank the many fine men and women who have attended my seminars and lectures over the years. Their insights, observations and experiences have been invaluable to me and indispensable to the writing of this book. You know who you are, and my gratitude to you is unbounded!

Specifically, I thank the late John Boyle for opening my eyes to the power of the mind in determining everything that happens to us. I thank Earl Nightingale for his wonderful insights into the potential of the average person and Denis Waitley for summarizing the principles of success in his *Psychology of Winning* audiocassette program. I've been greatly influenced in my thinking by many wonderful thinkers, writers, and speakers such as Stephen Covey, Ken Blanchard and Tom Peters, as well as by Zig Ziglar, Jim Rohn, Tony Robbins and Wayne Dyer.

I am extremely grateful to my friends at Nightingale-Conant Corporation, Vic Conant, Kevin McEneeley, Mike Willbond and Jill Schachter, who have worked with me over the years to assure the quality of the audio recordings of these ideas.

I'm especially grateful to my seminar sponsors, John Hammond, Dan Bratland, Jim Kaufman and Suanne Sandage, who have made these principles available to many thousands of people by conducting public seminars with me in every major city in North America over the years.

In my company, past and present, there have been, and are, several people who have helped me immeasurably. My heartfelt thanks to Victor Risling, who worked with me on the road for years, starting early and staying late, and who made a vital contribution to my career in its formative stages. I thank my friend and partner, Michael Wolff, my marketing director, Donna Villerilli, my executive assistants and secretaries, Mavis Hancock and Shirley Whetstone, without whose help in typing and retyping the manuscript, this book might never have been completed.

I thank my friends at Simon & Schuster, especially my editor Bob Bender, for their support and encouragement in the preparation of the manuscript, and without whom this book would not have been possible. Perhaps the most important person of all in this whole process has been Margaret McBride, my literary agent, whose faith and confidence in me and my work served as the critical spark that ignited the writing of this book in the first place. Thank you, Margaret.

One of the most important lessons I've learned in life is that no one ever does it alone. We are all dependent on others for virtually everything. I would like to thank so many people, but I would run out of space, so let me conclude these acknowledgments by thanking my wonderful wife, Barbara, for everything, but especially for patiently putting up with me over the months as I pounded away at this book. And to my dear children, Christina, Michael, David and Catherine, who were continually shortchanged for my time. I promise to make it up to you.

This book is lovingly dedicated to
my wonderful wife, Barbara,
the best friend, wife, mother and partner
I could ever have dreamed of.
God bless you and thank you for everything.
You make me a very lucky man.

CONTENTS

●

INTRODUCTION

•

The system you are about to learn can change your life. This book contains a unique synthesis of ideas, methods and techniques brought together in one place for the first time. The individual components of this system, however, are not new; they have been learned and relearned throughout all the ages of man. These principles and practices have been tested and proven by millions of men and women, and all great success is based on them.

By integrating these ideas and methods into your daily life, you will feel happier, healthier and more self-confident. You will experience a greater sense of power, purpose and self-direction. You will be more positive, more focused and more able to achieve your goals. You will get along better with the important people in your life. You'll be more successful in your career and you will feel wonderful about yourself.

You will learn how to unlock the great untapped reserves of potential that lie deep within you. By practicing the exercises that accompany each chapter, you'll get results out of all proportion to the effort you put in. You will propel your whole life onto a high-road of success, achievement and greater happiness than perhaps you've ever known.

To use a simple analogy, life is like a combination lock, only with more numbers. If you turn to the right numbers in the right sequence, the lock will open for you. It's not a miracle, nor does it depend on luck. It doesn't even matter who you are as long as you have the right numbers. By the same token, there is a proper combination of thoughts and actions that will enable you to accomplish almost anything you really want, and you can find that combination if you search for it.

Health, wealth, happiness, success and peace of mind are all amenable to the same principle. If you do the right things in the right way, you'll get the results you desire. If you can determine exactly what it is you want, you can find out how others have achieved it before you. If you then do the same things they have done, you'll achieve the same results they have.

This "secret of success" is so simple that it is overlooked by most people. Whatever you want you can have, if you want it badly enough, and if you are willing to persist long enough and hard enough in doing what others have done to accomplish similar things before you.

It doesn't matter if you're young or old, male or female, black or white. It doesn't matter if you were born with a silver spoon in your mouth or if you came from a deprived background. Nature is neutral. She is no respecter of persons. She plays no favorites. She gives you back what you put in, no more and no less. And you can determine what you put in.

Goethe once wrote, "Nature understands no jesting; she is always true, always serious, always severe; she is always right, and the errors and faults are always those of man. The man incapable of appreciating her, she despises and only to the apt, the pure, and the true, does she resign herself and reveal her secrets."

Unsuccessful people have a hard time with this idea because they are so accustomed to looking for the reasons for their lives outside themselves. But the proof is all around us. Everywhere you look, you see men and women from every background—young and old, black and white, educated and uneducated—accomplishing great things and making valuable contributions to the societies they live in.

At the same time, you see men and women with every advantage of background and education who seem to be going nowhere with their lives. They are working at jobs they don't like, staying in relationships they don't enjoy and functioning far below their potential for achievement and happiness.

The way for you to be happy and successful, to get more of the things you really want in life, is to get the combinations to the locks. Instead of spinning the dials of life hoping for a lucky break, as if you were playing a slot machine, you must instead study and emulate those who have already done what you want to do and achieved the results you want to achieve.

That's what this book is about. It contains the very best that has ever been discovered about individual achievement, in one place, free of jargon or complexity, ready to be put into action. This system gives you the combinations to the locks in virtually every area of your life.

I know these ideas work for two major reasons. First, I've tested and proven them by trial and error for many years. Second, I've taught this system to more than a million people and it has worked for every single person who has seriously applied these ideas in his or her life.

Some people study law and some people study engineering. Some read the sports pages and become authorities on football, baseball or basketball. Others invest many hours learning about cooking, history, stamps, computers or a thousand other subjects. I studied success in all its many forms.

From a young age, I wanted to know why it was that some people were more successful than others. I was mystified by the disparities of wealth, happiness and influence I saw all around me. Something deep inside me said that there must be reasons for this apparent inequality, and I was determined to find out what they were.

I came from a poor family and I didn't like it. My father was not always regularly employed and we never seemed to have enough money for anything but the bare necessities. For my first ten years, most of my clothes were from the Goodwill and the St. Vincent de Paul charities.

I was a behavior problem when I was growing up. I was always in trouble of some kind, angry and lashing back at life without knowing why. I was suspended several times and expelled from two high schools. I got more detentions than any other kid in any school I attended from the seventh to the twelfth grades.

I failed high school, dropping six out of seven courses in my last year. My first real job was washing dishes in the kitchen of a small hotel. After that, I drifted from laboring job to laboring job, living in boarding houses, small hotels or one-room apartments, and occasionally sleeping in my car, or on the ground next to it.

I worked in sawmills stacking lumber and on logging crews slashing brush with a chain saw. For a while, I dug wells. I worked as a construction laborer, and in a factory on the assembly line. When I was twenty-one, I got a job as a galley boy on a Norwegian freighter and went off to see the world. For the next few years, I traveled until I ran out of money, then worked until I could afford to travel again.

When I was twenty-three, I was still working as an itinerant farm laborer during the day and sleeping on the hay in the farmer's barn at night. When I could no longer get a laboring job, I got into sales, working on straight commission, getting paid every night so I could eat and pay for my rooming house, one day at a time.

Throughout these early experiences, which taught me a lot about life, I continued to seek the answer to the question, "Why are some people more successful than others?"

I was a voracious reader. I had a passion to know, to understand. I read everything I could find that would give meaning and order to what I saw going on around me. It was like a quest for me, like Don Quixote tilting at windmills, but with one big difference.

I am intensely practical. I was looking for clear explanations of specific things that I could do immediately to get better results. I had no patience for grand theory or abstract principles. My only question of each new idea was, "Does it work?"

When I got into sales, I spun my wheels for several months until I began asking, "Why is it that some salespeople are more successful than others?" I attacked the question wholeheartedly, reading everything I could find on selling, listening to every audiotape available and attending every training seminar that came along. I asked top salespeople how they sold and what they did to deal with the constant problems that salespeople face.

I tried everything that made sense and improved on it as I went along. My sales started to increase, bit by bit. In six months, I was the top salesperson in my company. I was soon teaching others what had worked for me, and many of them went on to be top salespeople as well.

When I got into management, I read everything I could find

that could help me to be more effective at getting results through others. I used what I learned to build a sales organization with ninety-five people in six countries producing millions of dollars in new business each month.

When I decided to get into real estate development, I hit the books once more. I got a real estate license and read everything I could find on the subject. For my first project, having never developed anything before, I optioned, financed, leased out, built and sold a three-million-dollar shopping center. And I learned everything I needed to know by studying and by asking questions of other successful developers.

Over the next five years, I was responsible for buying, annexing, planning, developing, building, leasing and selling millions of dollars worth of commercial, industrial and residential property.

I went from a tiny one-bedroom apartment with rented furniture to my own condominium, then to a house, then to an even bigger house with a swimming pool and a three-car garage.

I studied sales, management and business so I could learn how to make a good living. I completed high school at night and by taking correspondence courses. Based on my life experiences, and a high score on the Scholastic Aptitude Test, I gained admittance to an executive MBA program and spent three years studying business theory, majoring in strategic planning and marketing.

I subsequently became a management consultant and used my knowledge and experience to earn or save my clients millions of dollars.

I had always been fascinated with the subject of happiness, and why it was that some people were obviously happier and more fulfilled than others. To find the answers, I studied psychology, philosophy, religion, metaphysics, motivation and personal achievement.

To deal with my personality problems, I studied relationships, interpersonal psychology, communications and personality styles. When I got married, I read and listened to everything I could find on parenting and childraising. To improve the way I got along with people, I read books that helped me to better understand myself and the reasons I felt and acted the way I did.

I studied history, economics and politics to understand more about the past and present, and to learn why it is that some countries, and parts of countries, are more affluent than others.

In all, I probably put in more than twenty thousand hours of study over a period of twenty-five years. Many of these studies went on concurrently. Some took intense periods of two and three years, almost like obsessions. But these studies had one thing in common: They were all aimed at practical understanding. They were a continuous search for tested and proven ideas, insights and methods that could be applied to bring about improved results immediately.

And I made a great discovery. I found that I could learn anything I needed to know to become successful at anything that I really cared about. Knowledge made all things possible.

It took me twenty years to escape from poverty and from worrying about money all the time. I then concluded that if I put what I had learned about success together into a system of ideas that anyone could use, I could provide people with tools that would save them thousands of dollars and years of hard work.

In 1981, I sat down and assembled a "success system" for others to use. I designed it as a two-day seminar called The Inner Game of Success, and then offered it via direct mail and newspaper advertising.

I was on fire with the ideas in the seminar. I had an intense desire to share them with others. I knew these ideas worked and I was convinced that anyone who would apply even a small part of this system could bring about rapid, positive changes in his or her life.

Everything worthwhile takes time. The seminar took three years to catch on. During that time, I spent everything I owned fine-tuning the content and presentation of the course. Gradually, as I worked out the bugs, the seminar began to grow in popularity. More and more people attended, from farther and farther away.

From the beginning, people described the seminar with words like, "This is like getting a brand-new chance at life," or, "This seminar is like a blank check on the future." We eventually changed the name of the course to the Phoenix Seminar, naming it after the mythical symbol of transformation and new life.

In 1984, Nightingale-Conant Corporation, the largest distributor of audio and video learning programs in the world, released the seminar on audiotape as *The Psychology of Achievement*. It quickly became a best seller and has now sold almost five hundred thousand copies.

By 1985, the demand for the seminar outstripped my ability to present it personally. I recorded it on videotape with workbook accompaniment and trained people to present it professionally. We entitled it the Phoenix Seminar on the Psychology of Achievement. The video version became so popular that it has now been translated into twelve languages and is being presented in twenty-four countries.

This seminar is used as a core course in both personal and corporate transformation. Men and women who go through the program emerge more positive and optimistic about themselves, their families, their work and every aspect of their lives. They feel more confident, competent and capable of directing and controlling their lives in a more productive way.

Corporations use the Phoenix Seminar on the Psychology of Achievement to improve productivity, performance and output. They use it as a foundation course for both teamwork and total quality management programs, finding that when they build "total quality people," the people then build the company.

This book is my reply to the thousands of graduates who have asked me to present these concepts in written form. The system you will learn in the pages that follow is the same system taught in the Phoenix Seminar on the Psychology of Achievement. It is a complete and comprehensive approach to the business of living well, of living a life characterized by happiness, harmony, health and true prosperity.

One last point before we begin: Over the years, thousands of my graduates have come back to me, sometimes within a few hours of learning this system, and said, "You won't believe what's happened to me!"

They've then gone on to tell me about wonderful things that have taken place in their work and personal lives since they began applying these ideas.

So, I want you to know, in advance, that I will believe it, whatever it is. I know that when you begin practicing these principles in your life, you will experience successes you may never have dreamed possible before, and the more you use these ideas, the better they will work for you. Your future will become limited only by your imagination!

Make Your Life a Masterpiece

This is the age of achievement. Never have more people accomplished more things in more different fields than they are accomplishing today. More people are becoming successful at a faster rate than at any other time in history. There have never been more opportunities for you to turn your dreams into realities than there are right now.

Leading futurists and prominent businesspeople are predicting that mankind is entering a Golden Age. The Western ideals of democracy, individual liberty and free enterprise are sweeping the globe and bringing prosperity, growth and human freedom wherever they are seriously tried. There has probably never been a better time for you to achieve greater success, freedom, happiness and financial independence than at this very moment.

This book will show you how to improve your life, achieve your goals and realize your full potential for success and happiness. No matter who you are or what your situation, you have within you, right now, the ability to accomplish more than you ever have before. You have the potential to exceed all your previous levels of accomplishment. You can be, have and do more than perhaps you have ever imagined. All you need to do is to learn how, and then put what you learn into action.

Everything in this book has been tested and proven in the crucible of real life. My own experience has made me a sort of guinea pig for these ideas. If I had designed my early life as an ideal test case, I probably couldn't have done better. I started so far behind that no one could have blamed me for not amounting to anything.

MY OWN STORY

I was born in Canada in 1944. My parents were good people and hard-working but we never seemed to have enough money. I still remember my parents saying over and over as I was growing up, "We can't afford it, we can't afford it, we can't afford it." No matter what it was, we couldn't afford it. They had been through the Great Depression and they had never fully recovered from the experience of worrying about money all the time.

When I entered my teens, I became aware for the first time that many other families seemed to be doing far better than we were. They had nicer homes, newer clothes and better cars. They seemed not to worry as much about money as we did, and they seemed to be able to afford a lot of things that our family couldn't even dream of. It was about this time that I began asking the question, "Why is it that some people are more successful than others?"

I began wondering why it was that some people seemed to earn more money, have happier relationships and families, live in more beautiful homes and generally get much more joy and satisfaction out of life than others did.

As it happened, I had a lot of time to think about this question, because I spent a lot of time by myself. I was what was called a "loser." I fooled around in class. I ran around with a bad bunch of kids. I was always shooting my mouth off trying to get attention, and I eventually became very unpopular.

It's said that everyone is good for something, even if it's just to set a bad example. That was me. I was the kid that parents and teachers pointed to as a warning. "If you don't straighten up," they said, "you'll end up like Tracy."

When I was sixteen, I had the first revelation that led to changing the course of my life. It dawned on me one day that if I ever wanted things to change for me, then it was up to me to change. If I didn't like being unhappy and unpopular, and in trouble all the time, then it was up to me to do something about it. This began in earnest my lifelong search for the answer to the question, "Why are some people more successful than others?"

After dropping out of high school and working as a laborer for a couple of years, I finally saved a little money and went off to see the world.

I have since traveled or worked in more than eighty countries on six continents. I have been in situations and had experiences that most people could not imagine. I have been dirt poor, going without food and sleeping on the ground countless times in far and foreign lands.

I have also stayed in beautiful hotels and dined in fine restaurants in the great cities of the world. In time, I became a senior executive of a $265 million development company. I've met four presidents and three prime ministers. My wife and I even had dinner with the president of the United States less than six months after setting it as a goal.

Over the years, mostly in retrospect, I learned a variety of lessons, and one of the most important is this: You can't hit a target you can't see. You can't accomplish wonderful things with your life if you have no idea of what they are. You must first become absolutely clear about what you want if you are serious about unlocking the extraordinary power that lies within you.

Every success I've ever enjoyed came after I had taken the time to think through what my goal would look like when it was accomplished. I have since met and spoken with many men and women who have achieved great success and they all had that one trait in common. They knew exactly what they wanted. They all had a clear picture of what their ideal lives and accomplishments would look like. This vision of the kind of future they wanted to create for themselves became a powerful motivator that drove them onward. The realization of their goals seemed to flow from the exercise of establishing them in the first place.

Goal setting is an important element of this system, and I'll be explaining it in detail in Chapter Five. But well before you do that, you have to do something that very few people ever do. It is absolutely essential to making this system work, and it is this: You have to decide exactly what "success" means to you. You have to decide what your life would look like if you made it into a masterpiece.

Here's how you begin. Use "zero-based thinking." Imagine you could go back to the beginning in every situation in your life and start over. Like holding up a picture frame and viewing different parts of your life and relationships through it, ask this question: "If I had this decision to make today, knowing what I now know, what would I do?"

Refuse to compromise on your answers. Be perfectly honest with yourself. Define your ideal in each situation before you allow yourself to get bogged down with all the reasons it isn't possible for you. All great achievement begins with your deciding what it is you really want and then dedicating yourself wholeheartedly to attaining it.

THE SEVEN INGREDIENTS OF SUCCESS

Anything that you could ever want more of, or any factor that you would consider important to your happiness, can be placed in one of seven categories. These Seven Ingredients of Success are consistent with everything ever written or discovered on success and happiness. They characterize the life and accomplishments of all high-performing men and women. They include everything you could ever want.

Your ideal life is a blending of these seven ingredients in exactly the combination that makes you the happiest at any particular moment. By defining your success and happiness in terms of one or more of these seven ingredients, you create a clear target to aim it. You can then measure how well you're doing. You can identify the areas where you need to make changes if you want your life to improve.

You must start with your ideal, your vision of a perfect future. You begin unlocking your inner powers by lifting up your eyes and "seeing" your life exactly as if it were already perfect in every respect. Your first job is to create a blueprint, a clear picture of where you are going and what it will look like when you get there. This image will then serve as an organizing principle, a guide, a benchmark, against which you can measure and compare everything you do in the process of turning it into your reality.

PEACE OF MIND

The first of these seven ingredients of success, and easily the most important, is peace of mind. It is the highest human good. Without it, nothing else has much value. Because of this, you strive for it all your life. You usually evaluate how well you are doing at any given time by how much inner peace you enjoy.

Peace of mind is your internal gyroscope. When you are living in harmony with your highest values and your innermost convictions—when you are perfectly balanced in life—then you enjoy peace of mind. If, for any reason, you compromise your values, or go against your inner guidance, your peace of mind is the first thing to suffer.

Peace of mind, or harmony, is essential for the optimal performance of all human groupings, from your relationships with your friends and family members to the businesses and organizations in which you work. All interactions among people thrive on harmonious relationships. All manners, morals, etiquette and diplomacy are organized around the desire each person has to assure his or her peace of mind by not disrupting the peace of mind of others.

In corporations, peace of mind can be measured in terms of the amount of harmony that exists among coworkers. Productive, profitable companies are those in which people feel good about themselves. They feel safe and happy at work. They may be busy, even frantic with activity, but they are at peace inside.

The wonderful truth about peace of mind is that it is your normal, natural condition. Happiness is your birthright. It belongs to you. It is not something you experience occasionally if you're lucky. Peace of mind is central to your very existence. It is the basic precondition for enjoying everything else.

Achieving inner peace must be a central organizing principle of your life. It must become the overarching goal to which all your other goals are subservient. In fact, you are only successful as a person to the degree to which you can achieve your own happiness, your own contentment, your own sense of personal well-being—in short, your own peace of mind.

The very idea of specifically aiming at the achievement of my own happiness caused me a good deal of confusion and anxiety at one time. My religious background had drummed into me the idea that my own personal happiness was not a valid consideration for my choices and behaviors.

If anything, I was told that happiness was merely a by-product of living my life to make others happy. If I got any happiness, I was informed, I was just lucky. And if I didn't, then that was my lot in life. The very idea of setting happiness as a specific goal for myself was described as selfish and uncaring.

A major turning point came for me when I learned two things. First, I learned that if I didn't commit to achieving my own happiness, no one else would. If my aim in life was only to make others happy, I would always be at the mercy of the feelings of others, whoever they might be. And I found that trying to organize my life around making others happy was an unending exercise in frustration and disappointment, because it just wasn't possible.

Second, I discovered that I couldn't give away what I didn't have. I couldn't make someone else happy by being miserable myself. As Abraham Lincoln once said, "You can't help the poor by becoming one of them." I found that I couldn't make others happy unless I could make myself happy first.

Peace of mind is so important to everything else you accomplish that it must be subjected to rigorous analysis. Where does it come from? Under what conditions does it exist for you? How can you get more of it?

In the simplest terms, you experience happiness and peace of mind whenever you are completely free from the destructive emotions of fear, anger, doubt, guilt, resentment and worry. In the absence of negative emotions, you enjoy peace of mind naturally, effortlessly. The key to happiness then is to systematically eliminate, or at least minimize, the parts of your life that cause you negativity or stress of any kind.

This idea bowled me over when I first came across it many years ago. Imagine! The way to live a happy, productive life is to achieve your own peace of mind by systematically eliminating the negative people, situations and emotions that make you unhappy.

Wow! Could happiness in life be that simple? And herein lies the rub. The major obstacle to eliminating the negativity that interferes with your happiness is your attachment to the negative people and situations that cause it. Your rational mind comes up with all kinds of clever reasons why you must continue in your existing situation. Instead of working for you, instead of providing you with solutions to your problems, your amazing brain works frantically to keep you mired in them.

Later in this book, I'll show you a variety of ways to control, and eventually eliminate, your negative emotions. I'll show you powerful techniques you can use to neutralize anger and worry in moments. I'll show you how to take complete control of your emotions and how to keep them positive most of the time.

For the moment, though, your job is to engage in what is called "mountaintop thinking." Project forward in thought and imagine your ideal life. What combination of ingredients would have to exist for you to be perfectly happy? Don't worry about what's possible or not possible for you at the moment. Free your mind from all limitations and be perfectly selfish. Just define your life exactly as it would have to be for you to enjoy the peace of mind you desire.

What would you be doing? Where would you be living? Who would be there with you? How would you spend your time, day in and day out? Remember, you can't hit a target you can't see. But if you can envision it clearly, there's a very good likelihood that you can achieve it!

If you're in business, create this ideal future vision of what your job or work would look like if it was absolutely excellent in every respect. What would you do more of (or less of) to achieve higher levels of harmony and cooperation in your work environment?

In your family, what would your life look like if you and the people you care about were living in a state of complete peace and contentment? What sort of things would you do to help others to be happy in the process of achieving your own happiness?

When you set peace of mind as your goal and plan everything you do in terms of whether it helps or hinders your attainment of that goal, you'll probably never make another mistake. You'll do and say the right things. You'll find yourself operating from a higher set of principles. You'll feel wonderful about yourself. Peace of mind is the key.

HEALTH AND ENERGY

The second ingredient of success is health and energy. Just as peace of mind is your normal and natural mental state, health and energy is your normal and natural physical state.

Your body has a natural bias toward health. It produces energy

easily and in abundance in the absence of mental or physical interference. And radiant health exists in the absence of any pain, illness
or disease. Wonderfully enough, your body is constructed in such
a way that if you just stop doing certain things to it, it often
recovers and becomes healthy and energetic all by itself.

If you achieve all kinds of things in the material world, but you
lose your health or your peace of mind, you get little or no pleasure
from your other accomplishments.

Imagine yourself enjoying perfect health. Think of how you
would be if you were your ideal image of physical fitness. How
would you look? How would you feel? How much would you
weigh? What sort of foods would you eat and what kind of exercises
would you do? What would you be doing more of, and less of?

A businessman in one of my seminars came up to me after he
had thought about this "ideal image" and told me that, if he was in
perfect health, he would be able to run a marathon. His problem
was that he was forty years old, twenty pounds overweight, and
not particularly fit. He doubted that it was possible for him, but
the thought process had begun.

The more he thought about himself as he could be, rather than
as he was, the more excited he became about the very idea of
training for a marathon. He began to see himself as lean and fit. He
became more and more convinced that he could do it.

He bought a couple of books on jogging and started running a
little each day. He got the right clothes and the right running shoes.
He increased his distance each week and soon began doing "fun
runs" and mini-marathons. Within one year, he ran his first marathon, 26.4 miles. He fulfilled his vision and became the person he
had imagined he could be. Most important, he felt fitter, thinner,
stronger and more energetic than he had felt for many years.

LOVING RELATIONSHIPS

The third ingredient of success is loving relationships. These are
relationships with the people you love and care about, and the
people who love and care about you. They are the real measure of
how well you are doing as a human being. Most of your happiness
and unhappiness in life comes from your relationships with others,
and it is your relationships with others that make you truly human.

A key quality of the fully functioning person is that he or she has the ability to enter into and maintain long-term friendships and intimate relationships with other people. The very essence of your personality is demonstrated in the way you get along with others, and the way they get along with you.

At almost any time, you can measure how well you are doing in your relationships by one simple test: laughter. How much two people, or a family, laugh together is the surest single measure of how well things are going. When a relationship is truly happy, people laugh a lot when they're together. And when a relationship turns sour, the very first thing that goes is the laughter.

This is true for companies as well. High-performance, high-profit organizations are those in which people laugh and joke together. They enjoy one another and their work. They function smoothly and happily as teams. They are more optimistic, more open to new ideas, more creative and more flexible.

I used to think that people were an important part of any business. Then I learned a great truth; people are the business.

The furniture and fixtures can be replaced. The products, services and customers will change over time. But if you have the right people, the company will continue to prosper.

The most important single responsibility of the executive is to ensure harmony and happiness among the people he or she is responsible for, to create a climate of optimism, enthusiasm and high morale. This "esprit de corps" is the distinguishing quality of all world class organizations.

What is your ideal relationship? Who would it be with and what would it look like? If you could design your important relationships in every detail, what would you want more of, or less of? What could you do, starting today, to create these conditions in your own life?

Without a clear idea of what you really want in a relationship with another person, you will probably find yourself in situations not of your own choosing. Problems in life are almost invariably "people problems." They come with hair on top, and talk back.

People problems do more to disrupt your peace of mind and undermine your health than perhaps any other factor. One of your chief aims in life must therefore be to create a human environment in which you can be happy, contented and fulfilled. You must examine your relationships, one by one, and develop a plan to make each of them enjoyable and satisfying.

Only when you have your relationships under control and functioning harmoniously can you turn your thoughts toward the self-expression and self-actualization that enable you to fulfill your true potential.

FINANCIAL FREEDOM

The fourth ingredient of success is financial freedom. To be financially free means that you have enough money so that you don't worry about it continually, as most people do. It is not money that lies at the root of all evil; it is lack of money. Achieving your own financial freedom is one of the most important goals and responsibilities of your life. It is far too important to be left to chance.

Fully 80 percent of the population are preoccupied with money problems. They think about and worry about money when they wake up in the morning, while they're having breakfast, and throughout the day. They talk and think about it during the evening. This is not a happy, healthy way to live. This is not conducive to being the best you can be.

Money is important. While I put it as number four on the list of ingredients of success, it is an essential factor in the achievement of the first three. Most worry, stress, anxiety and lost peace of mind are caused by money worries. Many health problems are caused by stress and worry about money. Many problems in relationships are caused by money worries, and one of the main causes for divorce is arguments over money. You therefore owe it to yourself to develop your talents and abilities to the point where you know that you can earn enough money so that you don't have to worry about it.

A feeling of freedom is essential to the achievement of any other important goal, and you cannot be free until and unless you have enough money so that you are no longer preoccupied with it. One of your main aims in life must be to provide for your own financial independence, without self-delusion, procrastination or trusting to luck.

Imagine that you had a magic wand and you could wave it to

design your financial life in any way you wanted. What would your life look like if you achieved all your financial goals? What difference would it make in your day-to-day activities? What would you be doing more of, or less of?

How much would you like to be earning one year, five years, ten years from today? What kind of lifestyle would you like to be enjoying? How much would you like to have in the bank? How much would you like to be worth when you retire?

These are very important questions! Most people never ask and answer them in their entire lives. But if you can be perfectly clear about where you want to go financially, you can learn what you need to know and do to get there. Many graduates of my seminars have gone out and changed their lives from rags to riches. They have become presidents of large corporations. Some have become millionaires. They have started and built their own successful businesses, or been promoted rapidly in their companies or industries, but only after they decided what they wanted.

When you decide exactly what you want your financial picture to look like, you will be able to use this system to achieve your goals faster than you might have imagined possible. It all starts with your defining your financial future clearly and then making a plan to realize it. Everything will follow from that, as you'll learn later in this book.

WORTHY GOALS AND IDEALS

The fifth ingredient of success is worthy goals and ideals. Perhaps your deepest subconscious drive, according to Dr. Viktor E. Frankl, author of *Man's Search for Meaning*, is the need for meaning and purpose in life. To be truly happy, you need a clear sense of direction. You need a commitment to something bigger and more important than yourself. You need to feel that your life stands for something, that you are somehow making a valuable contribution to your world.

Happiness has been defined as "the progressive realization of a worthy ideal." You can only be happy when you are working step by step toward something that is really important to you.

Think about what sort of activities and accomplishments you most enjoy. What were you doing in the past when you were the happiest? What sort of activities give you your greatest sense of meaning and purpose in life?

SELF-KNOWLEDGE AND SELF-AWARENESS

The sixth ingredient of success is self-knowledge and self-awareness. Throughout all of history, self-knowledge has gone hand in hand with inner happiness and outer achievement. The phrase "Man, know thyself" goes all the way back to ancient Greece. To perform at your best, you need to know who you are and why you think and feel the way you do. You need to understand the forces and influences that have shaped your character from earliest childhood. You need to know why you react and respond the way you do to the people and situations around you. It is only when you understand and accept yourself that you can begin moving forward in the other areas of your life.

PERSONAL FULFILLMENT

The seventh ingredient of success is a sense of personal fulfillment. This is a feeling that you are becoming everything that you are capable of becoming. It is the sure knowledge that you are moving toward the realization of your full potential as a human being. Psychologist Abraham Maslow called this "self-actualization." He said it was the primary characteristic of the healthiest, happiest and most successful men and women in our society.

A major benefit of this book is that it will show you how to be your own psychologist. You will learn how to achieve and maintain a positive, optimistic and cheerful mental attitude under almost all circumstances. You will learn how to develop a fully integrated, fully functioning, fully mature personality.

Defining the seven ingredients of success gives you a series of targets to aim at. When you define your life in ideal terms, when you have the courage to decide exactly what you want, you begin the process of unlocking your hidden powers to succeed. In the chapters ahead, you will learn a proven system of thought and action you can use to achieve whatever goals you can set for yourself. But knowing where you want to end up is the first and most important step.

· · ·

In Chapter Two you learn the *Seven Laws of Mental Mastery* and how to use them to create whatever life you can imagine for yourself. In Chapter Three, you learn about your *Master Program* and how it controls every aspect of your thoughts and feelings about yourself. You learn how to reprogram it, to bring it into alignment with what you really want in your life.

In Chapter Four, you learn about your *Master Mind* and how to harness your mental powers for maximum achievement. You learn methods and techniques practiced by the most successful men and women of our age to achieve their goals.

In Chapter Five, you learn the *Master Skill* of success. You learn perhaps the most powerful process of goal-setting and goal-achieving ever organized and presented in one place. This Master Skill will enable you to accomplish more in the next one or two years than many people accomplish in a lifetime.

In Chapter Six, you learn about the *Master Power,* the Super-conscious Mind that is always available to you. Proper use of this mind enables you to accomplish virtually any goal you can set for yourself. The discovery and application of the superconscious faculty underlies all great success in the human experience, and you will learn to use it as naturally as breathing in and breathing out.

In Chapter Seven, you learn the *Master Decision* you must make before you can activate your higher powers for personal and business success. You learn the critical difference between high achievers and low achievers. You learn how to take complete control over every aspect of your experience and how to make your life into something truly wonderful.

In Chapter Eight, you learn about the *Master Goal,* inner peace, and how to organize every aspect of your life to assure the greatest happiness for yourself and the people around you. You learn the root causes of stress and negativity, and how to eliminate them from your life. You learn how to be more positive and optimistic in everything you do.

In Chapter Nine, you begin drawing together everything you've learned in previous chapters into a focus on achieving greater effectiveness with the people in your life. In *Mastering Human Relationships,* you learn the foundation principles of interpersonal psychology and how to get along better with others in almost any situation.

In Chapter Ten, *Mastering Personal Relationships,* you learn how to be happier in your romantic relationships. You learn why relationships succeed and why they fail. You learn a series of simple things you can do, or stop doing, that can transform your relationships overnight, and sometimes even faster.

In Chapter Eleven, *Mastering the Art of Parenting,* you learn how to be an excellent parent. You learn how to interact with your children, at any age, in such a way that they grow up happy, healthy and self-confident. You learn how to neutralize mistakes of the past and build loving relationships that endure for the rest of your life.

Finally, in Chapter Twelve, *Mastery: The Power of Love,* you learn the "secret of the ages," the most powerful force in the universe, the shaper of character and destiny, and the one thing that really matters. You learn the key to becoming fully human, to fulfilling your potential. You learn how to incorporate the principles of love into everything you do and into everything you are.

When you begin to practice what you learn in this book, you'll enjoy greater peace of mind, better health and energy, more and better loving relationships, greater financial freedom, exciting goals and ideals to which you can commit yourself, enhanced self-knowledge and self-awareness, and a wonderful feeling of personal fulfillment and personal achievement.

The ideas, insights and practical guidance contained in the pages ahead will bring you greater health, happiness and prosperity than you have ever experienced. As you apply these principles to your life, you will see improvements in yourself, your situation and the people around you that will appear amazing. Your whole life will open up and expand toward the horizon of your possibilities as you move onto the high road of Maximum Achievement.

APPLICATION EXERCISE

This system is intensely practical. Each chapter contains exercises for you to do. They are designed to empower you with the tools you need to take complete control of your life, and for these tools to work, you must practice with them. You must discipline yourself to do the exercises in sequence so you receive the full benefit of their cumulative effect.

Your first exercise has been described throughout this chapter.

It is for you to take the brush of your imagination and begin painting a masterpiece on the canvas of your life. It is for you to decide clearly what would make you the happiest in everything you are doing.

Decide what's right for you before you decide what's possible. Create your ideal life in every detail. Don't be concerned about the process of getting from where you are to where you want to go. For now, just focus on creating a vision of your perfect future. In the chapters ahead, you will learn how to turn your visions into your realities.

The Seven Laws of Mental Mastery

There is more practical information available today on how to achieve success in any field than there has ever been at any time. Yet, only 5 percent of the population are financially independent at the end of their working lives. Fully 80 percent of people working today would rather be doing something else, and 84 percent of them, by their own admission, feel that they are working below, even far below, their potential. Only 5 percent feel that they are producing at their full capacity in their jobs.

More people are sick, overweight, unfit and unhealthy than ever before. The United States spends more of its gross national product on health care than any other nation, and the costs are increasing. Today, we know that an enormous amount of illness and disease is caused by negative mental attitudes and unhappiness of various kinds. People actually make themselves sick and poison their relationships with their own thinking.

America is a free society. All choices are open to the individual. People can do anything, be anything, go anywhere, change any part of their lives for the better, whenever they want. Why is it then that so many people persist in their negativity and pessimism when they are free to think anything they want? Why is it that so few people are living up to their potential?

THE SEARCH

When I was growing up, it never occurred to me that if you wanted to be good at something, you had to study it thoroughly and practice it diligently. I had the idea that things just happen. Health, happiness, peace, prosperity and high achievement just occur in the course of human destiny if you happen to be in the right place at the right time.

Living with this idea, as the great majority do, puts a person under the Law of Accident. This law, which becomes a law to the degree to which it is accepted by default, is the governing principle for most people. In its simplest terms, it says that failing to plan is planning to fail.

If you want to be a doctor, you study and practice medicine. If you want to be a good cook, you study cooking by getting cookbooks and using proven recipes. If you want to live a life full of joy, happiness and self-fulfillment, you study the happiest and most successful people you can find and then do what they do until you get the same results in your own life.

This was an amazing thought to me. It seemed so simple! Surely it couldn't be as easy as that. And of course, it's not. Nothing really worthwhile is easy. It's an erroneous belief that, if a thing is right, it should be easy, like a relationship. If you have to really work at it, some people say, then there's probably something wrong with it. This kind of thinking is fatal to happiness.

As I began my quest for the holy grail of the good life, I formulated three basic operating principles that helped me immeasurably.

First, life is hard. It always has been and it always will be. It's never been any different for you or me or anyone else. The good thing is that if you accept this basic truth, life somehow becomes a little easier because you don't suffer so much from feelings of frustration and injustice.

Second, everything you are or ever will be is up to you. You are where you are today because that is where you have chosen to be. You are always free to choose your actions, or inactions, and your life today is the sum total of your choices, good and bad. If you want your future to be different, you have to make better choices.

Third, and perhaps most important, you can learn anything you need to learn to become anyone you want to become, to achieve anything you want to achieve. There are very few limitations and most of them are on the inside, not on the outside.

If necessity is the mother of invention, then pain seems to be the father of learning. We seem to need the prod of frustration and distress before we open ourselves up to new ideas and ways of doing things. This was certainly true for me in my early twenties.

To move ahead, you have to both learn and unlearn a few things. You are locked in place at your current level of knowledge and skill. You can go no further with what you now know. Your future largely depends on what you learn and practice from this moment onward.

I began to study success, happiness and achievement based on the preceding principles. They became the foundation upon which I built the superstructure of the system I'll be sharing with you as we go along. Each part of this book complements each other part of this book, very much as a magnificent building goes up, piece by piece, until the structure is complete in all its glory.

Thought by thought, action by action, you will learn how to make your life a masterpiece. You will learn how to create something truly beautiful out of your efforts. You will learn how to take complete control of your destiny. You will learn how to accomplish more than you might have ever dreamed possible. Just don't expect it to be easy.

BRICK BY BRICK

When I began to study the psychology and science of human achievement, I used myself and my own situation as the test of what was true or not. You must do the same. Listen to your inner voice. Irrespective of anything else you may have learned, or chosen to believe, simply ask, "Is this true for me?"

As you'll more fully understand in Chapter Six, superior men and women trust themselves at a deep level. They are very sensitive to whether something feels right. You should be the same. You should find that everything in this book has a good feel to it, but if it doesn't, put it aside for the time being and come back to it later when it makes more sense.

Theodore Roosevelt once said, "Do what you can, with what you have, right where you are." That's what I did. When I began asking why some people were more successful than others, I plunged in. Even though I had been a poor student, I was a voracious reader, and I wasn't afraid of hard work. While other people around me were dating and dancing, I was studying, making up for lost time.

One thing I learned was that if all it took to live a wonderful life was books and ideas, then we'd all be rich and happy. There are more and better books, tapes, videos and courses on how to be successful in every area of life today than there ever have been in all of human history. And I've never read or seen or listened to one that didn't have something valuable to offer. But all of them together is not enough.

You have to have a system. Without a system you can use to integrate the ideas you learn, you are like a person trying to assemble a jigsaw puzzle without a picture. And almost any system is better than no system at all. But you've got to learn the system and then discipline yourself to stay at it until you get the results you want.

No one would seriously try to master any complex subject without learning everything possible from those who had gone before and demonstrated mastery in that area. This is true in law, medicine, engineering and business. It is equally true in human relations, happiness, health, wealth and peace of mind. Virtually anything you could ever want to be, have or do is amenable to learning and hard work. But you have to have a system, and you have to work the system.

BASIC OPERATING PRINCIPLES

The main reason for so much underachievement and frustration is simply that people do not know how to get the most out of themselves. They don't know how to apply themselves for maximum performance and happiness. They don't know their basic operating principles and as a result, they waste many hours, even years, functioning far below their potential.

For example, imagine that someone gave you an expensive, sophisticated personal computer. It was delivered to your home, and when you took all the parts out of the boxes, you found that there was only one thing missing: the instruction manual. Now imagine that you had no training at all in computers or in computer language. Then imagine that you now had to figure out how the computer worked, how to set it up, how to operate it, how to program it and how to get it to produce something of value. How long do you think it would take you, working without help or guidance, to figure out how to use a personal computer on this basis?

The answer is that, even if you were highly motivated and determined, it would probably take you years to figure out how to operate a computer on your own. And it's a certainty that long before that, you would have turned your mind to other things and gone back to doing your work in the same old, slow fashion.

Now, let's imagine instead that you received the same computer, but this time it came complete with an instruction manual that was user-friendly and, in addition, a computer expert came along and showed you, step by step, how to set up the computer, how to operate it, how to program it and how to run it at maximum efficiency.

With the instruction manual and expert training, you could have the computer up and running in an afternoon. From then on, you would get better and better at using it, and the quality and quantity of what you produced would increase rapidly.

The point is this: You come into this world with no instruction manual. You are born with an amazing brain, the complexities and possibilities of which are so vast that we cannot yet comprehend them. This marvelous, three-pound organ of yours contains as many as 100 billion cells and processes 100 million bits of information per hour. It maintains a perfect chemical balance in every one of your body's billions of cells through your autonomic nervous system. Properly used, your incredible brain can take you from rags to riches, from loneliness to popularity, from sickness to radiant health, and from depression to happiness and joy—if you learn how to use it properly.

This entire book can be viewed as an instruction manual designed to help you get the most out of yourself. It will show you how to harness the amazing power of your mind to bring you anything you really want in life.

YOUR MULTIDIMENSIONAL MIND

Your mind is like a central processing unit in a large computer network. It is accessed, influenced and programmed by several operators, or sources. All data inputs affect and influence other data. All incoming information is immediately available to influence data being processed by any of the individual users. New information, whether true or false, can immediately alter operations in every other area.

Your subconscious mind is your central processing unit. Your main job in achieving any goal is to reprogram this unit so that what you think, feel and believe becomes the mental equivalent of exactly what you want to experience and enjoy.

The access ports to your subconscious are both internal and external. Internally, you are affected by your thoughts, your mental pictures or imagination and your feelings. Externally, you are influenced by your suggestive environment, by everything that registers on your conscious mind. You are affected by what you do, say, hear, see, read, watch, listen to and, especially, by the people you associate with and the conversations you participate in. Each of these influences can trigger or stimulate one or more of the other influences. All of them in combination have created, and are creating, the person you are today, and every aspect of your life.

When you think a thought, for any reason, it often triggers another thought, or even a stream of consciousness that takes you far away from the original thought. Your mind rushes on, like a torrent, carrying you toward your goals or away, depending on the amount of mental control you choose to exert.

Your thoughts trigger images or pictures consistent with them, and these images can lead from one to another and away from the thought that triggered them in the first place, or back toward it.

Thoughts or images trigger emotions of all kinds. Your feelings themselves trigger thoughts and images, which can then trigger additional feelings, and so on.

The thoughts you think, the images you hold, the feelings you experience trigger words and actions consistent with them. If you are thinking about your goals, if you can see your goals as already realized, and if this thought makes you feel positive and enthusiastic, you will speak positively and act effectively as you go through your day.

What you read can affect your thoughts, images, feelings, words and actions, and these can in turn influence what you read next. The people around you, your conversations, will influence how you speak, walk, talk and behave.

The tapes you listen to in your car, the shows you watch on television, the seminars you attend and the things you do each day will all affect the person you become and they will, in turn, affect, multiply, diminish, increase and alter other influences and other stored information.

In addition to all of these factors, your past experiences, your reinforcement history, good or bad, colors your attitudes and perceptions toward everything that happens to you, and around you.

If this sounds a little complicated, it is. Your mind and your life are like a room full of musicians, all playing different instruments and different tunes, and all trying to get your attention. Amidst all this confusion, is it any wonder that the great majority feel that they are not in control of their lives? Is it any wonder that most people would rather be doing something else, somewhere else, and in many cases, with someone else? Is it any wonder that most people feel that they could be doing much better than they are, but they feel helpless to make a change? This situation is both the great challenge and the great opportunity of your life.

Your main job, in taking control of your life and your future, is to become the conductor of your own orchestra. You must take control of the internal and external aspects of your life and get them all playing in harmony around a central theme of your own choosing. Your job is to play beautiful music with your life, to make your life a great performance.

UNDERSTANDING DIFFERENT LAWS

You may already know that there are two types of laws in the universe: man-made laws and natural laws. You can violate man-made laws, like traffic laws, and you may or may not get caught. But if you attempt to violate natural laws, you get caught every single time, without exception.

Natural laws, in turn, can be divided into two categories: physical laws and mental laws. The operation of physical laws, like those governing electricity or mechanics, can be proven in controlled experiments and practical activities.

Mental laws, however, can only be proven by experience and intuition, and by seeing them work in your own life.

Some mental laws were written about as far back as 2000 B.C., or four thousand years ago. In the ancient world, these laws or principles were taught in what were called the "mystery schools." Students would enter these schools and undergo long periods of training, taking many years, during which they would be gradually introduced, one at a time, to these principles.

In those days, such principles were never meant to be shared with the general public. The heads of these ancient schools felt that the average person would misunderstand and misuse these laws, and at that time, they were probably right.

Today, most of these laws are discussed and written about quite openly, although only a tiny fraction of the population is even aware of them. In studying the lives and stories of successful men and women, I found that almost all of them used these laws, consciously or unconsciously, and as a result they were often able to accomplish more in two or three years than the average person accomplishes in a lifetime. In fact, all real and lasting success comes from organizing your life in harmony with these general principles.

Here's an important point: Mental laws are like physical laws in that they are in force 100 percent of the time. The Law of Gravity, for instance, works everywhere on planet Earth twenty-four hours per day. If you jump from a ten-story building, you will fall to the sidewalk with equal force whether you are in downtown New York or downtown Tokyo.

It doesn't matter whether you know about gravity, or whether you agree with gravity, or whether anyone ever told you about gravity when you were growing up. The law is neutral. It works for you everywhere, regardless of whether you know about it or whether it is particularly convenient for you at that moment.

Mental laws, although their physical effects cannot be seen quite so easily, also work 100 percent of the time. Whenever your life is going well, it means that your thoughts and activities are aligned and in harmony with these invisible mental laws. Whenever you are having problems of any kind, it is almost invariably because you are violating one or more of these laws, whether you know about them or not. Because they are central to your happiness, it is essential that you become familiar with them and integrate them into everything you do.

1. THE LAW OF CONTROL

The Law of Control says that you feel positive about yourself to the degree to which you feel you are in control of your own life, and you feel negative about yourself to the degree to which you feel that you are not in control, or that you are controlled by some external force, person or influence.

This law or principle is widely recognized in psychology. It is called "locus of control" theory. It is generally agreed that most stress, anxiety, tension and psychosomatic illness comes about as a result of the person feeling out of control, or not in control of some important part of his life.

For example, if you feel that your life is controlled by your debts, or your boss, or your ill health, or a bad relationship, or the behavior of others, you will suffer stress. This stress will manifest itself in irritation, anger, and resentment. If not dealt with, it can progress to insomnia, depression or illness of various kinds.

You can have either an internal or an external locus of control. That is, you can feel that you are in charge of your own life, happy, positive and confident, or you can feel controlled by others, helpless, trapped, very much like a victim.

In every case, control over your life begins with your thoughts, the only thing over which you do have complete control. How you think about any situation determines how you feel, and your feelings determine your behavior.

Self-discipline, self-mastery, self-control all begin with you taking control of your thinking. No person or situation can make you feel anything—it is only the way you think about a situation that makes you feel the way you do. And you can control the way you think. As Eleanor Roosevelt said, "No one can make you feel inferior without your consent."

There are basically two ways you can get control of any situation that is causing you stress or unhappiness. First, you can take action. You can move forward and do something to change it. You can assert yourself in the situation and make it different somehow. And second, you can simply walk away. You can often regain control by letting go of a person or situation and getting busy doing something else.

Sometimes the very best thing to do in a situation if you feel out of control is just to leave. If you have ever ended an unhappy relationship or quit an unpleasant job, you will remember how much better you felt when you stopped struggling. By deciding not to resist anymore, you took back your sense of control.

The law of control explains why it is so important for you to be decisive. It explains why it is so important for you to know exactly what you want. The self-confidence that comes with feeling in control is why a person with a clear purpose and a plan always has an edge over someone who is vague or unsure.

Examine the various areas of your life with a mental checklist and decide where you feel positive and in control, and where you don't. Then begin thinking of the specific things you could do to get control in those parts of your life causing you stress. Think also of the situations you might be better off walking away from.

One of your major responsibilities is to get and keep your life under control. This sense of control becomes your foundation for building greater happiness and success in the future. Make sure it's rock solid.

2. THE LAW OF CAUSE AND EFFECT

The Law of Cause and Effect says that for every effect in your life there is a specific cause. It is so important it has been called the "Iron Law of the Universe." It says that everything happens for a reason, whether or not you know what it is. There are no accidents. We live in an orderly universe governed strictly by law, and this understanding is central to every other law or principle.

The Law of Cause and Effect says that there are specific causes of success and there are specific causes of failure. There are specific causes for health and for illness. There are specific causes for happiness and for unhappiness. If there is an effect in your life that you want more of, you merely need to trace it back to the causes and repeat the causes. If there is an effect in your life that you do not enjoy, you need to trace it back to the causes and get rid of them.

This law is so simple that it is baffling to most people. They continue doing, or not doing, things that are causing them unhappiness and frustration, and they then blame everyone else, or society, for their problems.

Insanity has been defined as "doing the same things in the same way and expecting to get different results." To some degree, we're all guilty of this. We need to face this tendency squarely and deal with it honestly.

There is a Scottish proverb that says, "It is better to light one wee candle than to curse the darkness." It is better by far to sit down and carefully analyze the reasons for your difficulties than to get upset and angry about them.

In the book of Proverbs, it says, "Whatsoever a man soweth, that also shall he reap." This version of the Law of Cause and Effect is called the Law of Sowing and Reaping. It says that whatever you sow, you will reap. It also says that whatever you are reaping *today* is the result of what you have sown in the past. If you wish to reap a different harvest in any area of your life in the future, you need to plant different seeds today, and of course, this refers primarily to mental seeds.

The most important application of the Law of Cause and Effect, or sowing and reaping, is this: "Thoughts are causes and conditions are effects."

Your thoughts are the primary causes of the conditions of your life. Everything in your experience has begun with a thought of some kind, yours or someone else's.

Everything you are or ever will be, will be as a result of the way you think. If you change the quality of your thinking, you change the quality of your life. The change in your outer experience will follow the change in your inner experience. You will reap what you sow. You are doing it right now.

The beauty of this immutable law is that by accepting it, you take full control over your thinking, your feelings and your results. By applying the Law of Cause and Effect, you bring yourself into harmony with the Law of Control. You immediately feel better and happier about yourself.

Every aspect of business success or failure can be explained by this basic law. If you sow the right causes, you reap the desired effects. If you produce quality products or services that customers want and need and are willing to pay for, and then promote them vigorously, you'll be successful in selling them. If you don't, you won't.

If you do high-quality work and achieve the results that your company needs to grow and prosper, you'll be successful and happy in your career. If you treat others well, they'll treat you well. You'll always get out of life what you put in—and *you* control what you put in.

3. THE LAW OF BELIEF

The Law of Belief says that whatever you believe, with feeling, becomes your reality. The more intensely that you believe something to be true, the more likely it is that it will be true for you. If you really believe something, you cannot imagine it to be otherwise. Your beliefs give you a form of tunnel vision. They edit out or cause you to ignore incoming information that is inconsistent with what you have decided to believe.

William James of Harvard said, "Belief creates the actual fact." In the Bible, it says, "According to your faith [belief] it is done unto you." To put it another way, you do not necessarily believe what you see but you *see* what you believe.

For example, if you absolutely believe that you are meant to be a great success in life, then no matter what happens, you will continue to press forward toward your goals. Nothing will stop you.

On the other hand, if you believe that success is a matter of luck or accident, then you will easily become discouraged and disappointed whenever things don't work out for you. Your beliefs set you up for either success or failure.

People generally have one of two ways of looking at the world. The first is what is called a *benevolent* world view. If you have a benevolent world view, you generally believe that the world is a pretty good place in which to live. You have a tendency to see the good in people and situations and to believe that there is plenty of opportunity around you and that you can take advantage of it. You believe that although you may not be perfect, you are a pretty good person overall. You believe in the future, for yourself and others. You are primarily optimistic.

The second way of looking at the world is with a *malevolent* world view. A person with a malevolent world view has a generally negative and pessimistic attitude toward himself or herself and toward life. He or she generally believes that "You can't fight City Hall," that "The rich get richer and the poor get poorer," and that no matter how hard you work, you can't get ahead anyway because the deck is stacked against you.

This type of person sees injustice, oppression and misfortune everywhere. When things go wrong for them, as they usually do, they blame it on bad luck or bad people. They feel like victims. Because of this attitude, they don't really like or respect themselves very much.

Needless to say, people with optimistic beliefs tend to be the movers and shakers, the builders and the creators of the future. They tend to be positive and cheerful, and they see the world as a good and bright place in which to live. They have upbeat mental attitudes that enable them to respond positively and constructively to the inevitable ups and downs of day-to-day life. A key part of your journey toward success is the development and maintenance of this benevolent or positive world view.

Perhaps the biggest mental roadblocks that you will ever have to overcome are those contained in your *self-limiting beliefs*. These are beliefs you have that limit you in some way. They hold you back by stopping you from even trying. They often cause you to see things that simply aren't true.

You may feel that you are limited in intelligence because you got average or mediocre grades in school. You may believe you are limited in creative capacity, or in your ability to learn and remember. Perhaps you feel that you are not very outgoing, or very smart about money. Some people feel that they cannot lose weight, quit smoking or be attractive to members of the opposite sex.

But whatever your belief, if you believe it strongly enough, it becomes your reality. You walk, talk, behave and interact with others in a manner consistent with your beliefs. Even if your beliefs are totally false, if you believe them, they will be true for you.

I held myself back and sold myself short for years, as many people do, because I didn't graduate from high school. I looked on university graduates with awe and respect. I unconsciously assumed that my future was limited. Because of this belief, I set only limited goals for myself, and I wasn't surprised if I didn't achieve them. After all, I did poorly in school—what could you expect?

One day, I read a true story about a young man from a small town who graduated from high school with straight A's. He then applied to the state university for admission. As part of the admissions procedure, he had to take the Scholastic Aptitude Test, like all the applicants to universities nationwide. A few weeks later, he received a letter from the admissions department informing him that he had scored in the 99th percentile on the test and he was accepted for the fall semester.

He was happy to be accepted but there was one problem. He didn't know about percentiles and he concluded mistakenly that the 99th percentile was his IQ score. He knew that the average IQ is 100 and he felt he could never do university-level work with his "limited" intelligence.

For the entire fall semester he failed or nearly failed every course. Finally, his counselor called him in and asked him why he was doing so poorly.

"Well," he said, "you can't blame me. I've only got a 99 IQ." The counselor had the student's file in front of him. "Why do you say that?" he asked.

"That's what it said in my letter of admission to the university," he replied.

When the counselor realized what had happened he explained the difference between an IQ and a percentile.

"A 99th percentile means that you scored equal to or higher than 99 percent of all the students in America who wrote this test. You're one of the brightest kids on this campus."

When the young man realized his error and changed his belief about his intelligence, he became a different person.

He went back into his classes and went to work with a new sense of competence and confidence. By the end of the semester he was on the honor roll and he eventually graduated in the top ten of his class.

This story holds a valuable lesson for you, as it did for me. We too easily accept that we are limited in some way. Then we ignore or reject any evidence that contradicts what we've already decided to believe.

A teacher asked a young boy, "Can you play a musical instrument?"

"I don't know," he replied. "I haven't tried yet."

In a way, you're like that young boy. You don't know either what you can really do. Don't be so quick to sell yourself short. Refuse to accept limitations on your potential. You can probably do far more than you've ever done before.

Most of your self-limiting beliefs are not true at all. They are based on negative information that you have taken in and accepted as true. Once you have accepted it as true, your belief makes it a fact for you. As Henry Ford said, "If you believe that you can do a thing, or if you believe you cannot, in either case, you are right."

In Chapter Three, you will learn how to build a strong, confident belief system, one that is completely consistent with what you want to achieve with your life. In the meantime, you should begin to identify any self-limiting beliefs that might be holding you back. Often, your spouse or a trusted friend can help you recognize and identify self-limiting ideas and beliefs that you are unaware of. Remember, they do just as much harm if you don't know about them as if you do.

4. THE LAW OF EXPECTATIONS

The Law of Expectations says that whatever you expect with confidence becomes your own self-fulfilling prophecy. To put it another way, what you get is not necessarily what you *want* in life, but what you *expect*. Your expectations exert a powerful, invisible influence that causes people to behave and situations to work out as you anticipated.

In a way, you are always acting as a fortune-teller in your own life by the way you talk about how you think things are going to turn out. Successful men and women have an attitude of confident, positive self-expectancy. They *expect* to be successful, they *expect* to be liked. They expect to be happy, and they are seldom disappointed.

Unsuccessful people have an attitude of negative expectations, of cynicism and pessimism that somehow causes situations to work out exactly as they expected.

In his book *Pygmalion in the Classroom,* Dr. Robert Rosenthal of Harvard University describes how the expectations of teachers have an enormous impact on the performance of their students. He also found that if students felt that they were expected to do well, they did much better than they would have in the absence of those expectations.

In a famous experiment conducted in the San Francisco Bay Area by Dr. Rosenthal in the late 1960s, at the beginning of a school year, three teachers were called into the principal's office. The principal told them, in effect, "We have been observing your teaching styles and we have concluded that you are the three best teachers in this school. As a special reward for teaching excellence, we are going to give you each one classroom of the brightest children in this school. These children have been selected on the basis of recent IQ tests, and we expect them to make jumps of 20 to 30 percent in academic achievement over the course of the coming year. But, because we don't want to be accused of discrimination, we want you to keep this confidential. We won't tell the parents, and you are not to tell the students that they have been specially selected for this advanced class."

The teachers were delighted. A teacher's dream is to have an entire classroom full of gifted children to teach. They went back to their classes with renewed enthusiasm.

For the entire school year, the classes were monitored, and the teachers were observed. The teachers seemed to teach with greater commitment. They seemed to be more patient with students who did not catch on to a new subject right away. They spent more time after school tutoring students. When a child was having difficulty grasping something, the teacher assumed that the problem was in the teaching, not the student.

At the end of the school year, the three classes led not only the school but the entire school district in grades on standardized tests. They had achieved a leap of 20 to 30 percent in academic achievement over the previous year, just as had been predicted.

When the results of the tests were in, the principal brought the teachers back into his office and sat them down. He congratulated them on having had such a wonderful year with their students. The teachers were unanimous in thanking the principal for giving them so many gifted young people to teach. They said that the teaching was easy when you had such fine students, and that they had enjoyed teaching that year more than in any other.

The principal then explained to them that it had all been an experiment. The students were not exceptional at all. Their names had been chosen by lottery out of the school population at large. They had been assigned randomly to the classes of the three teachers. In fact, they were just average students.

Needless to say, the teachers were surprised. How could the students have done so well, just as had been predicted? Then it occurred to them that the reason was that they were such excellent teachers. It was their expertise as teachers that was responsible for the results.

The principal then explained to them that they also had been chosen at random. At the beginning of the school year, the names of all the teachers in the school had been put into a hat and they were the first three that were drawn.

This is what is called a double-blind experiment. The experimenters held constant for everything except expectations. The expectations the principal had of the teachers were clear and explicit. He said, "You are excellent teachers and we expect you to get excellent results from these classes of superior students."

The expectations the teachers had of the students were implicit and unspoken. They simply treated the children as though they were highly intelligent and expected them to perform in a way consistent with the information they had been given.

In both cases, the expectations were based on false information. However, in both cases, the expectations, because they were created by a believable source, became self-fulfilling prophecies.

This is very important. Your expectations are shaped in direct proportion to your respect for the validity of the source. The more you look up to another person, the greater influence he or she will have on your expectations of yourself.

The teachers taught in an excellent fashion and the students learned at a higher rate than they had ever done before. One of the students in the experiment went from an IQ of 90 to an IQ of 115, a jump of 25 IQ points, by test, in one year under the influence of a teacher who had positive expectations. In experiment after experiment, it has been demonstrated that when teachers expect their students to perform well, the students work hard and live up to their teachers' expectations.

Many parents who have been through our seminars have transformed their children's academic lives by asking their children's teachers to start treating their children as if they were especially intelligent. They have found that the teachers have been, in most cases, more than willing to go along with this idea. The parents have then done the same thing at home.

The results have been astonishing. Children who were getting C's and D's have jumped to A's and B's in as little as two months. Children who were unmotivated and bored with school because they were doing so poorly have become enthusiastic and excited about learning under the influence of parents and teachers who confidently, positively expected them to do well.

Four Kinds of Expectations

There are four sources of expectations that have an impact on your life. The first is the expectations of your parents. We are all unconsciously programmed to try to live up to, or down to, the expectations that our parents expressed of us when we were growing up. The need for the approval of our parents goes on even after our parents are no longer with us. If your parents expected you to do well, and confidently, positively encouraged you to do your best and be your best, this will have had an enormous influence on the person you have become. If, as happens in many cases, your parents expressed negative expectations of you, or no expectations at all, you may still be unconsciously saddled with the burden of trying not to disappoint your parents.

In one study, 90 percent of prisoners interviewed by psychologists reported that they had been told over and over again by their parents when they were growing up that "Someday, you're going to end up in jail."

The second source of expectations that affects your behavior is the expectations that your boss has of your performance. People who work under bosses who have positive expectations are always happier, perform better, and get more done than those who work under bosses who are negative or critical. Because you are inordinately influenced by the expectations of people you are dependent upon for your income, it's not likely that you will ever be happy or successful working for or with people with negative attitudes and behavior.

The third source is the expectations that you have of your children, your spouse and your employees or staff. You have an enormous impact on the personality, the behavior and the performance of the people who look up to you for guidance and feedback. The more important you are in the life of someone else, the more powerfully will your expectations affect their performance. Perhaps the most consistently effective and predictable motivational behavior you can use is to confidently and constantly expect the best from others. People will always try not to disappoint you.

I always tell my children, "You're the best in the West; you're the best little boy (or girl) in the world." I tell them that I love them and that I think they are wonderful children and they are going to do great things with their lives.

Does this have an impact on their personalities? You'd better believe it! Try it yourself and see. Many successful people attribute much of their advance in life to the influence of someone they respected who constantly expressed confidence in their ability to be more than they were. Perhaps the kindest thing that you can do for another person is to say, "I believe in you. I know you can do it."

The fourth source is the expectations that you have of yourself. The wonderful thing about expectations is that you can manufacture your own. You can create your own mental set, your own way of approaching the world, confidently, expecting the very best of yourself in every situation. Your expectations of yourself are in themselves powerful enough to override any negative expectations that anyone else may have about you. You can create a force field of positive mental energy around you by confidently expecting to gain something from every situation.

W. Clement Stone, the multimillionaire, is famous for being an "inverse paranoid." This is someone who believes that the universe is conspiring to do him *good*. An inverse paranoid sees every situation as being heaven-sent either to confer some benefit or teach some valuable lesson to help make him successful. This form of inverse paranoia is the foundation of a positive mental attitude. This is the most outwardly identifiable quality of a high-performing man or woman.

One of our seminar graduates, who was unemployed at the time, told me that he began saying to himself every morning, "I believe something wonderful is going to happen to me today."

He repeated this over and over until he developed an expectant attitude that caused him to look forward to every event of the day. The amazing thing was that a series of wonderful things began to happen to him. After being unemployed for six months, he received two job offers within the first week after beginning this exercise. His financial problems and legal difficulties seemed to clear themselves up miraculously. Wonderful things began to happen to him at every turn.

Just imagine if you went around all day believing that something wonderful was about to happen to you. Think how much more positive, optimistic and cheerful you would be if you were absolutely convinced that everything was conspiring to make you happy and successful.

I can promise you this: If you try this exercise for just three days, at the end of the third day, so many wonderful things will have happened to you that you will not be able to recount them all.

You can never rise any higher than your expectations of yourself. Since they are completely under your control, be sure that your expectations are consistent with what you want to see happen. Always expect the best of yourself.

When you start consciously working with this mental law, you will have a power for good that is virtually unlimited. The power of positive expectations alone can change your whole personality, and your life as well.

5. THE LAW OF ATTRACTION

Many books have been written about this law, and many people feel that it is central to understanding the human condition. The Law of Attraction says that you are a *living magnet*. You invariably attract into your life people and situations in harmony with your dominant thoughts. Like attracts like. Birds of a feather flock together. Everything in your life you have attracted to yourself because of the person you are, and especially because of your thoughts.

Your friends, your family, your relationships, your job, your problems and your opportunities have all been attracted to you because of your habitual way of thinking in each area.

There is an example of this in music, called *the principle of sympathetic resonance*. If you have two pianos in a large room and you strike the note C on one piano and then walk across the room to the other piano, you will find that the string of C on the other piano is vibrating at the same rate of vibration as the C string on the first piano. By the same principle, you will tend to meet and become involved with people and situations that are vibrating in harmony with your own dominant thoughts and emotions.

As you look around you at every aspect of your life, positive or negative, you will see that your entire world is of your own making. And the more emotion you attach to a thought, the greater will be the rate of vibration and the more rapidly you will attract people and situations in harmony with that thought into your life.

You see this law in action all around you. You think of a friend and just then, the phone rings with him or her on the other end. You will decide to do something and immediately afterward you start getting ideas and assistance. You become like a magnet attracting iron filings.

Many people hold themselves back because they don't know how to get from where they are to where they want to go. But because of the Law of Attraction, it's not necessary for you to have all the answers before you begin. As long as you're clear about what you want and the kind of people you want to be associated with, you'll draw them into your life.

Your thoughts are a form of energy that vibrates at a speed determined by the level of emotional intensity accompanying the thought. The more excited, or scared, you are, the more rapidly your thoughts radiate out from you and attract similar people and situations back into your life.

Happy people seem to attract other happy, pleasant people. A person with a prosperity consciousness seems to attract money-making ideas and opportunities. Optimistic, enthusiastic salespeople attract bigger and better customers. Positive businesspeople attract the resources, customers, suppliers and bankers they need to build successful businesses. The Law of Attraction works everywhere all the time.

Like the other mental laws, the law of attraction is neutral. It can help you or hurt you. Actually this law could be considered a variation of the Law of Cause and Effect, or sowing and reaping. That is why the philosopher says:

> Sow a thought and you reap an act;
> Sow an act and you reap a habit;
> Sow a habit and you reap a character;
> Sow a character and you reap a destiny.

You can have more and be more and do more because you can change the person you are. You can change your dominant thoughts by exercising rigorous mental mastery. You can discipline yourself by keeping your thoughts on what you want and refusing to think about what you don't want.

People who use the Law of Attraction in a positive way are often called lucky. This is just another way of attempting to explain why so many good things and helpful people are drawn into the lives of those who are clear about their goals and consistently optimistic about achieving them.

6. THE LAW OF CORRESPONDENCE

The Law of Correspondence is one of the most important laws of all, and is in many ways a summary law that explains many others. It says, "As within, so without." It says that your outer world is a reflection of your inner world. This law declares that you can tell what is going on inside you by looking at what is going on around you.

In the Bible, this principle is explained in the words, "By their fruits, ye shall know them." Everything in your life is from the inner to the outer. Your external world of manifestation corresponds with your internal world of thought and emotion.

Your outer world of relationships will correspond to the person you really are inside, your true inner personality. Your outer world of health will correspond to your inner attitudes of mind. Your outer world of income and financial achievement will correspond to your inner world of thought and preparation. The way people respond and react to you will reflect your attitude and your behavior toward them.

The car you drive and the condition that you keep it in will correspond to your state of mind at any given time. When you are feeling positive and confident and in control of your life, your home, your car and your workplace will tend to be well-organized and efficient. When you feel overwhelmed with work, or frustrated and unhappy, your car, your workplace, your home, even your closets will tend to reflect this state of disarray and confusion. You can see the effects of this Law of Correspondence everywhere.

Everything is from the inner to the outer. My big mistake when I was younger was concentrating on doing rather than on being. I felt that I could get the things I wanted by practicing certain methods and techniques. I eventually learned that proper practice was necessary but not sufficient.

The German philosopher Goethe said, "One must *be* something to be able to *do* something." You must change yourself. You must become a different person on the inside before you see different results on the outside. And you can't fake it for very long, if at all.

Most people try to improve or change aspects of their lives by trying to get other people to change. They don't like what they see reflecting back to them in the mirror of their lives so they work at polishing the mirror instead of going to the source of reflection.

Emerson wrote, "What you are shouts at me so loudly, I can't hear a word you're saying." You always come across to others as you really are. You seldom fool anyone. And the only way you can permanently change the outer things is to change the inner things.

William James wrote, "The greatest revolution of my life is the discovery that individuals can change the outer aspects of their lives by changing the inner attitudes of their minds."

One of the most important questions you can ask yourself is, "What kind of a person do I have to be to earn the respect of the people I care about and live the kind of life I want to live?"

7. THE LAW OF MENTAL EQUIVALENCY

The Law of Mental Equivalency is also called the Law of Mind and could actually be considered a restatement of the previous laws. Essentially, it says that *thoughts objectify themselves*. Your thoughts, vividly imagined and repeated, charged with emotion, become your reality. Almost everything that you have in your life has been created by your own thinking, for better or for worse.

Put another way, thoughts are things. They take on a life of their own. First you have them, then they have you. You act in a manner consistent with what you are thinking most of the time. You eventually become what you think about. And if you change your thinking, you change your life.

Everything that happens in your life first begins and takes place in the form of thought. This is why *thoughtfulness* is a key quality of successful men and women. Becoming a skilled thinker in your own life means using your mental powers in such a way that they serve your best interests all of the time.

. . .

When you begin thinking in a positive, confident way about the main aspects of your life, you take *control* over what is happening to you. You bring your life into harmony with *cause and effect*. You sow positive causes and reap positive effects. You begin to *believe* more intensely in yourself and your possibilities. You *expect* more positive outcomes. You *attract* positive people and situations, and soon your outer life of results will begin to *correspond* to your inner world of constructive thinking.

This entire transformation begins with your thoughts. Change your thinking and you will, you must, change your life. The one thing you must do is to create the *mental equivalent* of what you want to experience in your reality. Everything else will follow from that.

PUTTING THESE IDEAS TO WORK

In Chapter One, you began the transforming exercise of painting a mental masterpiece by defining your ideal goals and aspirations in each major area of your life. Now, take some time, based on the action of these mental laws, to think about how your habitual modes of thought have created every aspect of your life today.

First, your relationships. What is it in your attitudes, beliefs, expectations and behaviors that is causing your problems with other people?

Second, your health. What are your ideas and beliefs about your weight, level of fitness, personal appearance, diet and rest? How do these beliefs help or hinder you?

Third, your career. How do your thoughts affect your position, your progress, the quality of your work and the amount of satisfaction you get from what you do?

Fourth, your level of financial achievement. What would you like to increase or improve? What are your beliefs and expectations concerning your material well-being? How much would you like to earn, and why?

Fifth, the quality of your inner life—your thoughts, feelings, peace of mind and happiness. What beliefs, attitudes and expectations are creating your world today? Which of them do you need to change?

If you are honest with yourself, you will find that you have self-limiting ways of thinking in one or more of these areas. This is quite normal. Honestly facing the facts about yourself is the starting point of rapid self-improvement.

CHAPTER 3

The Master Program

Everything that happens to you, everything you become and accomplish is determined by the way you think, by the way you use your mind. As you begin changing your mind, you begin changing your life. But how did you get to where you are today? What formative influences have combined to make you the person you are right now? Why do you think and feel the way you do, and what are the factors that have brought you to your current situation?

In this chapter, you will learn about your "master program" and how you have been put on a form of autopilot, starting from an early age. You will learn how to begin taking control of your internal guidance system, and how to remove influences and obstacles that have been interfering with your happiness without your even knowing about it. You will learn how to alter your master program to make it more consistent with the results you want.

When I was twenty, I was living in a small apartment with no job. It was the middle of winter and it was thirty-five degrees below zero. I was alone in a new city, thousands of miles from where I grew up.

Eleven years later, when I was thirty-one, I was again living alone in a small apartment. Again it was cold outside, thirty-five degrees below zero. I was deeply in debt, unemployed and a thousand miles from my family and friends.

After eleven years of working and traveling very little had changed. I was older and wiser but I still felt that I was spinning my wheels.

I felt frustrated. I felt that I was making very little progress. I had always harbored a secret belief that I had the potential to do more with my life, but I had no idea how to tap that potential.

I had heard that the average person uses only 10 percent or less of his or her potential in the course of a lifetime. Albert Einstein, one of the great geniuses of the twentieth century, was estimated to have only used about 15 percent of his.

Research at Stanford University concluded that the average person uses only about 2 percent of his or her mental abilities, based on studies of the neocortex, the "thinking brain" of the human being.

This subject fascinated me. What was the potential of the average person? What was my real potential? How could I get more out of myself? I was trying to open a combination lock without the right numbers. So I read and reflected, and I eventually discovered the answers, one by one. I learned the combination to the lock on the door of human potential. This combination enabled me to change my life, as it will enable you to change yours.

To begin with, in the entire history of the human race, there never has been, and never will be, anyone just like you. The odds that another person with your unique combination of characteristics and qualities will ever be born are more than 50 billion to one. You have the potential to do something special, even extraordinary, with your life, something that no one else can do. The only real question you have to answer is: Are you going to do it?

It's true that some people are born with extraordinary gifts, but most of us start off with talents and abilities that are more or less average. Most men and women who achieve great success in any field do it by developing their natural talents and abilities to a very high degree in some special area of interest. Your individual potential is there, inside you, but it has to be identified and developed if you want to get more of what is really possible out of yourself.

A SIMPLE EQUATION

One definition of individual potential is contained in the equation [IA + AA] × A = IHP. The first two letters, IA, stand for *inborn attributes*. These are what you are born with, your natural tendencies, your temperament, and your general mental ability.

The next two letters, AA, stand for *acquired attributes*. These are the knowledge, skill, talent, experience and ability that you have gained or developed as you have grown and matured.

The next letter, A, stands for *attitude,* or the kind of mental energy that you bring to bear on your combination of inborn and acquired attributes. IHP stands for *individual human performance*. So the formula is *Inborn Attributes plus Acquired Attributes multiplied by your Attitude equals your Individual Human Performance*.

Your inborn attributes, your natural talents and abilities, the "inner aspects" of your personality are largely fixed at birth. They are your genetic heritage. You can't do much to change them.

Your acquired attributes are the skills and abilities you develop by channeling your natural talents through your education and experience. These are your areas of competence and potential mastery.

You can develop, improve and change your acquired attributes over time through study and practice, but the process is slow and deliberate, requiring patience, discipline and considerable effort.

The only wild card in the equation is A, or attitude. And here's one of the insights that changed my life.

Since the quality of your attitude can be improved almost without limit, even a person with average *inborn attributes* and average *acquired attributes* can perform at a high level if he or she has a very *positive mental attitude*. And your attitude can be improved immediately and almost without limit. This is why it is your attitude as much as your aptitude that determines how much you accomplish. And your attitude is under the direct control of your will. You can decide what it is going to be every minute of every day.

Earl Nightingale referred to *attitude* as the most important word in the language. We know we should have a *positive* mental attitude. We've heard that for years. But what is that exactly?

Your attitude is the way you approach life. It is your "angle of attack." It is your general mental tone and the outward expression of your thoughts and feelings. A positive mental attitude is a generally optimistic and cheerful way of greeting the people, problems and events that you encounter throughout your day.

Your attitude is one of the best indicators of the person you really are inside. And people reflect back to you your attitude toward them. This is why happy, cheerful people seem to get along well wherever they go.

Developing this kind of positive attitude toward yourself and your life is the first step to unlocking your full potential. And the only way you can tell what kind of attitude you really have is by observing how you react when things go wrong. As Epictetus wrote, "Circumstances do not make the man; they merely reveal him to himself." You can tell best what you're made of by watching the way you behave when you're under pressure. Your real self comes out, for better or worse.

But where does your attitude come from? What causes one person to be positive and another to be negative? Your attitude is determined by your *expectations*. Your expectations about yourself and your life are very powerful. They exert an immense influence on your personality.

If you expect good things to happen to you, you'll be positive and optimistic in your approach to people and situations. If you look for the good in others, you'll probably find it. If you expect something wonderful to happen to you today, it probably will.

Positive expectations are the mark of the superior personality. They create in you an attitude of positive expectancy that goes hand in hand with happiness and self-confidence. They give you a form of mental resilience, a nonchalant optimism that enables you to respond constructively to the challenges you face every day. And as I said in Chapter Two, you can manufacture your own expectations by deciding to do so.

Where then do your expectations come from? Penetrating the layers of personality one by one is the only way to get right to the root cause of the way you think and feel. It is the only way to bring about rapid and permanent changes in your life and in your performance. Everything is from the inner to the outer. What you are doing and saying on the outside always has its roots in your inner life.

Your expectations are determined by your *beliefs* about yourself and the world you live in. Your expectations about people, work and every part of your life are generated by what you believe to be true in that area. Even if you have false or self-limiting beliefs, they will manifest themselves in your expectations, your attitudes and ultimately, in your results.

According to the law of belief, if you have a *benevolent* world view, if you believe that the world is a good place and that you are a good person, then you will expect the best from yourself, from others and from the situations you encounter. Your positive expectations will be expressed in a positive mental attitude and, by the Law of Correspondence, people will reflect back to you your attitude toward them. You will get back what you give out.

Your beliefs therefore determine the quality of your personality. And where do your beliefs come from? This brings us to perhaps the greatest breakthrough in psychology in the twentieth century —the discovery of the "self-concept."

THE MASTER PROGRAM

Your self-concept is your bundle of beliefs about yourself and about every part of your life and your world. It is the "master program" of your subconscious computer. The Law of Belief says that your beliefs determine your reality because you always see the world through a screen of prejudices formed by your belief structure. Your self-concept, your belief structure, precedes and predicts your performance and behavior in every area of your life. You always act in a manner consistent with your self-concept, consistent with the bundle of beliefs that you have acquired from infancy onward.

In other words, you are where you are and what you are because of what you believe yourself to be. Whether you are rich or poor, happy or unhappy, fat or thin, successful or unsuccessful, your beliefs make you this way.

If you change your beliefs in any area of your life, you begin immediately to change in that area. Your expectations, your attitudes, your behavior and your results all change.

Your outer world is an expression of your inner world, and cannot be otherwise. "You are not what you think you are, but what you *think,* you are."

Each of us has been programmed to walk, talk, think and act the way we do today. You cannot think, feel or behave any differently on the outside unless you change your master program, your self-concept, on the inside. A negative or erroneous idea in your self-concept will be expressed in negative attitudes and behavior in your life and relationships.

But you can change your program, your self-concept, by replacing self-limiting ideas and beliefs with self-liberating thoughts. You can begin to think of yourself as you want to be rather than as you are. You can decide to make every part of your life positive, exciting and uplifting. You can create your life as a masterpiece. And when you do, these new constructive thoughts begin immediately to clothe themselves in their physical realities.

<u>ASPECTS OF YOUR SELF-CONCEPT</u>

There is a direct relationship between how well you do anything and your self-concept in that area. You perform as well as you believe yourself capable of performing. You are as effective as you believe yourself to be in whatever you do. You can never be better or different on the outside than you believe yourself to be on the inside.

Whenever you feel good about yourself and are doing well at your job, or in your relationships, or at a sport, you are demonstrating a positive self-concept in that area. Whenever you do poorly or feel inferior or clumsy, or behave badly in some situation, your negative beliefs about yourself are being demonstrated in your behavior. As within, so without.

What makes positive change possible for you is that your self-concept is largely subjective, not objective. Your beliefs about yourself, especially your self-limiting beliefs and doubts, are not based on fact at all. Negative ideas about yourself and your abilities are usually based on false information and impressions you have taken in and accepted as true.

As soon as you begin to reject these self-limiting ideas, they begin to lose their power over you. By deliberately changing your self-concept, your true potential becomes unlimited.

A young man, about twenty-five, who came to my seminar was working as a construction laborer. During our discussion of the influence of the self-concept, he had a mental shock. The lights went on for him. He was stunned.

He told me that his father, an uneducated working man, had told his children continually, "Our family has always been laborers and we always will be. It's our lot in life. That's just the way it is." As he grew up hearing this, he accepted it as a fact, a belief, and when he left school, he went to work as a laborer.

In the seminar, he suddenly realized that he had bought his father's limited outlook on life without question. He had swallowed his father's belief system whole. He looked at himself and the world the way his father had.

Now, seven years later, he was still "working by the sweat of his brow." He had inadvertently allowed his father to shape his self-concept with regard to his work and his possibilities. He saw how his beliefs about himself had shaped his expectations and his attitude. He realized that he had continually attracted only laboring opportunities and that his outer world, his relationships and his lifestyle had all been determined by his beliefs.

He decided at that moment that he didn't like being a laborer. He had always felt he could do much more, but he had also felt trapped. Now, he experienced a new sense of freedom and control. He realized for the first time that his limitations were on the inside, not on the outside.

After the seminar, he quit his laboring job and got into sales, starting at the bottom. He did poorly at first, but he was determined. He read every book he could find on selling. He listened to every audiocassette program. He attended every sales seminar available in his area and he even traveled to seminars in other cities.

We kept in touch. Within one year, he had doubled his income. In two years, he was making four times as much. He went to the top of his sales force and was soon hired away for more money and greater opportunity.

Within five years he was making more than one hundred thousand dollars per year, had a beautiful home, a lovely wife, two children and an exciting future lying before him. He was the master of his own destiny.

The turning point for him, as it was for me and thousands of others, was learning how his self-concept controlled his life and then deciding to change it. Everything followed from that.

Not only do you have an overall self-concept, which is a general summary of your beliefs about yourself, but you also have a series of "mini-self-concepts." These parts of your self-concept control your performance and your behavior in each individual area of your life that you consider important.

You have a self-concept for how much you weigh, for how much you eat, for how much you exercise or for how fit you are.

You have a self-concept for how you dress and how you appear to other people. You have a self-concept of yourself as a parent, and as a child to your parents. You have a self-concept for how popular you are, at work and among your friends.

You have a self-concept for how well you play each sport and even for how well you play each part of each sport. A golfer may have one self-concept as a great driver and another self-concept as a poor putter, and that's the way he or she will play.

If you are in sales, you have an overall self-concept for how good you are as a salesperson, which determines how well you do in sales. You also have individual self-concepts for how good you are at prospecting, identifying needs, presenting solutions, answering objections and closing. In each of these areas, you will be relaxed and competent, or tense and unsure, depending upon how you think of yourself performing those tasks.

You have a self-concept for how well-organized and efficient you are, in both your personal and your work life. And you will always behave in a manner consistent with your self-concept. You cannot behave in a way that is different from your subconscious programming any more than a computer could decide to disregard its programming.

You have an overall self-concept for how competent you are in your field and for how much money you are capable of earning. You can never rise much higher than your self-concept level of ability or earn much more or less than your self-concept level of income.

In fact, if you earn more than 10 percent above or below what you feel you are worth, you will feel very uncomfortable. You will immediately begin engaging in compensatory behavior. If you earn 10 percent too much, you will begin to spend the money, lend it, invest it in things you know nothing about or even give it away or lose it. Such "throw-away" behavior is practiced by anyone who suddenly finds himself or herself with more money than is consistent with his or her self-concept.

There are many stories of men and women who have won large sums of money in various lotteries. In most cases, if they were working at laboring jobs when they won the money, in two or three years they were back working at the same jobs, their money was gone, and they had no idea where it went.

If you earn 10 percent or more below your self-concept level of income, you begin to engage in "scrambling" behavior. You begin to think more creatively, work longer and harder, look at second-income opportunities or think about changing jobs in order to get your income back up into your self-concept range.

Where money, weight or anything else is concerned, you gradually get into your various "comfort zones," and once there, you do everything possible to stay there. You resist change of any kind, even positive change.

The comfort zone is the great enemy of human potential. Your comfort zones become habits of living that are hard to break. And any habit persisted in over time eventually becomes a rut. Then, instead of using your intelligence to get out of your rut, you use most of your energies making your rut more comfortable. You justify and rationalize your situation as being unchangeable. You feel and say, "There's nothing I can do."

But there is a lot you can do to change your future. In the pages to come, you will learn how to break out of your comfort zones. You will learn how to step up to the keyboard of your own mental computer and input a new belief system for yourself. You will learn how to redesign your self-concept so you can get more of whatever you really want in life.

THE THREE PARTS OF YOUR SELF-CONCEPT

Your self-concept is made up of three parts, like three layers of a cake. The first of these three parts is your *self-ideal*. This is the vision or ideal description of the person that you would most like to be in every respect. This ideal image exerts a powerful influence on your behavior and on the way you think about yourself.

Your self-ideal is a combination of the qualities and attributes that you admire most in other people, living and dead. It is the sum of your dominant aspirations. It is your vision of what the perfect person should be.

Exceptional men and women have very clear self-ideals, toward which they are constantly striving. They set high standards for themselves and strive to live up to them. And so can you. The more clear you are about the person you want to become, the more likely it is that, day by day, you will evolve into that person. You will rise to the height of your dominant aspirations for yourself. You will become what you most admire.

Sadly, unsuccessful and unhappy men and women have very fuzzy ideals, or in most cases, no self-ideals at all. They give little or no thought to the person they want to be or to the qualities that they would like to develop in themselves. Their growth and evolution eventually slows and stops. They get stuck in a mental rut and they stay there. They lose all impetus for self-improvement.

When one looks up to, and respects, the qualities of integrity, purposefulness, courage and action orientation in others, one begins to incorporate those values in oneself.

As you clarify your fundamental values and work to integrate them into everything you do, your personality improves, and because your outer life reflects your inner life, your work, your relationships and every aspect of your outer life improves as well. More about this later.

The second part of your self-concept is your *self-image*. Your self-image is the way you *see* yourself, and the way you *think* about yourself, as you go about your daily activities. Your self-image is often called your "inner mirror," into which you look to see how you are supposed to behave or perform in a particular situation. You always behave consistently with the picture that you hold of yourself on the inside. Because of this, you can improve your performance by deliberately changing the mental pictures that you hold about yourself in that area.

This process of self-image modification is one of the fastest and most dependable ways to improve your performance. As you begin to see yourself and think about yourself as more competent and confident, your behavior becomes more focused and effective.

When you deliberately change your self-image, as you'll learn to do later in this chapter, you'll walk, talk, act and feel better than you ever have before. You will change both your personality and your results by changing your mental images.

The third part of your self-concept is your *self-esteem*. Your self-esteem is how you *feel* about yourself. It is the emotional component of your personality, and it is the foundation quality of high performance. It is the key to happiness and personal effectiveness. It is like the reactor core in a nuclear power plant. It is the source of the energy, enthusiasm, vitality and optimism that powers your personality and makes you into a high-achieving man or woman.

Your level of self-esteem is determined by two factors, which are like the opposite sides of the same coin. The first is how valuable and worthwhile you feel about yourself, how much you like and accept yourself as a good person. This is the "personal assessment" side of self-esteem. This is your rating of yourself, aside from what is going on in your life at the moment.

This first factor is not dependent upon external variables. A person with genuinely high self-esteem can have innumerable difficulties and setbacks in life and still retain a high, positive estimate of himself or herself as a human being. Unfortunately, there are very few people who have reached this state of evolution where they can retain a sense of inner value independent of external circumstances.

The second factor determining your level of self-esteem is your feeling of "self-efficacy," how competent and capable you feel you are in whatever you do. This is the "performance-based" side of self-esteem. It is the bedrock upon which most real and lasting self-confidence and self-respect are built.

These two parts of your self-esteem reinforce each other. When you feel good about yourself, you perform better. And when you perform well, you feel good about yourself. Both are essential. Neither can endure without the other.

The best measure of self-esteem is *how much you like yourself*. The more you like yourself, the better you do at everything you put your mind to. The more you like yourself, the more confidence you have, the more positive is your attitude, the healthier and more energetic you are and the happier you are overall.

And since how you feel is largely determined by how you talk to yourself, silently or aloud, you can raise your self-esteem at will by saying, over and over, with enthusiasm and conviction, the words "I like myself! I like myself! I like myself!"

Or, better yet, you can say "I love myself! I love myself! I love myself!" This may sound corny when you first hear it, but it is extremely powerful. As an experiment, look up from this page and say to yourself, as if you meant it from the bottom of your heart, "I like myself!" several times. Better yet, look in the next mirror you pass and say "I like myself." You'll find that you can't say this five or six times without feeling genuinely better about yourself.

We have taught this to our children. Whenever they are unhappy or misbehaving, we coax them into saying, "I like myself," and they soon break out in smiles and cheer up. It seems that the more open and receptive a person is to this message, the greater the impact it has on his or her personality.

Liking yourself is very healthy. In fact, it is the key to personal effectiveness and to happy relationships with others. The more you like and respect yourself, the better you perform in everything you do. You are more relaxed and positive. You are more confident about your abilities. You make fewer mistakes. You have more energy and you are more creative.

Some people have been taught to believe that liking yourself is the same as being conceited or obnoxious. But exactly the opposite is true. Both the "superiority complex," behaving in an arrogant or conceited way, and the "inferiority complex," behaving in a self-deprecating way, are manifestations of low self-esteem, of not liking oneself very much at all. People with genuine self-esteem get along easily and well with just about everyone.

THE RULES OF SELF-ESTEEM

There are two rules of self-esteem and self-liking: Rule number one is that you can never like or love anyone *else* more than you like or love *yourself.* You can't give away what you don't have.

Rule number two is that you can never expect anyone else to like or love you more than you like, love or respect yourself.

Your own level of self-liking and self-acceptance is the control valve on the quality of your human relationships. It is the problem or the solution in every human situation. Everything you do to build and reinforce your own self-esteem increases the amount of satisfaction and happiness you enjoy with the other people in your life.

If your self-concept is the *master program* of your subconscious computer, where does it come from? How is it formed? What is it composed of? And most important, how can you reprogram it to improve yourself and increase your effectiveness in everything you do?

SELF-CONCEPT FORMATION

You were not born with a self-concept. Everything that you *know* and *believe* about yourself today, you have learned as the result of what has happened to you since you were an infant. Each child comes into the world as pure potential, with a particular temperament and certain inborn attributes but with no self-concept at all. Every attitude, behavior, value, opinion, belief and fear you have today has been learned. Therefore, if there are elements of your self-concept that do not serve your purposes, you can unlearn them.

For example, I read recently about a thirty-two-year-old woman who was involved in an automobile accident. As a result of hitting her head, she experienced total amnesia. At the time of the accident, she was married, with two children, eight and ten years old. She was extremely shy, she had a stutter and she was very nervous around other people. She had a poor self-concept and a low level of self-esteem. To compound this problem, she did not work and she had a limited social circle.

Because of her total amnesia, when she woke up in the hospital she did not remember a single thing about her past life. She did not remember her parents, and she did not remember her husband and her children. Her mind was a complete blank.

This was so unusual that various specialists, neurosurgeons and psychologists were brought in to talk to her and to examine her.

She was such a special case that she became very well known. When she recovered physically, she was interviewed on radio and television. She began studying her condition, and eventually she wrote articles and a book describing her experience.

She began traveling and giving lectures to medical and professional groups. Ultimately she became a recognized authority on amnesia.

With no memory of her previous experiences, her childhood and her upbringing, and as a result of being the center of attention and being treated as though she were a very important person, she developed a totally new personality. She became positive, self-confident and outgoing. She became gregarious and extremely friendly, and she developed an excellent sense of humor. She became popular and met and moved in an entirely new social circle. In effect, she developed a brand-new self-concept that was completely consistent with high performance, happiness and life satisfaction. She substituted one mental program for another. *And you can do the same thing.*

Once you understand how your self-concept was formed, you

will be able to bring about changes that make you into the kind of person you admire and want to be like. You will learn how to become the kind of person who can accomplish the goals and dreams that are most important to you.

Children come into the world with no self-concept. Children learn who they are, and how important and valuable they are (or aren't) by the way they are treated from infancy onward. Infants have a tremendous need for love and touching. The love in their environment is like their emotional oxygen. You cannot give children too much love and affection in their formative years. Children need love like roses need rain, almost as much as they need food and drink and shelter for healthy growth.

The foundation of personality is laid down in the first three to five years of life. The healthiness of the adult will be largely determined by the quality and quantity of unbroken love and affection that the child receives from parents and others during this time.

A child who is raised with an abundance of love, affection and encouragement will tend to develop a positive and stable personality early in life. A child who is raised with criticism and punishment will tend to grow up fearful, suspicious, and distrustful, with the potential for a variety of personality problems that manifest themselves later in life. Adults with low self-esteem and negative mental attitudes were invariably children who were deprived of the love and security they needed during their formative years.

THE QUALITIES OF CHILDREN

Children are born with two remarkable qualities. The first is that they are born largely *unafraid*. They come into the world with only two physical fears, the fear of loud noises and the fear of falling. All other fears have to be taught to the child through repetition and reinforcement while the child is growing up.

Anyone who has ever tried to raise a small child to the age of five or six knows that they are not afraid of anything. They will climb up on ladders, run out into traffic, grab sharp instruments, and generally do things that appear suicidal to an adult. They have no fears at all until those fears are instilled in them by their parents and others.

The second remarkable quality of children is that they are completely *uninhibited*. They laugh, they cry, they wet their pants. They say and do exactly what they feel like with no concern whatever for the opinions of others. They are completely spontaneous and express themselves easily and naturally with no inhibitions at all. Have you ever seen a self-conscious baby?

Wonderfully enough, this is your natural state, the way you come into the world, unafraid and uninhibited, completely fearless and able to express yourself freely and easily in all situations. You know this is true because, years later, whenever you are in a safe situation, with people you trust, you often revert to this natural state of fearlessness and spontaneity. You feel relaxed and comfortable, completely free to let your hair down and be yourself. These are some of the best moments of your life, your peak experiences, when you are truly happy. And they are your normal, natural condition.

HOW CHILDREN LEARN

Children learn in two primary ways. First, they learn by imitation of one or both parents. Many of your adult habit patterns, including your values, your attitudes, your beliefs and your behaviors, were formed by watching and by listening to your parents when you were growing up. The sayings "Like father, like son" or "Like mother, like daughter" are certainly true. Often the child will identify strongly with one parent and will be more influenced by that parent than by the other.

The second way children learn is by moving away from discomfort toward comfort, or away from pain toward pleasure. Sigmund Freud called this the "pleasure principle." His conclusion, and that of most psychologists, is that this striving toward pleasure or happiness is the basic motivation for all human behavior. The child's development, from toilet training to eating habits, to every aspect of his or her socialization, is shaped by this continual drive or motivation toward comfort or personal pleasure, *toward* what feels good and *away* from what feels bad.

Of all the discomforts that a child can suffer, the withdrawal of the love and approval of the parent is the most traumatic and frightening. Children have an intense need for emotional security, for their parents' love, support and protection. When the parent withdraws his or her love in an attempt to discipline, control or punish the child, the child becomes extremely uncomfortable and insecure. The child becomes afraid.

The perception of the child is everything. It is not what the parents meant or intended that counts, it is what the child perceives that affects the child's feelings and actions. When the child perceives that love has been withdrawn, the child immediately changes his or her behavior in an attempt to win back the parent's love and approval. The child feels like a drowning person reaching for a life preserver.

Without a continuous and unbroken flow of unconditional love, the child's security is threatened. Frustrated, the child loses his or her fearlessness and spontaneity.

Most personality problems in life are the result of "love withheld." Probably much of what we do in life, from childhood onward, is done either to get love or to compensate for the lack of love. Most of our unhappy memories of childhood are associated with a perceived lack of love. Most of our problems in adult relationships are rooted in these earlier experiences of love deprivation.

At an early age, as a result of mistakes parents make in raising their children, especially when they use destructive criticism and physical punishment, the child begins to lose his or her natural fearlessness and spontaneity. He or she begins to develop negative habit patterns, negative ways of reacting to life. All habits, positive or negative, are conditioned responses to stimuli. They are learned as the result of repetition, over and over, until they are firmly ingrained in the subconscious mind. Then they function automatically, whenever they're triggered by some stimulus.

Negative habits become customary behavior, parts of our self-concept. They become our comfort zones. Once they are programmed in and become part of our psychological makeup, we only feel comfortable when we're behaving or reacting in a particular negative way. We become fear-driven rather than desire-driven.

THE SABOTEUR OF SUCCESS

Destructive criticism is one of the most harmful of all human behavior. It lowers self-esteem, creates poor self-image, and undermines the individual's performance in everything he or she attempts. Destructive criticism shakes the individual's self-confidence so that he or she feels inferior, tenses up and makes mistakes whenever he or she attempts anything for which he or she has been criticized in the past. The individual may give up trying at all and simply avoid the area of endeavor altogether.

The average parent criticizes his or her children as many as eight times for every time he or she praises them. Parents criticize their children unthinkingly in an attempt to get them to improve their behavior. But exactly the opposite occurs. Because destructive criticism undermines the child's self-esteem and weakens his or her self-concept, effectiveness decreases rather than increases. The child's performance gets worse, not better.

Destructive criticism makes the individual feel incompetent and inadequate. He or she feels angry and defensive and wants to strike back or escape. Performance nosedives. All sorts of negative consequences occur. Especially, the relationship between the parent and child deteriorates.

Children who are criticized for their schoolwork soon develop a negative association between schoolwork and how they feel about themselves. They begin to hate it and avoid it whenever possible. They see schoolwork as a source of pain and frustration. And because of the Laws of Attraction and Correspondence, they begin to associate with other children with the same attitudes.

Often people make the mistake of thinking they are giving "constructive criticism" when they are really just tearing the other person down—and calling it "constructive" to rationalize their behavior. True constructive criticism leaves the person feeling better and more capable of doing a better job in the future. If criticism doesn't improve performance, by increasing the individual's feelings of self-esteem and self-efficacy, then it has merely been a destructive act of self-expression carried out against someone who is not in a position to resist.

Destructive criticism lies at the root of many personality problems and of much hostility between individuals. It leaves a trail of broken spirits, demoralization, anger, resentment, self-doubt and a host of negative emotions.

When children are criticized at an early age, they soon learn to criticize themselves. They run themselves down, sell themselves short and interpret their experiences in a negative way. They continually feel, "I'm not good enough," no matter how hard they work or how well they do.

The whole purpose of criticism, if you must give it, is "performance improvement." It is to help the other person to be better as a result. Constructive criticism is not done for revenge. It is not a vehicle to express your displeasure or anger. Its purpose is to help, not hurt, or you should refrain from using it at all.

Here are seven steps you can follow to ensure that what you are giving is "constructive feedback" rather than destructive criticism.

First, protect the individual's self-esteem at all costs. Treat it like a balloon, with your words as potential needles. Be gentle. With my children, I always begin the process of correction with the words "I love you very much," and then I go on to give them the feedback and guidance they require to be better.

Second, focus on the future, not the past. Don't cry over spilled milk. Talk about "What do we do from here?" Use words like "Next time, why don't you . . ."

Third, focus on the behavior or the performance, not the person. Replace the word "you" with a description of the problem.

Instead of saying, "You are not selling enough," instead say, "Your sales figures are below what we expect. What can we do to get them up?"

Fourth, use "I" messages to retain ownership of your feelings. Instead of saying, "You make me very angry," instead say, "I feel very angry when you do that," or, "I am not happy about this situation and I would like to discuss how we could change it."

Fifth, get clear agreement on what is to change, and when, and by how much. Be specific as well as future-oriented and solution-oriented. Say things like, "In the future, it's important that you keep accurate notes and double check before you make shipments final."

Sixth, offer to help. Ask, "What can I do to help you in this situation?" Be prepared to show the person what to do and how to do it. As a parent, or if you are in a position of authority, one of your key jobs is to be a teacher. You can't expect another to do something different without instructing that person how it is to be done.

Seventh, assume that the other person wants to do a good job and that, if he or she has done a poor job or made a mistake, it was not deliberate. The problem is limited skill, incomplete information or a misunderstanding of some kind.

Be calm, patient, supportive, sensitive, clear and constructive rather than angry or destructive. Build the person up rather than tearing him or her down. There's probably no faster way for you to build self-esteem and self-efficacy in others than by immediately ceasing all destructive criticism. You will notice the difference at once in all your relationships.

NEGATIVE HABIT PATTERNS

There are two major negative habit patterns that we all learn in childhood. There are those that push you forward and those that hold you back. They affect everything you think, feel and do. They control and determine your destiny in life, and you are only vaguely aware of them. They are called the *inhibitive* and the *compulsive*. Understanding their impact in your life and learning how to counteract their influence on your behavior is absolutely indispensable to your achieving the kind of success and happiness that is possible for you.

The *inhibitive* negative habit pattern is learned when the child is told over and over again, "Don't! Get away from that! Stop that! Don't touch! Watch out!" The child's natural impulse is to touch, taste, smell, feel and explore every part of his or her world. When the parents react to the child's exploratory behavior by shouting, by becoming upset, by spanking the child or with some other form of disapproval, the child is not old enough to understand what is going on. Instead, the child internalizes the message that "every time I try something new or different, Mommy or Daddy gets mad at me and stops loving me. It must be because I'm too small, I'm incompetent, I'm incapable, I can't, I can't, I can't."

This feeling that "I can't" soon crystallizes into the "fear of failure." And the *fear of failure* is the greatest single obstacle to success in adult life. The fear of failure wells up inside you whenever you think of taking any kind of risk, or doing anything new or different involving any risk of loss of time, money or emotion.

In my own case, because I had done poorly in school, I feared that I wasn't smart enough to do much better than I was doing. When I saw other people around me wheeling and dealing and taking risks and getting into and out of jobs and business deals, I just looked away. I assumed they had attributes of intelligence and daring that I lacked.

When I was a child, because I had been brought up to fear whippings from my father, I was afraid of bullies on the playground. When I got into selling, I was afraid of cold calls. When I got into management, I was afraid of asserting myself. When I made a little money, I was afraid of investing, and when I had the chance, I was afraid of starting my own business, for fear I would fail and lose my investment.

My parents had been fearful and they brought me up fearful. They did a good job. It was only later when I learned that my fears were all in my mind, that there was nothing to be afraid of, that my real life began.

You experience all negative habit patterns in your body. When you are in the grip of a negative habit pattern, you feel and react exactly as if you were in danger of physical harm. And the place you feel the inhibitive negative habit pattern, the fear of failure, is down the front of your body, starting in your solar plexus and spreading from there.

If, for example, you were afraid of public speaking, and you were told that you were going to be called up in front of a large audience, your first reaction would be a feeling of weakness, of fright in your solar plexus, the emotional center of your body. And the more you thought about the upcoming event, the more the fear would spread. Your heart would start beating faster. You would begin breathing more rapidly and with shallower breaths.

Your throat might go dry, and you might get a pounding in the front part of your head, similar to a migraine headache. Your bladder might also fill up, and you would have an irresistible urge to run to the bathroom. You would react as if you were about to get a spanking. All these physical manifestations of the inhibitive negative habit pattern are usually programmed into your subconscious mind before you are six years old.

Negative habit patterns also trigger feelings of anxiety and nervousness, accompanied by perspiration, rapid heartbeat and emotional responses such as irritation, impatience and angry outbursts. The more deeply entrenched the negative habit pattern, the more extreme will be your reaction to the situation.

You learn the fear of failure, of inhibition, characterized by the words, "I can't," in three different ways.

First, you learn it by repeated association with a particular event, coupled with destructive criticism or physical punishment. If a child is spanked every time he or she touches the piano, he or she will eventually develop a conditioned response of fear that can be triggered by the very thought of playing a piano.

A doctor in my seminar told me how he was beaten by an alcoholic father when he was a child. The father would jump up from his chair without warning and hit the boy. Now, fifty years later, if the doctor even sees someone on television jump up quickly, his whole body reacts exactly as if he's about to be attacked. His solar plexus tightens up. His heart rate jumps. He begins to perspire. He shakes all over. This is a conditioned response caused by childhood trauma, and he will probably never get over it.

Second, you can learn a negative habit pattern as the result of *subtle* negative influences that you may not be aware of. Some people accept criticism of themselves unquestioningly as if they were actually true. Others believe the negative qualities described in their horoscopes. Some people do things poorly the first time and conclude they have no aptitude in that area.

The important thing for you to do is to continually ask yourself, "What if I had the capacity to be really good in that area?" Then, assume that you do have the inherent ability and go to work on yourself. When you begin casting off the bonds of your self-limiting beliefs and fears, you'll find that there are very few obstacles in front of you. They're almost all in your mind, in your automatic responses.

The third way you can learn a negative habit pattern or fearful response is as the result of a single traumatic event of some kind.

One particularly frightening experience, such as almost drowning or falling as a child, can give you an "irrational" fear of water or heights for life. The very thought of doing that particular thing triggers in you a form of paralysis.

Sometimes these fears are called phobias, and they can be progressive. One negative experience, continually dwelled upon and relived, can become a major fear that affects much of your life and seriously interferes with your happiness.

The key word here is "irrational." The situation triggers feelings of extreme anxiety and you become angry about it—but you don't know why. The very thought of it upsets you and interferes with your work or your relationships.

One of your requirements for becoming a positive person is to clear your mental decks, to blow out your subconscious tubes, and this requires that you identify and deal with any fears that could be holding you back.

Talk out your fears with a good friend or spouse. Others often can see things that you can't. Consult a psychologist or psychiatrist if necessary. A professional therapist can often help you to free yourself of mental obstacles that have been blocking your progress for years.

The second major type of negative habit pattern that children learn is the *compulsive*. The compulsive negative habit pattern is learned by the child when he or she is told over and over again, "You'd better, or else." Parents say, "If you don't do, or stop doing, something or other, you are in big trouble." To the child, *trouble* with parents always means the withdrawal of love and approval.

When parents make their love *conditional* upon the child's performance or behavior, the child soon internalizes the message that "I am not loved and therefore I am not safe until and unless I do what pleases my mommy and daddy. Therefore, *I have to* do what pleases them. I have to do what makes them happy. I have to do what they want. I have to, I have to, I have to."

This compulsive negative habit pattern develops when parents make their love conditional rather than *unconditional*. It manifests itself in the *fear of rejection*. And the fear of rejection is the second major reason for failure and underachievement in adult life.

If you were raised with conditional love, you can tell because of the way you feel as an adult. You will be overly concerned, if not obsessed, with the opinions of others, especially with the opinions of your parents, spouse, boss or friends.

The word is "overly." It's normal and natural to be considerate of the thoughts and feelings of others. It is this concern for and respect for people's opinions that serves as the glue that holds society together. Otherwise, we would have chaos.

But carried to an extreme, like all fears, it can be paralyzing. It can reach the point where people are incapable of making a decision for themselves until they have received approval from someone else.

We need and strive for the respect of other people, but superior people, self-actualizing men and women, have sufficient confidence in themselves to consider the opinions of others and then make their own decisions based on what they feel is right for them.

Remember, we're all afraid. Especially, we fear criticism and disapproval. We will go to great lengths to earn the goodwill and acceptance of people we look up to. We will make sacrifices of all kinds to be liked. Soldiers will even risk their lives not to let others down.

But you need to be constantly aware of this insidious influence. It can, as Francis Bacon wrote, "make a man who can in no way be true to his own ends."

In each situation in which the opinions of others are involved, ask yourself, "What do I really want to do? What would make me the happiest?" Then make your decisions for the person who is going to have to live with them—yourself.

The compulsive negative habit pattern is experienced physically in the form of tension in the neck and shoulders and pain in the lower back. It is usually manifested whenever you feel overloaded, "under the gun," or when you have too much to do and too little time. These physical pains are a major result of stress and overwork. They can lead to serious psychosomatic illnesses.

Women tend to manifest the fear of rejection in depression, withdrawal and physical symptoms. Men tend to manifest this compulsive negative habit pattern in what is called "Type A behavior." This behavior usually stems from the relationship between the father and the son, or the father and the daughter. It is caused by the feeling of the child that he or she never got the proper quality and quantity of love from his or her father.

For men, this unconscious striving for love from their fathers is transferred, in adult life, to the boss in the workplace. Type A behavior is then manifested as an over-concern for the approval of the boss. In extreme cases, this can cause a man to become obsessive about his work, even to the point of ruining his health and his family.

I remember when my father died, I took it very badly. I felt that

I had never been able to get it right—that I had never done the things necessary to get his complete love and acceptance. Two years after his death, I still felt a great sense of loss and emptiness whenever I thought about him.

Then, one evening, I took my mother out to dinner and shared my feelings with her. She was surprised and told me that I had no reason to be sad or upset. She explained that my father had never had very much love to give to anyone.

Because of his childhood and early experiences, he had very little love for himself, and therefore very little for his children, including me. She told me that there was nothing that I could have done to get more love than I got.

Over time, I have found that most men who suffer from Type A behavior are still trying to earn the love and respect of their fathers. But what I learned after my father died was that, whatever love you get, or got, from your father, that was all he had to give. There is nothing that you could have done, and nothing that you can do now, to change it. Once you understand and accept that, you can relax a little and then get on with the rest of your life.

THE SELF-CONCEPT IN BUSINESS

Every group of people, from a couple to a large organization, forms a self-concept. It is the overall personality of the people when they're together, or when they think of themselves as part of a larger whole. It can be called morale, or the culture, but it is much more. It is the general psychological tone of the organization. Above all, it is how happy the individuals are as part of the larger group. It is how proud and confident they feel, or don't feel, in their membership in the greater entity.

Each couple has a self-concept. It is the way they see themselves and feel about themselves when they are together. It's expressed in the amount they laugh together, or don't laugh. Couples and families with positive self-concepts are happy and enthusiastic about each other and about being together. Couples and families with negative self-concepts are characterized by constant complaining, criticizing and arguing.

Corporations have self-concepts as well, as does each division, department, or human grouping within the corporation, right down to the personality of the clean-up crew that comes in after hours.

The self-concept of a business is made up of three basic ingredients. The first, the self-ideal, is a combination of the vision, values, ethics and mission of the organization. Wherever these are clear and positive and committed to by top management, the people in the company are happier, more positive and more confident about themselves and where they're going.

One of the most profound and unavoidable responsibilities of management (or parents) is to clearly articulate this self-ideal, and then to embody their values in their behavior toward others, to repeatedly tell others what they stand for and believe in and then lead by example.

The second ingredient of the company's self-concept is the collective self-image. This is the way the company's management and employees see themselves and think about themselves. This self-image is largely determined by how well they feel they are doing their job, performing their functions. It is especially affected by the quality of their products and services, and by the way they feel they are perceived in the marketplace by their customers and suppliers.

When I work with companies whose sales are up, whose market share is growing and whose profits are respectable, everyone seems happy, outgoing and confident. When I deal with companies that are struggling, in the marketplace or for internal reasons, the employees are often like members of a team that is losing too many games. They are unhappy, unsure and negative about their prospects. They take it out on each other by criticizing, complaining and backbiting.

One of the jobs of the executive or team leader is to keep people's spirits up by continually telling them how good they are. Everyone looks upward for guidance on how to interpret what's happening. The executive's job is to keep morale high by putting the best possible spin on events and by keeping people focused on the possibilities of the future, rather than the problems of the past.

The final ingredient of the organization's self-concept, self-esteem, is the sum total of the ideals of the corporation, the current performance of the organization and how well each person feels he or she is being treated by superiors and coworkers. Managers who continually praise and encourage their people build high self-esteem in them. This high self-esteem is demonstrated in optimism, energy, creativity, cooperation and commitment. It is the hardest ingredient of all to build and maintain, but people who like and respect themselves as part of a first-class team become a powerful force in a competitive marketplace. They become a victory just looking for a place to happen.

A company, organization, department, division, work team or family with a positive self-concept is one in which people feel terrific about themselves. Creating such a group is the highest art of management. It is the supreme skill of the individual in society. With a high, positive self-concept people are more productive, more resilient, more confident and happier than they could ever be without it.

With this kind of team or family, you can do wonderful things. You can fulfill your potential as you help others to fulfill theirs.

LIFE'S GREATEST THREAT

The greatest problem of human life is fear. It is fear that robs us of happiness. It is fear that causes us to settle for far less than we are capable of. It is fear that is the root cause of negative emotions, unhappiness and problems in human relationships.

The only good thing about fear, if there is anything good, is that it is learned, and because of this, it can be unlearned.

The fear of failure and the fear of rejection are learned responses, programmed into you before the age of six. These fears usually set the upper and lower limits of your comfort zone. Because of them, you do enough not to be criticized or rejected on the low side, and you stay well within your limits so you can avoid risk or failure on the high side. Once you've slipped into your comfort zone, you stay there, attempting to avoid any feeling of fear or anxiety. Your fears hold you back from most of what is possible for you.

The opposite of fear is love, starting with self-love, or self-esteem. There is an inverse or opposite relationship between self-esteem and fears of all kinds. The more you like yourself, the less you fear failure and rejection. The more you like yourself, the more willing you are to reach out and take the risks that will lead you on to success and happiness. The more you like yourself, the more willing you are to take the actions that propel you out of your comfort zone and toward the achievement of your real goals and desires.

You begin the process of raising your self-esteem and overriding your fears by repeating the powerful words, "I like myself! I like myself! I like myself!" over and over.

Start off each day by repeating "I like myself" fifty or one hundred times until the words penetrate your subconscious mind. You will soon see and feel the difference in your self-confidence, your competence and your relationships with others. You will start to feel wonderful about yourself.

PROGRAMMING YOUR MIND FOR SUCCESS

Because of your self-concept, you become what you think about most of the time. Your dominant thoughts and aspirations become your reality. The things you think about, and the way you think about them, determine your levels of health, wealth and happiness in every area of your life. You can tell how much you really want anything by how willing you are to discipline your thinking in such a way that you keep your mind on *only* the things you want, and off of the things you don't want.

You have created your life today by all of your previous thinking. You are where you are and what you are because of yourself. You can change your future at any time by taking control of your conscious mind from this point forward. You can make your life into something wonderful—an experience of freedom, joy, health, happiness and prosperity—simply by deciding to do so, and by refusing to entertain any contradictory thoughts at the same time. It's up to you.

Because of the nature of your multidimensional mind, you can rewrite your master program by deliberately bombarding your mind with a series of messages, framed in different ways and coming from several directions. If you wanted to become physically fit, you would do exercises that engaged your whole body. If you want to become mentally fit, positive and healthy, you ensure that the messages coming into your conscious mind are consistent with the ideal life you want to live.

This change in the person you are, so you can enjoy the life you really want, is not easy. It has taken you your whole life to get to where you are today, with your current state of mind. It will take considerable effort on your part to change. Fortunately, it's worth it, and the results you get will be both rapid and out of all proportion to the effort you put in.

HOMEOSTASIS

To achieve different results, you must become a different person. You must change your goals and ideals for yourself and develop a new self-image. By the Law of Correspondence, your outer world will reflect your inner world. You must become a new person on the inside to permanently experience the good you desire on the outside.

The first and for most people the most difficult obstacle you will face is within yourself. It is your unconscious striving to remain consistent with what you've said and done in the past that holds you back.

This "homeostatic impulse" is another term for your *comfort zone*. It is your unconscious tendency to be drawn irresistibly toward doing what you've always done. This inability to break free of the tentacles of the past is the reason most people accomplish far less than they are capable of and remain unfulfilled and dissatisfied for most of their lives.

Homeostasis is neither good nor bad. It is a natural mechanism built in to you as part of your "standard equipment" to enable you to function automatically in a great number of areas. This mechanism keeps your body at 98.6 degrees Fahrenheit. It maintains chemical balance in your billions of cells and governs your autonomic nervous system. It is indispensable to the proper physical functioning of your body.

Whenever you think, say or do something contrary to your current habits, your homeostatic impulse attempts to pull you back into your comfort zone by making you feel uncomfortable and uneasy. Because you always move from discomfort toward comfort, you tend to move back toward what you're comfortable doing and move away from things that are new and challenging.

This is quite normal. Doing something different from what you're accustomed to makes you feel tense and uneasy. Even thinking about doing something different can be stressful. Moving out of your comfort zone can be so nerve-wracking, in fact, that most people never do it until they are forced to.

Your natural tendency, if you are forced out of your comfort zone, even if you weren't happy in it, is to recreate a new comfort zone similar to the one you just left. You will actually work to recreate a situation you didn't like in the first place.

Many people have had the experience of losing a job they didn't like and then going out looking for the identical job somewhere else. I remember losing my job as a dishwasher in the kitchen of a hotel, which was not a great job, and then spending the next few months applying for dishwashing jobs in other hotels.

It's vital that you be aware of this homeostatic mechanism. It's nature's way of keeping you consistent with the way you've been in the past. But all growth and progress requires you to move out of your comfort zone in the direction of something bigger and better. Greater success and happiness are only possible for you when you are willing to feel awkward and uncomfortable during the process of creating a new comfort zone at a higher level of effectiveness.

Beware the siren song of old habits, of the comfort zone, luring you to stay where you are, holding you back from all the great things that are possible for you. You must consciously and deliberately counter the pull of the comfort zone as you move upward and onward toward ever higher levels of accomplishment.

PSYCHOSCLEROSIS

The second major obstacle to change is a "hardening of the attitudes." This is rooted in fear, as is much of the homeostatic impulse. Psychosclerosis is your natural tendency to fall in love with your own ideas, and then to vigorously defend them against anything new.

The opposite of psychosclerosis is flexibility, the willingness to consider other points of view, other ideas, with the very real possibility that you could be wrong.

This mental flexibility is the mark of the superior person. The very act of considering all options in a particular situation enables you to see much more of what is possible for you. Instead of using your intelligence to find fault with alternative approaches, you suspend judgment long enough to see if you can't find something beneficial in a different idea, or in a new way of doing things.

This approach is essential in mental programming, in changing your mind for the better. A major reason people fail to move forward in life is that they become too rigid and inflexible in their ideas, especially in their ideas about themselves and what is possible for them. They then dwell on all the reasons why something would *not* work for them, rather than why it would. They act as their own prosecuting attorneys, building the case against themselves, and you as well, if you let them.

A major turning point in your thinking comes when you change your language from "whether" to "how." When you start thinking about *how* you are going to accomplish something you want, and you simultaneously refuse to consider whether it's possible or not, your entire mentality begins to change. You *do* get what you think about most of the time, and if you continually think in terms of *how* you can achieve it, and the specific actions you can take to move toward it, you are much more likely to be successful in the end.

THE POWER OF LOVE

Much of what you do is done either to get love or to compensate for lack of love, beginning in early childhood. The emotion of love exerts an enormous influence on your every choice and decision. Your self-ideal, the guiding mechanism of your self-concept and the regulator of your behavior, can be understood as your idea of the kind of person you need to be to earn the love and respect of the people you care about. Your self-esteem, what Dr. Nathaniel Branden calls "your reputation with yourself," is largely determined by how lovable and valuable you appear in your own thinking.

Many personality problems are rooted in "love withheld." Your adult personality is largely formed by the amount and quality of love you received during your formative years. Almost everything you do today—the goals you set, the dreams you have, the commitments you make—is influenced by the power of love in your life.

In fact, you are inevitably drawn toward the people whose love you both want and need, and you are inordinately influenced by their opinions. When you begin the process of reprogramming your mind, everything you do must be consistent with increasing the amount of love and respect you have for yourself, and that others have for you. Only in this way will you be continually motivated to make the effort necessary to become the person you are capable of becoming.

Who are the people whose love and respect are most important to you? What do you have to do and who do you have to become for them to love and respect you? These are core questions for a happy life.

THE POWER OF SUGGESTION

Second only to the power of love in determining how you think and feel is the power of suggestion. Your multidimensional mind is affected by everything that is going on around and within you. Your suggestive environment has an immense impact on everything you become and on everything that happens to you. Any change in your physical, mental or emotional environment can change the way you think, feel and act *in moments,* and thereby change your results.

You are immediately influenced by changes in temperature or noise level. You are instantly affected by conversations or confrontations with other people. One unkind remark can put you off for the whole day. One bit of good news can make you happy and cheerful for hours.

Unfortunately, unless you control them carefully, most of the suggestions in your environment will tend to be negative. The radio, television and newspapers are full of "negative sensationalism." Most conversations are filled with carping, complaining and condemning. Most people have developed the habit of "ain't it awful" thinking and talking. Their conversations are negative and critical.

The key to your mental programming is for you to take systematic and purposeful control of your suggestive environment. It is for you to create a mental world that is predominantly positive and consistent with the person you want to be and the life you want to live. Controlling your suggestive environment requires that you decide the ingredients of your "mental diet," for the indefinite future.

There are three additional mental laws you need to understand to effectively reprogram your mind and change your future. They are the Law of Habit, the Law of Practice and the Law of Emotion. They contain vital answers to questions about success and happiness, and they point to many of the solutions that you are seeking.

THE LAW OF HABIT

Virtually everything you do is the result of habit. The way you talk, the way you work, drive, think, interact with others, spend money and deal with the important people in your life are all largely habitual. Your behavior in every area of life is based on the accumulation of all your experiences, starting in infancy. Probably 95 percent of your actions and reactions are automatic, unconscious responses to your physical and human environment.

Your habits are major obstacles to your becoming the kind of person you want to be. Your habitual ways of thinking, feeling, talking and behaving are often roadblocks that stand between where you are today and where you really want to go. They keep you "running in place."

The Law of Habit is a vitally important mental law. It explains the comfort zone and success and failure as well as any other single principle. It has its counterpart in physics in Newton's first law of motion, which states that a body at rest tends to remain at rest, and a body in motion tends to remain in motion, unless acted upon by an outside force.

Your thinking and behavior are subject to the same principle. In the absence of an outside force, or a definite decision on your part to do something different, you'll keep on doing very much the same thing indefinitely.

You'll work in the same job, associate with the same people, eat the same foods, take the same route to work, engage in the same leisure activities, watch the same television, read the same books and live very much the same kind of life.

Habits are only good as long as they serve you, as long as their effect is to continually enrich and improve your life. It is when your habits become the major obstacles to your happiness that you have to modify them or change them completely.

Some people have developed the habit of being late for appointments or late completing assignments. But successful people are invariably punctual and dependable. People can rely on them. Successful people keep their commitments. And they respect the time of others by not inconveniencing them.

Others have the "television" or "newspaper" habit. They spend inordinate amounts of time each day watching television or reading the newspaper. Often they do both at the same time.

The most dangerous habits you can form, however, are mental habits. Because of the fact that whatever you think about continually you create in your life, your negative or self-limiting thoughts hurt you more than almost anything else you can engage in.

Your habitual modes of thinking are absolutely the most important things in your life. As Shakespeare wrote, "There is nothing either good or bad, but thinking makes it so." You live in a mental world. Nothing around you has any meaning except the meaning you give it with your thoughts. If you change your ways of thinking, you change your life.

Success and failure, happiness and unhappiness, are largely the result of habit, of the automatic ways you respond and react to what's going on around you. Changing habits that are no longer consistent with your higher purposes is one of the hardest things you'll ever do, and one of the most essential to the quality of your life. But unless you've already reached some level of excellence or perfection, you are living today with habits that you *must* discard if you are going to move forward. Remember, bad habits are *easy* to form, but hard to live with; good habits are *hard* to form, but easy to live with. Your job is to form good habits and make them your masters.

THE LAW OF PRACTICE

The good news is that all habits are learned, and they can therefore be unlearned. You are today, in every respect, the result of your conditioning, almost like a laboratory animal. You have been trained, or have trained yourself, to be the person you are, and to get the results in life that you're getting. Your training began before you were old enough to know what was going on, and you are today the result of the training you have engaged in over the years.

You can change if you *want* to. The Law of Practice states that whatever thought or action you repeat often enough becomes a new habit. You can develop any habit you consider desirable or necessary. You can become the kind of person you want to be if you can discipline yourself to think and act in a way that is consistent with your new, higher ideals long enough for them to become new habits. This is how you become a new and better person.

Because your outer world corresponds to your inner world, as you begin to develop more constructive ways of thinking and behaving, people and situations around you will begin to change, sometimes in the most remarkable and unexpected ways.

A friend of mine was involved in a messy lawsuit over a business matter. The more angry he became, the more determined and unreasonable became the other party, and so did his lawyers.

He finally decided to change his thinking. He deliberately let the whole situation drop out of his mind. He began to think charitably and compassionately about the other party. When the subject came up, he refused to allow himself to become involved or upset. He let it go.

Within a few days of his deciding to change his thinking about the lawsuit, the other person called, apologized for any misunderstanding or bad feeling, and proposed a reasonable solution. Instead of their going to court, the matter ended peacefully.

The new president of a fast-growing company was convinced that one of the executives he had inherited was playing politics and deliberately manipulating people and situations so he would appear to be more competent and more valuable to the organization than he really was.

The new president was on the verge of letting the executive go when he decided to change his thinking. He deliberately chose to reinterpret the behaviors of the executive in a favorable way. He then examined every action of the executive from the viewpoint of his being a loyal employee acting in the best interests of the company.

Somewhat to his surprise, he found that the executive's behavior was much easier to both understand and appreciate from this perspective. He saw that the executive, far from being political in his behaviors, was extremely competent and was running interference for the new president in areas in which he was not yet familiar. The relationship between the two changed immediately, for the better, right after the president changed his thinking and began assuming the very best of intentions on the part of the other man.

Your ability to take control of your mind and begin thinking the kind of thoughts that lead to the outcomes you desire is the starting point of the process that leads to complete freedom, happiness and self-expression.

THE LAW OF EMOTION

Your emotions are the energizing forces behind your thoughts. The more intensely you *feel* something, the greater effect that thought or circumstance will have on your life. Emotion is like an electric current, or fire, which can be either constructive or destructive, depending on how it is used.

The Law of Emotion states that 100 percent of your decisions and subsequent actions are based on emotion. You are not largely emotional, or 90 percent emotional and 10 percent logical, as has been assumed. You are *completely* emotional. Everything you do is based on an emotion of some kind.

Before I understood this point, I used to think I was doing the logical thing, the practical thing, the thing that "made sense" in a variety of situations. When I learned about the Law of Emotion, I realized that I was really a slave to my emotions, especially if I didn't take time to think about which emotions had the upper hand in a particular situation or decision.

Here's the key point: There are only *two* main categories of emotions: desire and fear. Most of what you do, or don't do, is determined by one or the other. And the things you do, or refrain from doing, because of *fear* greatly outweigh the number of things you do because of *desire*.

Most people are immobilized by fears of all kinds. They fear poverty or loss. They fear criticism or disapproval. They fear ill health. They fear being taken advantage of. Above all, they fear failure and rejection to the point where they are willing to "lead lives of quiet desperation" rather than to risk having any of their fears realized. Most of the population lives this way, most of their lives.

The more you desire or fear something, the more likely you are to attract it into your life. A thought without an emotion behind it has no power to influence you one way or the other. An emotion with no thought to guide it causes frustration and unhappiness. But when you have a clear thought, positive or negative, accompanied by an intense emotion of either fear or desire, you activate the various mental laws and begin drawing whatever it is toward you.

This is why it is so important for you to keep your thoughts on the things you want and keep them off the things you fear. Happy, effective men and women recognize the power of their thoughts and they are very emphatic about keeping them positive and constructive. Your mind is so powerful that you must control it with great firmness so that it is continually moving you in the direction you want to go, or it will move you away from your desires.

Changing your self-concept is not easy. It may be the hardest thing you ever do. And the most valuable. But it is not a matter of choice. Once you have made the decision to do something important and valuable with your life, to achieve your own ideal of personal greatness, you absolutely must go to work on changing your own mentality.

THREE ESSENTIAL CONDITIONS FOR CHANGE

There are three requirements for developing a new self-concept. These are the keys to changing the direction of your life. First, you must sincerely *want* to change. You must really want to become totally positive toward yourself and your possibilities. You must have an intense, burning desire to be more than you've ever been before.

Often, people ask me what they can do to get *others* to change. I remind them that the starting point of change, of accomplishing anything different or better, is *desire,* and desire is always personal. You can't want something for someone else, just as you can't set goals for someone else. It isn't that change isn't possible, it's just that it requires desire on the part of the person who expects to change, or it won't take place.

It's like the question, "How many psychiatrists does it take to change a light bulb?" The answer is, "Only one, but the light bulb must really *want* to change."

The starting point of your becoming a new and better person is for you to feel that the change is desirable or necessary, or both. The change, the goal, the new personality quality must be consistent with your values, your ideals and the person you would really like to be.

Second, you must be *willing* to change. Many people say they want to change, but, in their hearts, they are not really willing to give up the old life, the old associations and everything else that goes with them. One person may want to be healthy but may not want to give up cigarettes. Another person may want to be financially successful, but may not want to give up having a good time every night with his or her friends.

You must be willing to let go of the old person in order to become the new person. You must be willing to *stop* doing certain things, even if your friends disapprove, in order to *start* doing the things that are consistent with the new you. You must overcome the twin obstacles of *homeostasis* and *psychosclerosis,* of the comfort zone and of inflexible thinking.

Third, you must *be willing to make efforts*. You must be willing to persevere for a long time without much evidence of progress. What you are aiming for is a fundamental long-term improvement in your life. It's taken you many years to become the person you are. You must be willing to work very hard to become someone different.

MENTAL POWER IN TWENTY-ONE DAYS

One of the most powerful ways to change your mental habits and the future direction of your life is for you to go on a twenty-one-day Positive Mental Attitude (PMA) diet. For twenty-one days you keep your thoughts, words and actions consistent, all day, every day, with the goals you want to achieve and the person that you would like to become.

You need to stay on this diet for twenty-one days for two reasons. First, it takes an adult between fourteen and twenty-one days to develop a new habit of thought, a new "neural groove" in the brain, like a cow path across a pasture. Sometimes you will notice definite changes in yourself and your results much faster. But usually, habits that have taken a lifetime to form take longer than a few days to change or override.

The second reason you need to practice these methods for twenty-one days is for you to learn patience and persistence. It takes twenty-one days of calm, patience and warmth for a hen to hatch an egg. If a hen, with a brain the size of a pea, can discipline itself to sit on an egg for twenty-one days without seeing any change at all, then it is probably not too much to ask *you* to persevere patiently for the same period of time before expecting to see any changes. Patience in self-development is the key.

The wonderful thing about your self-concept is that it is in a continual state of evolution. You are continually evolving and growing and developing in the direction of your dominant thoughts. If you change your dominant thoughts about yourself for any period of time, your self-concept and your beliefs will begin to change and evolve in that direction as well.

The reason the self-concept of most people does not change appreciably over time is that they continue to think about the same things in the same way day after day, year after year. William James wrote, "If I see myself today as I was in the past, my past must resurrect itself and become my future."

But when you set big, exciting goals for yourself and the person you want to be, and then think about these things every day, you take full control of your mental evolution and the direction of your life. You become what you think about.

SEVEN WAYS TO CONTROL YOUR MENTAL LIFE

There is a series of actions you can take every day to saturate your mind with positive influences and to assure that you are continually bombarding yourself with suggestions that are consistent with the person you want to become.

Think about yourself, in a casual and relaxed way, as the person you would like to be, with the qualities you would like to have. Begin imagining what *life* would be like, what your *home* would be like, what your *work* would be like, what your *health* would be like, and the *standard of living* that you would most enjoy. Allow yourself to fantasize and luxuriate in the daydream and in the feeling of achieving your goals. This activity is the first signal that a new direction is being programmed into your subconscious computer.

1. Visualization

The first of these actions is visualization. This is perhaps the most powerful technique of self-image modification available to mankind. Your visual images become your reality. They intensify your desires and deepen your beliefs. They increase your willpower and build your persistence. They are enormously powerful.

There are four elements of a visualization. An increase in any one of them will accelerate the rate at which you create the physical equivalent of that mental picture in your life.

The first of these elements is *frequency*. How often you visualize a particular future event, goal or behavior has a powerful impact on your thinking, feeling and acting. People who accomplish extraordinary things visualize their desired results continually. They think about what they want to accomplish all the time. They replay the ideal image of their futures over and over, like projecting a slide on the screen of their minds. In fact, the frequency with which you visualize not only tells you how much you want to realize that picture but also intensifies your desires and your belief that it is achievable.

The second element in visualization is *vividness*. This refers to the clarity with which you see something in your imagination. There is a direct relationship between how vividly you can see a desired goal or result and how rapidly it appears for you.

You have often had the experience of thinking about something you wanted. Your first thoughts were vague and fuzzy, but as you thought about it more and more, and perhaps gathered information, your mental picture of what you wanted became clearer and clearer. Finally, when you could close your eyes and see it in complete detail, it materialized in your world. This is the way you achieve most goals.

Successful people are very clear about what they want, and of course, this refers to the clarity of their mental pictures. Unsuccessful people are unsure of what they want to be and do. Their fuzzy mental pictures are too vague to motivate them, or to activate the various mental laws to work in their behalf.

The third dimension of visualization is *intensity*. This refers to the amount of emotion that you combine with your mental pictures. When you intensely desire something, when you are excited and enthusiastic about your goals, or when you have a deep faith that you will realize a goal that you are working toward, whatever it is occurs much faster. Increasing the amount of emotion with which you accompany your visualizations is like stepping on the accelerator of your own potential. This is perhaps why Ralph Waldo Emerson wrote, "Nothing great was ever achieved without enthusiasm."

Unsuccessful people, on the other hand, are usually unmotivated and unexcited about what they are doing and where they are going. They have a general attitude of pessimism that keeps them functioning at a low level of energy. They tend to be more passive and accepting of things as they are, rather than being excited about things as they could be.

The fourth part of visualization is *duration*. This refers to the length of time you can hold the picture of something you want in your mind. The longer you imagine a desired future event, the more likely it is to appear. Whenever you can, you should get actual pictures of things or conditions you desire and look at them repeatedly, until they are accepted as commands by your subconscious mind. Your self-concept soon changes to be consistent with your new visual commands.

Do you want a new car? Then go to the dealership and take it for a test drive. Bring the brochures home, cut them up and put pictures of the car wherever you can see them. A friend of mine started doing this when he was broke and driving an old car. He test drove a new BMW every weekend. He even put a picture of the car he wanted on his steering wheel so he could imagine he was already driving the car of his dreams. And within one year, he had started a new job, learned a new set of skills, increased his income and was able to buy the car.

When you combine the elements of *frequency, vividness, intensity* and *duration* with your visualizations of anything you want to be, have or do in the future, you actually *supercharge* yourself and *accelerate* your movement toward it. You unleash your hidden powers to succeed and tap resources that enable you to accomplish things beyond anything you've ever done before.

Most successful people have developed this ability, through practice, to create clear, vivid mental pictures of themselves being the persons and doing the things they really want. And since your external performance is always consistent with your internal image or picture, if you *see* yourself as an excellent parent, spouse, executive or salesperson, you will *feel* more relaxed, confident and capable in that role. If you *see* yourself as awkward or clumsy in any role, you will *feel* tense and uneasy whenever you find yourself in that particular situation.

A PRACTICAL APPLICATION

For example, most people are terrified of public speaking, of standing up in front of an audience. If this is a fear of yours, here is how you can overcome it by using mental programming techniques with creative visualization.

First, you begin to think about how your life would be different if you were an accomplished public speaker. You think of how much more confident you would feel, and how much more you would be respected and admired by others when you gave an excellent talk. You then create a clear mental picture of yourself speaking to an audience. Recall an occasion when you were speaking to your friends, or members of your family, at a party, for example. See yourself relaxed and happy. Get the feeling of calmness, confidence and pride that goes with this image of effectiveness.

Each time you think of yourself speaking in public, recall this positive mental picture and see yourself as calm, relaxed and in control, with the people in your audience responding to you in a positive, supportive way.

To accelerate your self-image modification, you purchase books on public speaking and, as you read, you think of yourself doing what the author is describing. Perhaps you listen to an audiocassette program that instructs you on how to prepare and organize a talk. It tells you how to design the opening, the body of the talk and the closing. Perhaps you attend seminars and meetings and watch other speakers. As you do, you imagine yourself up there speaking to the audience. Over time you gradually find your fear diminishing and your desire to speak increasing.

Does this process work? It certainly does! It has worked for more than 3 million members of Toastmasters International since that organization was formed in 1923.

The Toastmasters process was designed for men and women who felt their careers were being held back because of their fear of speaking to groups, giving group presentations or even speaking up at meetings.

At a typical Toastmasters meeting, everyone gets an opportunity to stand up and speak, if only for a few seconds. The audience is made up of others who also want to be able to speak on their feet. They are positive and supportive of one another. When a member goes home, he has a mental image, or picture, of a positive speaking experience. And every time he goes to a meeting and speaks, that image is reinforced.

Here's a remarkable discovery: Your subconscious mind cannot tell the difference between a real experience and one that you vividly imagine. Every time that you recollect, remember and re-experience an event in your conscious mind, your subconscious mind accepts it and stores it exactly as if you had just repeated it.

What this means is that, if you have just one positive experience, in any area of your life, and you think about this positive experience over and over, you actually program yourself to do it again. And if you haven't had such a positive experience yet, you can *imagine* or create one in your mind and dwell on that. Your subconscious won't know that you made it up.

The power of visualization works with negative experiences as well. *One* negative experience, dwelled upon repeatedly, will de-motivate and discourage you in that area. So choose your thoughts and your mental pictures with care.

If you've had even one *positive* experience of speaking well before a supportive audience, you can recall and relive that experience whenever you think of public speaking. This process of repeated visualization enables you to actually program yourself for self-confidence and excellent performance in speaking in the future.

If you have a mental picture of yourself as fit and healthy, in a slim, trim body, and you visualize that picture over and over, your subconscious mind will gradually begin to adjust your appetite, your metabolism and your desire for exercise and healthy living. The excess weight will fall off and stay off. You will be "thinking thin," and it is the only known method for permanent weight loss that seems to work.

If you find yourself lacking confidence in any situation, cancel the negative thought by repeatedly visualizing yourself as calm, confident and relaxed when you're in that situation. Recall a situation in which you had a terrific time with a group of other people. Whenever you feel nervous around others, change your mental picture and think instead of a previous positive experience. Eventually, your subconscious mind will transfer the positive feeling associated with the positive situation over to the situation that usually causes you to feel tense and uneasy. Your fears will gradually diminish and disappear.

Use visualization to *flood* your mind at every opportunity with pictures of your ideal life. One way of doing this is to create a "treasure map" to look at. Design a poster for your wall with either your photograph or a picture of the goal that you wish to achieve in the center. Then cut out pictures, headlines and quotations from magazines and newspapers and paste them all over the poster. Create a powerful visual representation of the ingredients that symbolize success and achievement for you.

Take some time each day to stand in front of this poster and *drink in* the images, letting them soak into your subconscious mind. In each important area of your life, *dwell* upon your success experiences, real and imagined. Recall and relive them vividly. If you are in sales, for example, and you have had a successful sale, dwell on that sale repeatedly. Think about it vividly in every detail as often as you can. Each time you dwell on a success experience, your subconscious records it as though you are having yet another success experience of the same kind.

Using visualization, you can convince your subconscious mind that you are repeating the success experience over and over. Your subconscious mind will then make your words, your actions and your emotional responses fit a pattern consistent with the images of success that you have supplied to it.

The mistake that most people make is that they dwell upon and vividly imagine their failure experiences, what went wrong and how they goofed. Then they are surprised when they feel tense and anxious the next time they are in a similar situation.

All improvement in your life begins with an improvement in your mental pictures. Your mental pictures trigger thoughts, feelings, words and actions consistent with them. Visualization activates all the mental laws, including the Law of Attraction, drawing people and resources into your life to help translate your images into your realities.

2. Affirmations

The second technique of mental programming is the use of affirmations. Affirmations are based on the three "P's." They are *positive, present tense and personal*. Affirmations are strong statements or commands from your conscious mind to your subconscious mind. They override old information and reinforce new, positive habits of thought and behavior.

The affirmation "I like myself" is positive, present tense and personal. When you repeat it continually, it is eventually accepted as a valid description of the reality you desire. You actually begin to feel better about yourself in everything you do. This affirmation soon overrides old data you may have taken that is inconsistent with high self-esteem.

With affirmations, your potential is unlimited. Strong, affirmative statements, emotionalized and repeated with conviction, often bring about immediate personality changes. You can increase your enthusiasm, boost your courage, assert control over your emotions, and build up your self-esteem by repeating statements that are consistent with the person you want to be.

One of the most powerful influences on your subconscious mind is what you say to yourself and believe. Affirmations like "I can do it!" or "I earn $XXX per year" or "I weigh XXX pounds" can bring about lasting changes in your self-concept and in your results.

All change is from the inner to the outer. All change begins in the self-concept. You must become the person you want to be on the inside before you see the appearance of this person on the outside.

Your subconscious mind is very literal, and the simpler the command, the more impact it has on your thinking. For example, a powerful affirmation I use regularly to condition my mind is, "I *believe* in the perfect outcome of every situation in my life."

This affirmation makes you feel calm, positive and relaxed in dealing with any difficulty. It is a wonderful antidote to worry. "I believe in the perfect outcome of every situation in my life." It is an excellent antidote to worry.

It is also simple, clear and in the present tense. Your subconscious mind responds only to this type of command, to affirmations and mental pictures that are presented in the "now," as though the goal or quality already existed.

For example, instead of saying, "I am not going to smoke anymore" (both negative and in the future tense), you would say, "I am a nonsmoker."

This is a way of "telling the truth, in advance." This is how you convince your subconscious mind that the condition you desire already exists. Your subconscious then makes whatever changes are necessary, internally and externally, to align your inner world with your desired outer reality.

We have had a variety of interesting experiences with people quitting smoking. One of our graduates repeated, "I am a nonsmoker," several times a day for two months. Simultaneously, he visualized himself as a nonsmoker. Over that time, he gradually found himself reaching for a cigarette less and less often. By the end of the two months, he was down to one cigarette a day, and he finally quit and had no further desire to smoke even two years later.

Another seminar graduate did the same thing. He repeated, "I am a nonsmoker," over and over, but nothing happened. He continued to smoke two packs a day. He affirmed and visualized himself as a nonsmoker every single day, patiently trusting that the process of mental reprogramming would eventually work.

At the end of eight weeks, he woke up one morning, reached for a cigarette, lit it and almost choked. He said that he thought he had gotten hold of a "rotten" cigarette, whatever that is. He tried a second cigarette and a third. Each one of them made him retch. He suddenly realized that he had programmed himself into believing that smoking was a totally distasteful habit. He never touched a cigarette again.

You cannot change habits overnight. You must be patient and persistent in affirming and visualizing, confidently believing and expecting that, when you are ready, the desired changes will occur, and not before.

3. Verbalization

The third technique is to verbalize, to affirm aloud, with others, or alone, in front of a mirror. Standing in front of a mirror and saying very clearly and emotionally, "I can do it, I can do it, I can do it!" is a powerful way to build up your confidence for a coming challenge. Anything that you say aloud with conviction and enthusiasm has double the impact of an affirmation that you make quietly to yourself.

When you insist to *others* that you can or will do something, it has powerful impact on your thinking and your subsequent behavior. Sports teams use this method of verbalization with others to get themselves mentally prepared before a game. They chant and cheer together before they go out into competition.

Keep your conversation throughout the day consistent with what you really want to happen. Refuse to discuss your fears and misgivings. Be positive and optimistic in everything you say. Be cheerful. You'll be amazed at how much better you feel and how much more confidently you behave when your language is upbeat and success oriented.

4. Acting the Part

The fourth technique of mental programming is to walk, talk and act exactly as if you were already the person you desire to be. Behave as if you have already achieved the goals you've set for yourself. Act as if you were recognized and respected by everyone. Act as though you had money in the bank already. The power of this technique is explained by the Law of Reversibility.

This law states that, when you feel positive and optimistic, your feelings will generate actions and behaviors consistent with them. The opposite is also true. If you do not feel positive, but you act enthusiastically or cheerfully anyway, despite how you feel, *your positive behavior will generate positive feelings, just as your positive feelings generate positive behavior*. Your feelings and behavior are reversible.

It is almost impossible to "act the part" of a happy, cheerful person for more than five or six minutes without actually having a "backflow" experience in which your actions create the emotions that are consistent with them. Another way to put it is, "Fake it until you make it." Behave positively and enthusiastically and you will soon feel positive and enthusiastic.

The reason this method is so powerful is that, even if you cannot control your feelings at any given moment, you can control your actions. And if you control your actions, by this Law of Reversibility, you will create the emotional state that you desire.

Using this technique, you can deliberately create in yourself the mental qualities of a high-performing man or woman. You can act with purpose, courage, confidence, competence and intelligence. You can pretend that you already have each one of these qualities, and surprisingly enough, you will soon feel these qualities in yourself. People will then accept you and respond to you exactly as if you were the person you see yourself as being.

These four techniques are enough in themselves to completely transform your self-concept and your personality: Begin by thinking of yourself as you would ideally like to be. Then *visualize* yourself in vivid detail, as though you already were the person that you intend to become. *Affirm* to yourself, and *verbalize* aloud, strong, positive statements consistent with your goals. Remember as you do this that words do create emotion and crystallize thought. And finally, *keep your behavior consistent* with your new messages of success, happiness, prosperity and a positive personality.

5. Feeding Your Mind

Technique number five in the PMA diet is to feed your mind continually with words and images consistent with the direction in which you are growing. Read books and magazines for personal and professional development. Listen to educational audiocassettes at every opportunity. Watch educational videocassettes. Attend seminars and lectures and take additional courses that accelerate your development of these new habit patterns of thought.*

The more you read, listen, watch and learn about any subject, the more confident and capable you feel in that area. If you are in management, and you are continually learning how to be a better and more effective manager, you will more and more often see yourself and think about yourself as excellent in your field. If you are in sales, and you continually feed your mind with information and ideas that help you to be better, you will feel better about your ability to perform, and you will actually make more sales. As you improve your inner understanding, you improve your outer results.

6. Associating with Positive People

Technique number six is to get around the *right* people. Associate with winners. Fly with the eagles rather than scratching with the

---

* For a free catalogue of audio and video learning programs, plus a list of recommended readings, write to Brian Tracy, 462 Stevens Ave., Solana Beach, CA 92075, or phone 619-481-2977.

turkeys. Because of the strong suggestive influence that other people have on you, for good or for ill, you must be extremely careful about who you choose to spend time with.

Dr. David McClelland of Harvard found, after twenty-five years of research, that the choice of a negative "reference group" was in itself enough to condemn a person to failure and underachievement in life. Your reference groups are the people you identify with— the ones you work with, socialize with, live with and get involved with in community or nonwork activities. Like a chameleon, you unconsciously adopt the attitudes, behavior and opinions of the people with whom you most closely associate.

In selecting the people that you will spend time with, follow Baron de Rothschild's advice and "make no useless acquaintances." To meet new, positive people, you usually have to *stop* associating with your old group. Especially, get away from negative people. They are the primary cause of most unhappiness in your life.

Staying in a bad relationship can be enough in itself to cut off your full potential for success and happiness. There is no suggestive influence more powerful than the people around you. Select them with care.

7. Teaching Others

The seventh technique for internalizing these ideas is for you to teach others what you are learning. *You become what you teach*. You teach what you *are*. When you attempt to articulate and explain a new concept to someone else in order to help him or her, you understand it and internalize it better yourself. In fact, you only really know something to the degree to which you can teach it to someone else and have them understand and apply it in their own lives.

Developing new, positive habits of thought and behavior is not easy. It requires eternal vigilance. You must launch your new habits strongly. Never allow exceptions until the new habit is locked in. When you slip from time to time, the important thing is that you don't *dwell* on it. Your job is to keep your mind focused intently on the direction that you are going, on your dominant goals, and on the new person you are becoming.

Whatever you can hold in your mind on a continuing basis, you can have. Forget the way you were in the past. Discard past labels. It is how you see yourself, how you talk about yourself and how you act *now,* in the present, that is creating your future.

If you see yourself now as you wish to be, and you walk, talk, and behave as the very best person you can imagine yourself being, your dominant thoughts and goals will materialize as your reality. You *will* become what you think about most of the time.

ACTION EXERCISE

Select *one* positive habit pattern or behavior that you would like to develop, and for the next twenty-one days, discipline yourself to think, visualize, verbalize, affirm and behave in a manner consistent with the new habit you want to develop.

Whatever your goals and ambitions, think and talk in terms of their accomplishment. Read, learn, visualize, affirm and dwell on your goal. Think in terms of "how" you can achieve it. Act as if it were already a reality, if you can. At the very least, behave in every respect as if achieving your goal were inevitable.

The key to making these methods work for you is for you to demonstrate to yourself, in a specific area, that you can develop one important habit or attitude of your own choosing. Once you have proved this to yourself, you will have the self-confidence and the conviction to make any change or to accomplish any goal that you could set for yourself. Instead of wishing or hoping, you will *know* that your possibilities are unlimited.

The Master Mind

Your outer world corresponds to your inner world. What happens to you depends to a great degree on what is happening inside you. Your external experience is a reflection of your internal thought patterns. Over time, you create in your life the mental equivalent of your innermost convictions about yourself and what is possible for you.

As I read story after story of famous men and women, as I reflected upon their biographies and autobiographies, I was struck by the common thread that ran through all of them. They all seemed to have, or to develop, an unshakable belief in their ability to overcome all obstacles and reach some great height.

This belief or conviction seemed to give them powers not possessed by the ordinary person. They went on to accomplish remarkable things, often against overwhelming odds and in defiance of the predictions of people around them.

When I left high school and began drifting from job to job, I had no central aim or purpose aside from somehow "seeing the world." Like most people, I slipped into the "reactive-responsive mode." I took whatever job came along. I associated with whoever happened to be around at the time. Instead of planning my life, I just reacted to my external environment and responded to my emotional and physical needs.

I assumed that this was "all there is." I came to accept, unconsciously, that what I knew and what I was doing constituted the upper limits of what was possible for me. The best I felt I could do was to react as intelligently and as constructively as possible and try not to make too many mistakes.

When my studies in psychology, religion and metaphysics mentioned the subconscious mind, I neither understood it very well nor attempted to use it to help me. However, the more I learned about the mental laws that govern our behavior and determine our results, the more I realized there was a hidden dimension of achievement that I was missing.

The more I understood the importance of the self-concept and learned that everything we do is predetermined by our belief systems, the more I felt I was coming closer to the combination that would open the lock.

Then I understood the meaning of human potential. If you and I are using only 10 percent or less of our potential for effectiveness and achievement, the other 90 percent or more must be contained in mental powers we have not yet tapped. I concluded that, to get the most out of myself, I needed the "access codes" that would enable me to get into and harness these enormous capabilities.

Your subconscious mind is enormously powerful. When you use it properly, it can help you to move more rapidly toward the achievement of your goals and desires than you ever dreamed possible. You can use your subconscious mind for creation or destruction, for good or for evil. You can be a prince or a pauper, depending on the way you use your subconscious mind. To fulfill your potential, you must learn how to access it at will and use it for your purposes intelligently and constructively.

My lawyer was showing me through his offices not long ago. He took me into the typing pool where there were several secretaries typing letters and legal documents. Each of the secretaries was hooked into a minicomputer that was available and accessible to all of them. As we left the room, he explained to me that he and his partners had spent more than one hundred thousand dollars on this computer installation, which they had purchased about two years ago. He told me that when it was installed, all the secretaries working there at that time were given training in how to use the computer to increase the quantity and quality of legal work they could produce.

Over time, he said, all of the original secretaries had left or gone on to other things. They were replaced, one by one, with legal secretaries who had no computer training. "Because we are so busy," he said, "no one has had a chance to go back and train these new secretaries on how to get the most out of our computer system, so now instead of using this computer for advanced information and word processing, our secretaries simply use it as a glorified typewriter, typing one letter or one document at a time and spending many hours to produce what the minicomputer could produce in a few minutes."

Unfortunately, most people are like those secretaries. They work every day with their minds—but they use their powerful mental computers only for the most rudimentary tasks and then wonder why their work is so hard and why they seem to produce so little.

When I was washing dishes, I was convinced that the only way I could make more money was by working longer hours and by washing even more dishes. I eventually learned that the belief that you can only improve your life with longer hours and harder work leads you down a blind alley. The answer I found was to work "smarter," to use more of my *mental* powers rather than more of my *physical* powers to achieve my goals.

Successful people are those who have learned how to operate their conscious and subconscious minds in harmony, enabling them to get the things they want far faster and with much less effort. This discovery changed the focus of my efforts and the direction of my life.

TWO MINDS WITHIN ONE

Here is a simple model to help you visualize your subconscious mind, how it operates, how you can control its functions and what it produces in your life.

Imagine two balls stuck together, a golf ball and a basketball, with the golf ball on top. This picture represents the relative power and capability of your conscious and your subconscious minds, with the basketball being your subconscious. The two minds are essential to each other, but they have their own separate areas of operation.

In computer terms, your conscious mind is the programmer, inputting data very much like a computer operator, by what it decides to allow in to your thinking. Your subconscious mind is the hardware of your computer, the framework within which data operates. Your self-concept is the software program that determines what you produce in your life. All are necessary and interdependent, and everything that happens to you is determined by your understanding of this special computer language and also your skill at using it.

THE CONSCIOUS MIND

Your conscious mind is your objective or thinking mind. It has no memory, and it can only hold one thought at a time. This mind has four essential functions.

First, it *identifies* incoming information. This is information received through any of the six senses—sight, sound, smell, taste, touch or feeling.

Your conscious mind is continually observing and categorizing what is going on around you. To illustrate, imagine that you are walking along the sidewalk and you decide to cross the street. You step off the curb. At that moment, you hear the roar of an automobile engine. You immediately turn and look in the direction of the moving automobile to identify the sound and where it is coming from. This is the first function.

The second function of your conscious mind is *comparison*. The information about the car that you have seen and heard goes immediately to your subconscious mind. There, it is compared with all of your previously stored information and experiences with moving automobiles.

If the car, for example, is a block away, and moving at thirty miles per hour, your subconscious memory bank will tell you that there is no danger and that you can continue walking.

If, on the other hand, the car is moving toward you at sixty miles per hour and is only one hundred yards away, you will get a "danger" message that will stimulate further action on your part.

The third function of your conscious mind is *analysis,* and analysis always precedes the fourth function, *deciding*.

Your conscious mind functions very much like a binary computer, performing two functions: It accepts or rejects data in making choices and decisions. It can deal with only one thought at a time, positive or negative, "yes" or "no." It is continually sorting impressions, deciding which are relevant to you and which are not.

So, you are walking across the street, you hear the roar of the moving automobile, and you see that it is bearing down on you. Because of your knowledge of the speed of moving vehicles, your analysis tells you you are in danger and that some decision is required. Your first question is, "Do I get out of the way? Yes or no?" If the decision is "yes," then your next question is, "Do I jump forward? Yes or no?" If the decision is "no," because of cross traffic, then your next question is, "Do I jump backward? Yes or no?" If your decision is "yes," this message is instantly transmitted to your subconscious mind and in a split second, your whole body jumps back out of the way, with no additional thought or decision on your part.

You didn't have to use your conscious mind to think about whether you should put your right foot or left foot back first. Once you gave the command, from your conscious mind to your subconscious mind, all the necessary nerves and muscles were coordinated and put into action in a single instant to obey your decision.

The mathematician Peter Ouspensky, in his book *In Search of the Miraculous,* estimated that your subconscious mind functions at as much as thirty thousand times the speed of your conscious mind. You can demonstrate this speed of operation by holding your hand out in front of you and wiggling your fingers. By turning all coordination of movement over to your subconscious, you can do this easily. Then, try to thread a needle, this time using your conscious mind, and see how much mental effort and concentration you must exert to perform a few small movements of your hand, when your subconscious isn't operating.

Your conscious mind functions like the captain of a submarine looking at the surface through a periscope. Only the captain can see. Only the captain's perception of what is going on on the surface is available to the crew.

Whatever the captain sees, feels and decides is immediately relayed throughout the submarine and the entire crew swings into action to carry out his instructions.

You often feel limited in what you can do because you are so determined to be "in control." You are often convinced that the way to get better or different results is to "try harder." But this isn't the answer at all.

The way to really improve your life is to use more of your *master mind,* your subconscious powers, by understanding how to activate them. To do this, you need to know what your subconscious does and how it works.

YOUR SUBCONSCIOUS MIND

Your subconscious mind is like a huge memory bank. Its capacity is virtually unlimited. It permanently stores everything that ever happens to you. By the time you reach the age of twenty-one, you've already permanently stored more than one hundred times the contents of the entire *Encyclopaedia Britannica.* Under hypnosis, older people can often remember with perfect clarity events from fifty years before. Your unconscious memory is virtually perfect. It is your conscious recall that is suspect.

The function of your subconscious mind is to *store and retrieve data.* Its job is to ensure that you respond exactly the way you are programmed. Your subconscious mind makes everything you say and do fit a pattern consistent with your self-concept, your "master program."

Your subconscious mind is subjective. It does not think or reason independently; it merely obeys the commands it receives from your conscious mind. Just as your conscious mind can be thought of as the gardener, planting seeds, your subconscious mind can be thought of as the garden, or fertile soil, in which the seeds germinate and grow.

Your conscious mind *commands* and your subconscious mind *obeys.* Your subconscious mind is an unquestioning servant that works day and night to make your behavior fit a pattern consistent with your *emotionalized* thoughts, hopes and desires. Your subconscious mind grows either flowers or weeds in the garden of your life, whichever you plant by the mental equivalents you create.

Your subconscious mind has what is called a *homeostatic* impulse. It keeps your body temperature at 98.6 degrees Fahrenheit, just as it keeps you breathing regularly and keeps your heart beating at a certain rate. Through your autonomic nervous system, it maintains a balance among the hundreds of chemicals in your billions of cells so that your entire physical machine functions in complete harmony most of the time.

Your subconscious mind also practices homeostasis in your

mental realm, by keeping you thinking and acting in a manner consistent with what you have done and said in the past. All your habits of thinking and acting are stored in your subconscious mind. It has *memorized* all your comfort zones and it works to keep you in them. Your subconscious mind causes you to feel emotionally and physically uncomfortable whenever you attempt to do anything new or different, or to change any of your established patterns of behavior.

Your subconscious mind functions like a gyroscope or a homing beam, keeping you in balance and on track based on the data and instructions that you have previously programmed into it.

You can feel your subconscious pulling you back toward your comfort zone each time you try something new. Even thinking about doing something different from what you're accustomed to will make you feel tense and uneasy.

Applying for a new job, testing for a driver's license after several years, calling on new customers, taking up a new, challenging assignment or approaching a member of the opposite sex and feeling nervous or awkward—all are examples of your feeling out of your comfort zone.

A major difference between leaders and also-rans is that superior men and women are always stretching themselves, pushing themselves out of their comfort zones. They are very aware how quickly the comfort zone, in any area, becomes a rut. They know that complacency is the great enemy of creativity and future possibilities.

For you to grow, to get out of your comfort zone, you have to be willing to feel awkward and uncomfortable doing it the first few times. If it's worth doing well, it's worth doing poorly until you get a feel for it, until you develop a new comfort zone at a new, higher level of competence.

If you aren't willing to face feeling clumsy and inadequate initially—in sales, in management, in sports, in personal relationships—you will get stuck at a low level of achievement. Your biggest battle is almost always with yourself and your biggest challenge is in breaking free of your old habitual ways of thinking and acting.

In Chapter Two, I introduced seven mental laws and explained how everything that happens to you begins with your thoughts. In Chapter Three, I explained how your master program, your self-concept, determines how you think in the first place, especially the origination of your fears. Your subconscious mind contains the *hard disc* where the instructions for these laws are stored. In addition, there are three more laws that help to explain who you are today, and why things happen to you the way they do.

THE LAW OF SUBCONSCIOUS ACTIVITY

The Law of Subconscious Activity states that any idea or thought that you accept as true in your conscious mind will be accepted without question by your subconscious mind. Your subconscious will immediately begin working to bring it into your reality.

Your subconscious mind is the seat of the Law of Attraction, the sending station of mental vibrations and thought energy. When you begin to believe that something is possible for you, your subconscious mind begins broadcasting mental energies and you begin to attract people and circumstances in harmony with your new dominant thoughts.

Your subconscious mind regulates the type of information from your environment that you will see, hear and be aware of. It will sensitize you to any information that you've told it is important. And the more emotional you are about anything, the more rapidly your subconscious will alert you to things you can do to bring it into your reality.

For example, if you decide that you want to buy a red sports car, you will suddenly start to see red sports cars at every turn. If you start to plan a foreign trip, you will begin to see articles, information and posters on foreign places everywhere you go. Your subconscious mind works to bring to your attention the things you may need to make your desires a reality.

When you begin thinking about a new goal, your subconscious takes this new thought as a command. It begins to adjust your words and actions so they are more consistent with your achieving it. You begin to do and say the right things at the right time to help you move toward it.

As you change your self-concept, and your beliefs about your possibilities, your subconscious mind gradually makes you feel more comfortable, more confident as the new, better person you are becoming. You actually create a new comfort zone for a better, higher level of personal performance.

THE LAW OF CONCENTRATION

The Law of Concentration states that whatever you *dwell* upon, grows. The more you think about something, the more it becomes part of your reality.

This law explains much of success and most of failure. It is a paraphrase of the Law of Cause and Effect, or sowing and reaping. It says that you cannot think one thought and get a different result. You cannot plant oats and get barley. Successful, happy people are those who have developed the ability to concentrate single-mindedly on one thing, and to stay with it until it's complete. They discipline themselves to think and talk only about what they want, and to keep their minds *off* what they don't want.

Ralph Waldo Emerson wrote, "A man becomes what he thinks about most of the time." Effective people guard the doorways of their minds diligently. They remain focused on what's really important to them. They dwell on their desires for the future and refuse to entertain their fears and doubts. As a result, they seem to accomplish extraordinary things in the same amount of time that the average person spends just living from day to day.

When I became excited about my own personal development, I went from focusing on too little to reading and getting involved in too much. I scattered my energies everywhere. I diffused my focus. I was busy, committed and overactive. I was positive and excited about many possibilities and I was negative and critical about others. I was like a car careening from one side of the road to the other, often ending up in the ditch.

I eventually learned that "more is less." I learned that the Law of Concentration is very powerful and that I couldn't be working on several things at once and end up doing any of them particularly well.

So I cut back. I stopped every activity except for the one or two that were most important to me. Most of all, I disciplined my thinking and dedicated myself to concentrating on and talking only about what I really wanted.

Here is a test for you: For one day, twenty-four hours, see if you can think about and talk about only the things you want. Resolve to keep your conversation free of all negativity, doubt, fear or criticism. Discipline yourself to speak cheerfully and optimistically about each person and each situation in the world around you.

It won't be easy. It might not even be possible for you, at first. But this exercise will show you how much of your time and energy is spent thinking and talking about things you don't really want. This exercise, repeated, will open your eyes and prepare you to get the most from the ideas coming in the chapters ahead.

THE LAW OF SUBSTITUTION

This is one of the most important of all the mental laws. It is an extension of the Law of Control. It states that your conscious mind can hold only one thought at a time, and that you can substitute one thought for another. This "crowding out" principle allows you to deliberately replace a negative thought with a positive thought. In so doing, you take control of your emotional life. This law is your key to happiness, to a positive mental attitude and to personal liberation. It can change your relationships, your conversations and the predominant content of your conscious mind. Many people have told me this law alone has changed their lives.

Your conscious mind is never empty; it is always occupied with something. By using the Law of Substitution, you can replace any negative or fearful thought that may be troubling you. You can deliberately substitute a positive thought in its place.

This powerful method of mental control is how you keep your mind calm and at peace. You *choose* to think about something uplifting, like your goals, whenever you are faced with a situation that would normally upset you.

In using the Law of Substitution to change your mind from negative to positive, the fastest way is simply to stop talking and thinking about the *problem* and to start talking and thinking about the *solution*. Focus your mind on what can be done in the future rather than what has happened in the past.

Thinking about a solution is inherently positive. When you think about what you can *do,* what action you can take, rather than dwelling on what has happened, your mind becomes calm and clear in an instant. Thinking about someone you care about, or your next vacation, is another way to use this law. Your objective is to find ways to keep your mind positive by consciously choosing to replace negative thoughts with positive thoughts. And you are always free to choose your thoughts.

One of the most powerful things you can say, over and over, to build your self-esteem and improve your overall self-concept is, "I like myself! I like myself! I like myself!"

Whenever things go wrong, or you feel unhappy for any reason, you can neutralize the feelings with the words "I like myself."

Every time you say, "I like myself," and especially when you say it with enthusiasm and conviction, your subconscious mind accepts it as a command. It then works to override and cancel any previously recorded messages you may have taken in that are inconsistent with high self-esteem and peak performance.

Many of our seminar graduates have transformed their personalities by simply repeating "I like myself!" fifty or one hundred times every day. You'll feel good about yourself the first time you say it, and as you repeat it over and over, you'll feel better and better.

ACCELERATING SUBCONSCIOUS ACTIVITY

In Chapter Three, on the master program, we talked about several methods of self-concept development, and how you could take control over your own personal evolution by saturating your mind with messages and inputs that are consistent with the person you want to become.

The methods of visualization, affirmation, verbalization, acting the part, associating with the right people and feeding your mind with the appropriate books, tapes and articles are tested and proven ways to change your thinking about yourself and your possibilities. They work consistently and predictably. They should become as natural to you as you go through your day as breathing in and breathing out.

These techniques of mental programming are similar to the commands you use when you are operating a computer. They are straightforward and effective, and they enable you to get results faster than in any other way. They are indispensable to your personal and professional growth.

But they are not enough. They are "basic commands." There are even faster working methods. Just as there are "power commands" in computer programs that allow you to accelerate the process of generating output, there are a series of special techniques you can use to greatly speed up the process of subconscious reprogramming. These techniques enable you to change your self-concept and your attitudes of mind at a speed that is often amazing. And since your outer world quickly reflects your new inner world, you immediately begin to see changes in your external reality.

In times past, many of these principles and techniques were guarded and only made available to a small number of carefully selected people. Some of these methods of rapid reprogramming have only been developed in the last few years. The one thing they have in common is that they have been proven to work by countless thousands of people through the ages. They are the keys to the lock in the door of personal transformation.

To benefit the most from these techniques, you need intense, burning desire for personal improvement. You need the ability to trust, and to persist patiently, confidently, knowing that there is a cumulative effect to all of your efforts, and that you will ultimately achieve the riches and rewards that you desire.

THE DISCOVERY OF THE SUBCONSCIOUS

The first giant step in the field of personal transformation was made by Doctor Emile Coué in Geneva in 1895. His clinic was achieving recovery rates averaging five times faster than any other similar hospital or clinic in Europe. His technique was so simple that for a long time, it was not believed or accepted. He simply taught each of his patients to say, "Every day in every way, I'm feeling better and better."

The doctors and nurses would greet each patient by saying, "Every day, in every way, you are looking better and better." As simple as this sounds, it worked wonders in bringing about rapid healing and recuperation from a variety of major and minor illnesses.

The success of Dr. Coué led to further work by a German doctor, Johannes Shulz, on methods to accelerate healing. Dr. Shulz was a psychologist and was looking for ways to help people overcome depression, neurosis, anxiety and other mental conditions that were interfering with their happiness. What he discovered was that the more *relaxed* one was while talking to oneself and saying,

"Every day in every way, I'm feeling better and better," the faster one recovered.

Dr. Shulz eventually developed the process known as "autogenic (self) conditioning." He found that if you used a systematic process to relax the patient and then encouraged him or her to visualize and affirm positive, constructive messages, the new information seemed to go straight to the subconscious mind, and once it was accepted by the subconscious, rapid and noticeable improvements in physical and mental health could be seen.

Over the years, autogenic conditioning was developed extensively in Europe and it is now extremely popular in most European countries. It has reached such a sophisticated level today that it is now used to help people with a variety of things, from mental disorders of all kinds to sales effectiveness, public speaking and athletic training.

The East Germans developed autogenic conditioning to the highest level of any country in the world. Their techniques were so advanced that they were treated as state secrets. By using these techniques, the East Germans won more gold medals per capita in the Olympics than any other country in the world. Autogenic conditioning enabled them to program their athletes to perform at extraordinary levels.

One of the reasons autogenic conditioning works so well is that it uses a vitally important mental law, the Law of Relaxation. This law states that "in all mental working, effort defeats itself."

This is the opposite of the way things work in the physical world. If you wish to drive a nail into a board in the material realm, the harder you hit the nail, the faster and deeper it will penetrate.

However, if you wish to develop a new pattern of thought, the opposite is true. The more you relax, or "don't try," the faster the thought seems to be accepted by your subconscious mind and the faster the physical result of the thought or goal appears in your world.

Here is an example of a technique based on the principles of autogenic conditioning and relaxation that has had an incredible impact on my life and the lives of many others. It is so powerful it should be taught to everyone. It is almost infallible in enabling you to achieve your goals. It will enable you to conquer worry and fear and to generate feelings of calmness, confidence and self-control.

This technique is based on another application of the Law of

Reversibility. You recall the first application of this law. It states that, just as feelings generate actions, actions generate feelings. You can act your way into feeling, and the feeling will then generate the actions consistent with it. Either one can create the other. This is an essential aspect of accessing your master mind and unlocking your potential.

The second application of the Law of Reversibility is that, just as an *objective* state, an actual accomplishment or a success of some kind, creates a *subjective* state, the feeling of happiness and achievement, the subjective state will also create the objective state.

To put it another way, if you can create the feeling, or the emotion, that you would experience if you accomplished a goal or solved a problem, and you can hold that feeling, the feeling will create, in your physical world, the result that goes with it—the result that would trigger the emotion if the result had *actually* occurred.

THE END OF THE MOVIE

Here is an illustration. Imagine you go to a theater to see an exciting adventure movie. You arrive at the theater ten minutes before the earlier scheduled movie is over. Instead of waiting in the lobby, however, you go into the theater, sit down and watch the last ten minutes of the movie.

You see how the entire plot unfolds and how everything turns out for the principal actors. You see the problems resolved and what happens to everyone when the movie ends.

Then, when the next showing begins, you go back and sit through the entire movie from the beginning. Only this time, instead of being caught up in the suspense and drama of the unfolding plot, you relax and watch the movie objectively. You take time to appreciate the cinematography, the dialogue, the way that the scenes are connected and how the plot unfolds and develops. You are calm and relaxed. You are far less anxious or emotional than you would be if you had not already seen the last ten minutes. Because you *already* know how it ends.

SPEED UP THE PROCESS

This is exactly the same method you use to program your new self-concept, and your goals, into the deeper levels of your subconscious mind, where they "lock in" and take on a power of their own. The *emotional* component is critical. It is the calm, confident, expectant, positive emotion, combined with relaxation, that activates your subconscious and brings about rapid change. This mental state, self-induced, is followed very quickly, sometimes instantaneously, by the physical manifestation of your desired result.

Here is a five-step process you can use to implement this method to help bring about any desired mental, emotional or physical condition.

Step one, *verbalize and affirm* your desired outcome. For example, if you are wrestling with a problem involving someone else, you could say, calmly and confidently, "This situation is resolved happily with good for all concerned." Your statement should be a clear description of your desired outcome or end state. Don't get wrapped up in detail. Don't worry about the process.

Step two, *visualize* and clearly see the outcome you desire in this situation. See yourself, and everyone else involved, happy and at peace with the outcome. This will require effort and concentration.

Step three, *emotionalize* your combined affirmation and visualization by creating "the feeling" that you will actually experience when everything is resolved happily. Imagine yourself already successful, the goal already attained.

Step four, and this is the catalyst in the process, *release* the situation completely. Let it go just as you would if someone you trusted said that he would take care of it and that you need not ever think about it again.

Step five is *realization,* the appearance in your outer world of the solution. The realization or manifestation of your desire is in direct proportion to the extent to which you have completely released all concern for the outcome and turned your mind to other things. "According to your faith, it is done unto you."

Once more, the five steps to activating the Law of Reversibility are (1) verbalization, articulating in words the desired outcome; (2) visualization, creating a clear mental picture of what the outcome will look like; (3) emotionalization, creating in yourself the feeling of satisfaction that would accompany the resolved situation; (4) releasing all concern while you turn your mind to other things; and finally, (5) realization, the appearance of the solution, or the achievement of your goal.

This attitude of calm, confident expectation that all will be well is an experience of higher consciousness. Religious people refer to this as prayer, and it is said that prayer is the highest form of affirmation. Ralph Waldo Trine called this state of consciousness being "In Tune with the Infinite." It doesn't matter what you call it. All that matters is that it works with amazing reliability. The reason for this is that it activates your *superconscious mind,* which we'll discuss thoroughly in Chapter Six.

ACCELERATING THE PROCESS OF CHANGE

There are several additional mental techniques you can use to activate your master mind and accelerate the process of inner change and external realization. Each of these methods is a *combination* of the mental programming techniques for changing your self-concept explained in Chapter Three.

Each of them is extremely effective and when you use them regularly, alone or together, you can transform yourself and your life in wonderful ways.

Written Affirmation Technique

The first of these methods for accelerated change is "written affirmation technique." To use this technique, you sit down with a pad of paper or a notebook, preferably in the morning, and write out a clear, present-tense description of your major definite purpose or goal, exactly as you would like to see it in reality. The description can be as long or as short as you like. It can be brief or detailed. You can write a present-tense description of the way you would like to see the events of the day unfold, or you can describe how you would look and feel with the new personality qualities you desire.

Once you've written out your goals, put down your pen, close your eyes, breathe deeply, and visualize your goal as accomplished, or *see* the events of the day unfolding satisfactorily. As you visualize, create the *feeling* that would go with your imagined success. Smile and enjoy the pleasure that would accompany the achievement of your goals. Then, release it completely, let it go, open your eyes, and carry on with your day.

Writing is a powerful way to imprint your goals on your subconscious mind. Many people have had the experience of writing out a list of their goals for the year on January first, just once, and then rereading the list at the end of the year and finding that most of the goals have somehow been achieved.

The more often you write out your goals, the more rapidly they materialize. Use a spiral notebook and write them down every day. It only takes a few minutes, but it programs you for the hours ahead. Writing and rewriting your goals convinces you more and more that they are attainable. As your conviction deepens and your confidence grows, you become more alert and aware of opportunities to make them a reality. You activate the Laws of Attraction and Correspondence and the goals begin to materialize around you. Many of our seminar graduates have been astonished at how rapidly their lives began to improve once they began using this technique.

Standard Affirmation Technique

The second mental programming technique you can use is "standard affirmation technique." This consists of writing out your goals in bold letters on a series of three-inch by five-inch index cards. You write the things you want as affirmations, in the present tense and in words that are clear and definite.

This method is best used twice per day, morning and evening. Find a place where you can be alone and quiet for a few minutes. Take several deep breaths to relax your body and prepare your mind. Exhale slowly. Sit comfortably with your cards in your lap. Then read the first of your goals. Close your eyes and repeat it to yourself five times. Visualize your goal as it would be if it were already achieved. Imagine how you would walk, talk and act if the goal were a reality right now. Emotionalize your picture of the goal and create the feeling of pleasure and happiness that would accompany successful accomplishment of your desire.

Then take another deep breath, exhale and release the goal confidently. Do this with each of your goals. Your subconscious mind can work effectively in this way on ten to fifteen goals at a time. (You'll learn an advanced system for setting your goals in Chapter Five, The Master Skill.)

This entire exercise should not take more than thirty to sixty seconds for each goal, for a maximum of fifteen minutes for fifteen goals. By doing this in the morning before starting out, you send a strong set of signals to your subconscious mind. It then activates the Law of Attraction and heightens your awareness of anything going on around you during the day that could help you accomplish one or more of your goals. By reviewing your goals in this way again in the evening, immediately before sleeping, you set your subconscious mind to work on your goals during the night. Often, it will bring you ideas and solutions when you awake in the morning.

Quick Affirmation Technique

The third acceleration method is called "quick affirmation technique." You can use this technique before any *nonrecurring* event of importance, such as a sales call or a meeting with your boss. This method of mental programming is used by professional speakers, actors, entertainers and top business people. They use it to prepare themselves for upcoming events when it is important that they be at their best.

The quick affirmation technique consists of telescoping the steps to mental preparation we discussed earlier. It is like a mental warmup. You can do it in less than thirty seconds. You can use this technique in your car, in the elevator, or even in the washroom.

The way it works is simple. You get by yourself, close your eyes, affirm the ideal outcome, visualize it, emotionalize it and release it. See and feel the event working out successfully. Then go into the meeting (or whatever) with calmness and confidence.

If you have an important presentation or interview coming up in a few days, you should use this technique every time you think about it. Instead of looking forward with nervousness and anxiety, use the Law of Substitution and perform this quick affirmation technique. As you get closer and closer to the actual day and hour, you will feel yourself growing in confidence and self-assurance. By the time the actual event arrives, you will be mentally prepared to perform at your best.

Autogenic Conditioning: The Method

The fourth accelerating technique is the complete process of "autogenic conditioning" that we discussed earlier. This is a more elaborate exercise, in which you systematically relax your entire body before affirming, visualizing, emotionalizing and releasing.

In its simplest form, you can get most of the benefits of auto-

genic conditioning by assuming a comfortable position, either sitting in a comfortable chair or lying on a bed. You close your eyes,
breathe deeply and begin talking to the six parts of your body—
your left arm, your right arm, your left leg, your right leg, your
chest and your head.

These are the words that seem to work the best. Begin by
repeating six times, one breath to one repetition, "My left arm is
becoming heavy and warm." Then repeat six times, "My left arm is
now heavy and warm." Finally, say six times, "My left arm is *completely* heavy and warm."

Each time you inhale and exhale, you speak one command.
Repeat this process with each of the other five parts of your body,
going from your left arm to your right arm, then from your left leg
to your right leg, then to your chest and finally to your head and
neck.

In less than ten minutes, you will have talked your body down
into a deep state of relaxation. Your mind will be in the alpha state.
You will then be ready for deep programming.

This technique is sometimes called self-hypnosis or autosuggestion, and is extremely effective in two areas. First, you can use it to
overcome fears and build confidence in your relationships, work,
financial life, health and other activities. It can even help solve such
problems as call reluctance in salespeople, fear of public speaking
and nervousness in dealing with any challenge of daily life. Second,
you can use it to accelerate the development of motor skills and
sports ability in areas such as tennis, golf, skiing, hockey, figure
skating, football, and basketball.

It is a form of mental rehearsal. You practice the movements
over and over in your imagination, visualizing perfect performance
every time and programming that image of excellence into your
subconscious mind.

Your subconscious mind cannot tell the difference between a
real experience and one that you *vividly imagine,* especially one that
you vividly imagine when you are deeply relaxed. Your subconscious merely accepts the mental picture as a command to guide
future action. The next time you actually perform the activity you
will be much more relaxed and confident. You will be noticeably
better than you were before.

Most gold-medal-winning Olympic athletes use this technique

or something similar to it. Successful business people use it to give themselves the psychological advantage in any meeting, negotiation or confrontation. And it works better and better the more you practice it.

Heterogenic Conditioning

The fifth technique of rapid mental transformation is called "heterogenic conditioning." This is conditioning or programming by someone other than yourself.

Your self-concept has been formed largely as the result of two primary forms of suggestion: *autosuggestion,* the things that you have said to yourself and believed, and *heterosuggestion,* the things that other people have said to you that you have believed. Everything you believe to be true about yourself today is the result of one of these influences, especially the second.

You are already aware of some examples of heterogenic conditioning. These are the things that your parents, your older relatives, your teachers or other people you respect have told you about yourself. Other heterogenic examples are lectures or audiocassette programs in which the speaker uses the word "you" in making each recommendation.

Whenever you hear the word "you" attached to a message, it influences your subconscious mind. That is why you must never allow anyone to say anything to you about yourself that you do not sincerely desire to be true. You are dealing with a very powerful principle and you must use it deliberately in a positive and constructive way.

THE LOZANOV EXPERIMENTS

During the 1950s and 1960s in Bulgaria, psychologist Georgi Lozanov conducted extensive research on the process by which people learn and permanently record information. He was intrigued by examples of "superlearning" from around the world, such as the fact that Muslim students memorize and recite the entire Koran, a book the size of the New Testament, before entering any Muslim university.

Lozanov found entire religions in India with no written books or materials. The masters and disciples of these religions passed down their teachings *orally* from one generation to the next. He met people who could recite religious teachings for hours with no reference to notes.

As his research progressed, Lozanov became interested in the idea that each of us actually has *two* brains, a right and a left hemisphere, and they perform different functions.

For example, the left brain is the logical, linear, practical brain. It is responsible for reasoning, analysis and calculation. It is the mathematical, verbal, sequential, pragmatic and skeptical side of the brain. It is responsible for language and for processing facts and is concrete and straightforward. It is the "no-nonsense" or engineering side of the brain.

The right hemisphere of the brain is very different. It thinks in terms of pictures and stories. It is holistic, dealing with all aspects of an idea or situation simultaneously. The right hemisphere is intuitive, musical and creative. It is the artistic, abstract and imaginative side of the brain.

The left brain seems to be stimulated by intense, logical, linear presentation of information. The right brain seems to process information best in a state of relaxation. What Lozanov discovered was that it was when both brains were working together harmoniously that rapid learning took place.

Lozanov went on to pioneer research into the various levels of brainwave activity—beta, alpha, theta and delta. He found that in our normal waking state, *beta,* the brain functions at fourteen waves per second or faster. In *alpha,* the relaxed or meditative state just below beta, the brain functions at eight to thirteen waves per second. This seemed to be the ideal brain wave level for learning.

The third level of brain wave activity is theta, five to seven waves per second, and the fourth is delta, the state of deep sleep, where brain waves slow to one-half to four waves per second.

Lozanov was interested in accelerating the speed at which the brain absorbed and stored new information. He developed what is today called "accelerated learning" by combining all these findings into a new way to learn and retain information of any kind.

Lozanov discovered that if you could put a person into a deep state of relaxation, into alpha, and then present new information while gentle classical music played in the background, the right and left brains would synchronize and learning would take place at a rapid rate.

His experiments involved having classes of adults sit deeply relaxed with their eyes closed while music played softly in the room. The instructor would then read lists of words in a foreign language, repeating them in different ways.

Afterward, the students would be brought to full alertness and tested for retention. With this method, the students learned at a remarkable rate. They remembered 98 percent of what they had been taught.

In 1969, Lozanov was able to teach students 150 new words per three-hour session, easily three to five times the rate of learning in a traditional language school. Later, he increased the learning rate to 500 words per day and then to 1,000 new words in a single day, by using more advanced combinations of relaxation, music and repetition.

In 1974, with a special class of students, Lozanov increased the learning rate to 1,800 new words of a foreign language in one day, still maintaining a retention level of 98 percent.

In 1979, Lozanov was able to teach a special class 3,000 new words, the equivalent of fluency in a foreign language, in a single day. Six months afterwards, these students could still recall 60 percent of what they had learned, compared with the 10 percent average recall rate in an American university. The work of Lozanov demonstrated that rapid learning is possible—not only for facts and information, but also for new behaviors and new mental habits.

TAPED AFFIRMATIONS WITH MUSIC

By combining the discoveries of Lozanov with a combination of affirmations, music and relaxation, you can vastly accelerate the speed at which you achieve your goals and develop the personality characteristics you desire. This form of heterogenic conditioning is the use of *taped affirmations with music*.

There are two ways you can use this particular method. The first is by listening to subliminal tapes, which I do *not* recommend. You simply do not know what message is on the tape. Some of the expensive tapes sold in the mass marketplace have been found to have no messages on them at all.

The second method of taped affirmations with music is called "progressive relaxation." With this method, a clear voice counts you down into a state of deep relaxation against a background of gentle classical music. This combination of words and music activates your right brain and drops you into the alpha state. While you are in this state of relaxed awareness, the positive messages, combined with the music, bypass your critical, conscious mind and go straight into your subconscious, where they bring about rapid personality change.

Taped affirmation with music is healthy and refreshing in its own right. At the end of a series of positive messages, the voice on the tape counts you back to full alertness. You open your eyes feeling relaxed, refreshed and happy.

Taped affirmation is effortless and easy. A typical taped affirmation process is only about twenty minutes long. It is a form of *active* meditation. If you practice it twice a day, morning and evening, you will be more positive, more relaxed, more creative and in far better control of your emotions. Many of your minor ailments will clear up, and I am aware of cases in which major illnesses disappeared when people started using this technique regularly.

You can create your own affirmation tapes* and put your own goals onto them. You simply play relaxing music that you enjoy on one record or tape player, while you read your affirmations, with the music in the background, onto a second tape player. It is very hard to make a mistake, and even a homemade tape can be very effective in programming you to achieve your goals.

COMBINING DIFFERENT METHODS

Sometimes people ask me which of these methods they should use. My answer is that you should use as many of them as you feel comfortable with, and whichever one is most convenient for you at any given time. Ideally, your entire day should be one continuous affirmation. You should be walking, talking and behaving in a cheerful and positive manner, visualizing and feeling enthusiastic about everything you do.

Your mental movies, combined with emotionalization, are the previews of your life's coming attractions. Your biggest single job

---

* If you would like your own prerecorded Affirmation Tape, 22 minutes long, complete with ten powerful affirmations plus music, phone 619-481-2977, or see the instructions in Appendix C.

is to exert the self-control, self-mastery and self-discipline needed to keep your words, thoughts and pictures *off* what you don't want and focused squarely *on* what you do want. Add to this a dash of confident expectations and you are on your way to a positive mental attitude and a happy, satisfying life.

PUTTING THESE TECHNIQUES TO WORK

Take a specific situation in your life, an upcoming event or something that is worrying you and causing you stress. Each time you think of the situation, apply the quick affirmation technique and then release it. Do this until the event has passed successfully or the situation has been resolved satisfactorily.

Next, get yourself a package of three-inch by five-inch index cards. There are packages available with spiral binding that you can make into your own affirmation book. Write out your goals, one per card, in clear, present-tense language. Review them twice per day using the standard affirmation technique until you see your goals materializing around you.

Make your own relaxation tape with music and listen to it regularly, until the messages are firmly embedded in your subconscious mind and you begin to see the results in the world around you.

As you go through your day, behave as if you are already the kind of person you want to be, and as if you have already achieved the goals you want to achieve.

Get that "end of the movie" feeling and just relax. Carry yourself with calm confidence and positive feelings of success and happiness, knowing that if you can hold it in your mind, you can have it. And you will.

AN OLD FABLE

Many years ago, in ancient Greece, a traveler met an old man on the road and asked him how to get to Mount Olympus. The old man, who happened to be Socrates, replied by saying, "If you really want to get to Mount Olympus, just make sure that *every step you take is in that direction.*"

The moral of the story is simple. If you want to be successful and happy, just make sure that your every thought and action are taking you in that direction.

Sir Isaac Newton is generally considered to be the greatest scientist who ever lived. His breakthroughs in mathematics and physics laid the groundwork for the modern age. In his later years, he was asked how it was that he, one man, had managed to make such significant contributions to the world of science. He replied: "By thinking of nothing else."

In its simplest terms, success begins with you exercising your power of choice to take systematic, purposeful control over the thoughts you hold in your conscious mind. By rigorously disciplining yourself to think and talk only about what you want, and by refusing to dwell upon the things that you don't want, you begin your journey toward the stars.

THE POWER OF YOUR SUBCONSCIOUS MIND

The quality of *thoughtfulness* goes hand in hand with the evolution of character and the development of personal effectiveness. The mental laws we've discussed so far are tools to think with. They make you more aware of who you are, how you got that way, and more important, how you can get to where you want to go in the future.

Most people spend their lives in a form of sleep. They go busily about their daily activities almost totally preoccupied by a continuous stream of disorganized thought. You've experienced this phenomenon when you've gotten into your car and driven to work or across town, lost in thought, with almost no memory of the trip at all.

Many of your habitual routines and conversations take place with a low level of awareness, almost as if you were in a mental fog, and with your having little or no recollection of the particular flow of events.

Sometimes, this preoccupation and busyness is deliberate. You use it to avoid thinking about parts of your life that you would rather not confront or deal with. Sometimes it is simply automatic. You have been going through the motions for so long that your thought processes are automatic.

You only wake up temporarily when you are shocked or surprised, such as when you are cut off in traffic, or scared or caught off guard, but as soon as you recover your composure, you slip back into the warm, gentle stream of waking sleep and your thoughts just flow past amid a continual collage of feelings and images.

To become all you can be, you must live more *consciously*. You must become more alert, more aware and more awake. You must take more control over your thought processes so that the combined power of the various mental laws is moving you in a direction of your own choosing rather than steering you blindly on a form of mental autopilot.

AWAKENING FROM SLEEP

You begin this process of awakening by reflecting on parts of your life—past, present and future. As an exercise in awareness, start by imagining that, before you were born, somewhere on the other side of the cosmos, you had evolved over many lifetimes to become a particular type of person with a particular set of qualities, interests, talents and abilities. It doesn't matter what you think about the idea of reincarnation. This exercise is just that: an exercise with a point that will become clear.

Continuing this line of thought, imagine that you deliberately chose your parents, that you chose the situation you were born into and brought up in. You did this because, at your stage of personal growth and evolution, there were specific lessons about yourself, about life and about other people that you had to learn, and which you could learn in no other way.

Imagine also that the person you are today, especially the good qualities you've developed, evolved largely or partially as the result of the difficult experiences you had growing up and especially as the result of the problems you had with one or both of your parents.

Here is an important question: If you learned that you had *deliberately* chosen your parents and that the person you are today has come about as a direct result of your choice, how would this discovery change your attitude toward your parents and the experiences of your childhood? Would you be more positive and accepting of them? Would you see yourself and your past experiences in a different light? Would you become more philosophical and objective toward what might have appeared, up to now, to have been a difficult time of your life?

As you begin to think about this idea, about having deliberately chosen your parents, you begin to see possibilities that you had totally ignored up to now. Instead of seeing yourself as a passive agent or victim caught up in circumstances beyond your control, you begin to see yourself as an active participant in your own evolution.

Let's take this exercise a little further. Imagine that you are here on this earth to do something wonderful with your life, to become an exceptional person and to make an important contribution to your world. Imagine that this is all part of a great master plan that has been carefully designed with your best interests in mind, and that every event and circumstance of your life is an indispensable part of a big jigsaw puzzle, the outline of which you can only begin to see when you stand back and start to look at your life from a higher plane.

Assume, as a general rule, that whatever your current situation or difficulty, it is exactly what you require, right now, to teach you something you need to know before you can continue on your upward journey. With this perspective, you can see that every experience is a positive experience if you view it as an opportunity for growth and self-mastery.

Now, project backward, and with calmness, clarity and a positive mental attitude, think about how every previous experience and situation of your life might have been sent to you, at exactly the right time for you, to teach you something you needed to learn so that you could continue moving toward the wonderful life that awaits you.

Imagine that the events of your life could not have been otherwise than they were, especially if you were operating on autopilot most of the time. As you stand back and appreciate the incredibly complex, interconnected events that have brought you to where you are in life right now, you will begin to develop the perspective of the philosopher, of the superior intellect. You begin to superimpose on your experience what is called a "sense of coherence," an attitude and a feeling that your life is part of something greater than yourself and that everything fits together and happens for a reason.

As you think of your life as a series of events and experiences that are conspiring toward your achieving some great goal or making some great contribution to mankind, you begin to develop a "sense of destiny," the hallmark of potential greatness as a human being.

PUTTING THE LAWS TO WORK

These mental exercises enable you to begin unlocking the powers of your subconscious mind. They enable you to put these laws to work in a deliberate and systematic way.

You activate the *Law of Control* by choosing consciously to view yourself as an active creative influence in your own life. When you take mental control, you place your hands firmly on the steering wheel of your own destiny. You become the architect of your own future.

You free yourself from the *Law of Accident* when you become aware of the role of your own thoughts in directing the course of your life.

You activate the *Law of Cause and Effect* when you stand back from your day-to-day life and reflect upon the incredible number of coincidences that have shaped you into the person you are today. You see that nothing happened by accident. You realize that everything happened, and is happening, as the result of immutable law—even if you can't see clearly where your life is going at the moment.

You trigger the *Law of Belief* when you accept that your life and your experiences are leading you toward the accomplishment of something important. The more you think about this as inevitable, the more likely it is to come true for you. Your beliefs do become your realities.

You apply the *Law of Expectations* when you confidently expect to gain something worthwhile, if not invaluable, from everything that happens to you. This attitude of confident self-expectancy makes your life into more of an adventure, with unpredictable but happy events occurring to move you toward some positive outcome. You become more optimistic and cheerful, as well as calm and relaxed, and your expectations do become self-fulfilling prophecies.

Your positive, future-oriented thinking triggers the *Law of At-*

traction. You begin drawing into your life people and circumstances in harmony with your dominant thoughts of hope and optimism and confidence. The more you think of yourself and your life as uniquely blessed and important, the more you attract to yourself the ideas, opportunities and people that make your dreams come true.

Consistent with the *Law of Correspondence,* you see yourself as a special person put on this earth with a special purpose, and your outer world of relationships, health, work and material accomplishments begin to reflect your inner attitudes of mind.

As you plant these thought seeds into your subconscious by continually holding them in your conscious mind, by the *Law of Subconscious Activity,* your subconscious begins to make all your words, feelings, actions and even your body language fit a pattern consistent with your new self-concept and your new goals.

You use the *Law of Substitution* continually, knowing that your major responsibility in this process is to keep negative thoughts of fear, anger and self-doubt out of your mind. You do this by holding thoughts of faith, hope and love instead, until these new thoughts are firmly rooted and growing with a life and power of their own.

You apply the *Law of Concentration* by dwelling continually on thoughts of courage and confidence, of hope and love and on the wonderful future life has in store for you. You take time each day to sit and soak your mind in positive and uplifting thoughts, knowing that whatever you dwell upon long enough and hard enough will eventually materialize in the world around you.

YOU CAN DO IT

Your greatest need is to be patient, calm and trusting. These mental laws are the most powerful forces ever discovered. You will achieve what you are meant to achieve when you are ready for it, when your mind is thoroughly prepared. Whatever you want, wants you. Whatever you desire is moving toward you right now, just as you are moving toward it. Your primary job is to decide exactly what you want, which we'll discuss in Chapter 5, and then to get out of your own way, which we'll discuss in Chapter 7.

Developing a positive, constructive way of looking at your life requires thoughtfulness. Developing a superior way of thinking requires that you become more alert, more aware and more awake. Harmonizing all these mental laws so that your life improves in every way requires a new attitude toward yourself and your possibilities.

It may be difficult at first, but the payoff for you will be a heightened sense of self-control and self-mastery, a more positive mental attitude, and a tremendous feeling of empowerment in every part of your life.

ACTION COMMITMENT

Take a sheet of paper and make a list of all the things that you want to see in your life. Write down everything that you can think of. Happiness, health, good friends, travel, prosperity, financial success, popularity, recognition, the respect of others . . . let your imagination run freely.

Here is the hard part: For the next twenty-four hours, think and talk only about the things on your list. See if you can get through one entire day without criticizing, condemning, complaining or getting angry, upset or worried about anything. See if you have the willpower and strength of character to think about only what you want for one whole day.

This exercise will give you a real insight into where you are in your development, and it will also show you how far you have to go. In the next chapter, you will learn the master skill of success, and how to achieve virtually any goal you could ever set for yourself.

The Master Skill

The ability to set goals and to make plans for their accomplishment is the master skill of success. Developing this skill will do more to ensure your success than anything else you could ever do. In twenty-five years of study and experience, I've come to the conclusion that *success equals goals, and all else is commentary*. Intense goal orientation is an essential characteristic of all high-achieving men and women, in every study, in every field. It's not possible to realize even a fraction of your potential until you have learned how to set and achieve goals as normally and as naturally as you brush your teeth or comb your hair in the morning.

Everything we've talked about in this book so far has been intended to bring us to this chapter on goals. It has been part of the necessary preparation for you to put the *master skill* to work in every part of your life. All the material concerning the clearing of your mind and the development of a calm, optimistic attitude toward yourself and your possibilities has been essential. Learning how your mind works, and how the elements in your thinking, based on your past experiences, can affect your behavior and your outcomes today has gone to lay the foundation for what lies ahead.

I was twenty-three years old before I first learned about goals. I knew they existed in sports but the idea of mapping out my life using goals and plans had never occurred to me.

It wasn't that I didn't have goals, nor was it that I hadn't achieved any. I had already traveled three-quarters of the way around the world, including going from the West Coast of the

United States to Capetown, South Africa—by land and sea—and then traveling from London, England, to Singapore the same way.

I had just never given any thought to the process of goal attainment. I had never realized that it is a specific procedure that I could use to accomplish amazing things. Like most people, I was moving randomly through life, reacting and responding rather than focusing and concentrating. As motivational speaker Zig Ziglar says, I was a "wandering generality rather than a meaningful specific."

Then I discovered goals and was never the same again. My whole life has been different since I learned the master skill, and yours will be, too.

GOALS ARE THE FUEL

Goals are the fuel in the furnace of achievement. A person without goals is like a ship without a rudder, drifting aimlessly and always in danger of ending up on the rocks. A person with goals is like a ship with a rudder, guided by a captain with a map, a compass, and a destination, sailing straight and true toward a port of his own choosing. Thomas Carlyle wrote that "a man with a half volition goes back and forth and makes no progress on even the smoothest road, whereas a person with a full volition moves ahead steadily no matter how difficult the path."

Human beings, you and I, are goal-centered organisms. We are teleological in that we are motivated by purposes, by desired end states. We are engineered mentally to move progressively and successively from one goal to the next, and we are never really happy unless, and until, we are moving toward the accomplishment of something that is important to us.

Your brain has within it a goal-seeking mechanism that guides and directs you unerringly over time toward the accomplishment of your objectives. This cybernetic faculty is like the guidance system in a missile; it continually takes in feedback from the target and automatically corrects your course. Because of this mechanism in your brain, you accomplish almost any goal you set for yourself, as long as the goal is clear and you persist long enough. The process of achieving your goals is almost automatic. It is the goal setting in the first place that seems to be the big problem for most people.

It is a truism that each of us is achieving the goals we have set.

You are where you are and what you are because you have decided to be there. Your thoughts, your actions and your behavior have gotten you to your present position in life, and they could have brought you to no other place, rightly considered.

If your goal is to get through the day and then get home and watch television, you will achieve it. If your goal is to be fit and healthy and to live a long life, then you will achieve that, too. And if your goal is to be financially independent or even wealthy, if that is truly your goal, then there is nothing that can stop you from reaching it, sooner or later. Your only limitation is your desire: How badly do you want it?

YOUR SUCCESS MECHANISM

You are equipped with both a "success mechanism" and a "failure mechanism." Your failure mechanism is your natural tendency to follow *the path of least resistance,* your impulse toward immediate gratification with little or no concern for the long-term consequences of your actions. Your failure mechanism operates automatically twenty-four hours per day. Every minute, every hour, it ticks away, and most people allow their desire for what is fun, easy and convenient to determine most of what they do.

However, you also have a *success mechanism* built into your brain. Your success mechanism can override your failure mechanism. And your success mechanism is triggered by a goal. The bigger your goal and the more intensely you desire it, the more likely you will be to exert your powers of self-discipline and will-power, and the more capable you will be of *making yourself* do the things that you need to do to get where you want to go.

After a career of fifty years, during which he personally worked with and trained more than twenty thousand sales people, Elmer Letterman concluded that the one quality that was most predictive of success was what he called "Intensity of Purpose." Taking any two people with the same relative levels of intelligence, background, education and experience, the one with the greatest intensity of purpose will always win out over the other.

TWO REQUIREMENTS FOR SUCCESS

The famous oil billionaire H. L. Hunt, who went bankrupt raising cotton in Arkansas and then went on to build a fortune of several billion dollars and become one of the world's richest men, was once asked his formula for success.

He said that in America, you only needed two things to be successful: "First," he said, "decide exactly what it is you want. Most people never do that. Second, determine the price you're going to have to pay to get it, and then resolve to pay that price."

The great weakness of most people is that, even if they have some idea of what they want, they have never sat down and thought through what it will take to get it, and whether or not they are willing to pay that price.

We only know two things for certain about the price of success. First, in order to get whatever you desire, however you define it, you must pay the price in full. You must sow before you reap. And you may have to work a long time before you harvest the crop. This is the working of the Iron Law, the immutable Law of Cause and Effect. Most frustration in goal attainment comes from trying to violate this timeless principle.

Second, you have to pay the *full* price in advance. Success is not like going to a restaurant where you can pay the bill after you've enjoyed the dinner. The success that you desire requires payment in full, in advance, every single time.

And how can you tell if you have paid the full price of success? That's easy. When you have paid the full price, the success will be there in front of you for all to see. It will happen by law, not by chance. When you've sown, you will reap; cause and effect, action and reaction. The life you are enjoying today is a reflection of the price you've paid up to now. The life you enjoy in the future will reflect the price you pay between now and then.

GOALS MAKE THE LAWS WORK FOR YOU

I described several mental laws in earlier chapters. You may be a bit unsure about how you are going to remember to use and apply all of these laws. Fortunately, you don't have to. When you have a clearly defined goal toward which you are working every day, all these laws work automatically and in harmony with your purposes. You align yourself with the powers of the universe. You unlock the incredible reserves of potential that lie within you. When you organize your whole life in concert with these timeless principles, you begin accomplishing things that you never dreamed possible, and with less effort than you had believed necessary.

The greatest single enemy of your potential for greater success and achievement is your comfort zone, your tendency to get stuck in a rut and then to resist all change, even positive change, that would force you out of it.

Everyone naturally fears and avoids change. We want things to stay the same, but simultaneously to get better. However, all growth, all progress, all advancement requires change. And change is inevitable. In spite of anything you do, life never goes on the same way for very long. It is always changing in one direction or another. Things are either getting better for you or getting worse, but they never stay the same.

As you recall, the Law of Control states that you feel positive about yourself to the degree to which you feel you're in control of your own life. The first benefit of goal setting is that goals allow you to *control the direction of change* in your life, ensuring that change is predominantly positive and self-determined. No one fears a change that represents an improvement. With clear goals, backed by detailed plans of action, you ensure that the changes that are taking place represent improvements in your life and you eliminate a major cause of fear and insecurity.

The Law of Cause and Effect states that for every effect in your life there is a specific cause. Goals are causes: Health, happiness, freedom and prosperity are effects. You sow goals and you reap results. Goals begin as thoughts, or causes, and manifest themselves as conditions or effects. The primary cause of success in life is the ability to set and achieve goals.

That's why people who do not have goals are doomed forever to work for those who do. You either work to achieve your own goals or you work to achieve someone else's goals. The best work of all is when you are achieving your own goals by helping others to achieve theirs.

You trigger the Law of Belief by intensely believing that you will achieve your goals, and by taking actions consistent with those beliefs. This is the foundation of faith and self-confidence.

You trigger the Law of Expectations by confidently expecting that everything that is happening, positive or negative, is moving you toward the realization of your goals. You look for something beneficial in every event, a valuable lesson, something you can use to your advantage.

You activate the Law of Attraction by thinking continually about your goals. With your goals as your dominant thoughts, you invariably begin to attract into your life people and circumstances in harmony with those goals. You attract ideas, opportunities and resources that can help you.

The Law of Correspondence states that your outer world will correspond to your inner world. When your inner world is dominated by thoughts, goals and plans to achieve the things that are important to you, your outer world of manifestation and effect soon mirrors your inner hopes and aspirations.

The Law of Subconscious Activity says that whatever thoughts you hold in your conscious mind, your subconscious mind works to bring into your reality. More and more of your subconscious mind is dedicated to making your words and actions fit a pattern consistent with what you really want to achieve.

The Law of Concentration says that whatever you dwell upon, grows. What do you dwell upon continually? Your goals! The more you dwell upon, reflect upon, and think about the things you want and how you can attain them, the more sensitive and aware you become of opportunities to attain them.

The Law of Substitution says that you can substitute a positive thought for a negative one. What positive thought do you use to substitute for negative thoughts or experiences? Your goals! Whenever something goes wrong, *think* about your goals. Whenever you have a bad day, *think* about your goals. The very thought of a goal, something that you want to accomplish in the future, is inherently positive and uplifting. It is impossible to think about your goals continually without being optimistic and highly motivated.

When you begin using all these mental laws behind a clearly defined purpose to which you are totally committed, you become an unstoppable powerhouse of mental and physical energy that will not be denied. With clear, specific goals, you develop and use all your mental powers. You then accomplish more in a few years than most people accomplish in a lifetime.

With everything that we know about goal setting, you would think that everyone would be doing it. You have probably been told for years that you have to have goals. You've been told that you have to be working toward your goals on a regular basis. You know you can't hit a target you can't see.

Yet the sad fact is that very few people have any real goals at all. Less than 3 percent of men and women have their goals in writing. Fewer than 1 percent of them read and review their goals regularly. Most people seem to have no idea just how important goals are.

Many people have attended seminars, read books and listened to tapes on goal setting, and yet if you ask them if they have clear written goals, and plans for their accomplishment, they will confess sheepishly that they do not. They know that they are supposed to have goals, and they intend to set some goals fairly soon, but they just haven't yet gotten around to it.

When I began studying and applying these principles of goal setting, I got such extraordinary results that I eagerly shared these ideas with anyone who would listen. That's how I started speaking in public and giving seminars.

However, I was continually amazed at how readily people would agree with me, but then go away and do nothing. I began to question and try to figure out why it was that people don't set goals. I finally concluded that there are basically *seven reasons* why people don't set goals. It is important to be aware of them and to determine whether they apply to your situation. Ignorance is not bliss. Not knowing about these mental obstacles, and not learning how to counteract them, can be fatal to your prospects for the future.

WHY PEOPLE DON'T SET GOALS

The *first* reason people don't set goals is that they are simply *not serious*. They are talkers instead of doers. They want to be more successful, they want to improve their lives, but they are not willing to make the necessary effort. They do not have the "fire in the belly" that translates into a burning desire to make something of themselves, to make their lives bigger and better and more exciting.

The only way you can tell what a person *really* believes is by actions, not words. It is not what you say, or what you intend, or what you wish or hope or pray for, but only what you *do* that counts. Your true values and beliefs are only and always expressed in your behavior. One person who will take action is worth ten brilliant talkers who do nothing.

I get countless phone calls, letters and proposals from all kinds of people with all kinds of ideas during the course of a year. But the only ones who impress me, or anyone else, are the ones who actually do something. Remember, only action is action, and nothing else counts for much. Don't tell people what you are going to do, *show* them. Get serious!

The *second* reason people don't set goals is that they have not yet accepted responsibility for their lives. I used to think that goals were the starting point of success until I realized that, until people accept that they are fully responsible for their lives and for everything that happens to them, they will not even take the first step toward goal setting.

The irresponsible person is the person who is still waiting for real life to begin. Such a person uses up all his or her creative energies making elaborate excuses for his or her failure to make progress, and then buys lottery tickets and goes home to watch television. We'll talk about this in detail in Chapter Seven.

The *third* reason people don't set goals is their deep-seated feelings of guilt and unworthiness. A person who is so low mentally and emotionally that he or she has to "look up to see bottom" is not the kind of person who confidently and optimistically sets goals for the months and years ahead. A person who was raised in a negative environment, leaving him or her with feelings of undeservingness and the attitudes of "What's the use?" and "I'm not good enough," is hardly capable of serious goal setting.

The *fourth* reason people don't set goals is that they don't realize the importance of goals. If you are raised in a household in which your parents do not have goals and the setting and achieving of goals is not a regular topic of family discussion, you can reach adulthood without even knowing that there are such things as goals, outside of sports.

If you move in a social circle in which people do not have clearly defined goals toward which they are working, it will be natural for you to assume that goals are not a particularly important part of life. Since 80 percent of the people around you are going nowhere, if you are not careful you will end up drifting with the crowd, following the followers, and going nowhere as well.

If people knew that all their hopes and dreams and plans, all their aspirations and ambitions, are dependent upon their ability and their willingness to set goals—if people realized how important goals are to a happy, successful life—I think far more people would have goals than do today.

The *fifth* reason people don't set goals is that they don't know how. You can earn a university degree in our society, the equivalent of fifteen or sixteen years of education, and never once receive an hour's worth of instruction on goal setting, even though goal setting is more important to your long-term happiness than any other single subject that you could ever learn. An even worse mistake that people make is to assume that they *already* know how to set goals. A person who assumes that he or she has a critical skill when, in reality, his or her understanding of it is rudimentary at best, is in great danger of failing at life.

I have been studying and practicing goal-setting techniques for more than twenty years. I have taught hundreds of thousands of men and women how to set goals for their lives and I have done strategic planning and goal setting for billion-dollar corporations. I know very few people who have studied the subject and applied it as thoroughly as I have, and I still feel that I have an enormous amount to learn. If someone truly knows goal setting down cold, he or she is probably either very rich or very happy, or both.

The *sixth* reason people don't set goals is quite simply the *fear of rejection*, or the fear of criticism. From the time we were children, we have had our hopes and dreams slapped down by the criticism and laughter of others. Maybe our parents didn't want us to get our hopes up, or to be disappointed, so they quickly pointed out all the reasons we would not be able to achieve our goals. Our siblings and friends might have laughed at us and ridiculed us for thinking about being someone or doing something far beyond what they could imagine for themselves. These influences can affect your attitude toward yourself and goal setting for years.

Children are not dumb. They soon learn that "if you want to get along, you go along." Over time, a child who is constantly criticized or discouraged stops coming up with new ideas, new dreams, or new goals. He begins the lifelong process of playing it safe, of selling himself short, and accepting underachievement in life as inevitable and unavoidable.

The solution to this fear of criticism or sounding foolish is simple: *Keep your goals confidential.* Don't tell anybody. All effective goal-setters finally learn to keep their goals to themselves. No one can laugh at you or criticize you if he or she doesn't know what your goals are.

There are two exceptions to this practice of confidentiality. The first are the people, such as your boss or spouse, whose help you will need to achieve your goals.

And second, you can share your goals with other goal-oriented people, people who will encourage you in the direction you want to go. You should also make it a policy to encourage everyone you speak to who tells you about a goal they have. Tell them to "go for it!" Tell them, "You can do it." Encouraging others motivates you, as well. It is one of the best applications of the Law of Sowing and Reaping. If you would like others to encourage you, take every opportunity to encourage them.

The *seventh* and most predominant reason people do not set goals is the fear of failure. I cannot repeat often enough, *the fear of failure is the greatest single obstacle to success in adult life*. It is what keeps people in their comfort zones. It is what makes them keep their heads down and play it safe as the years pass by.

The fear of failure is expressed in the attitude of, "I can't, I can't, I can't." It is learned in early childhood as the result of destructive criticism and punishment for doing things your parents disapproved of. Once entrenched in the subconscious mind, this fear does more to paralyze hope and kill ambition than any other negative emotion in the human experience.

The major reason for the fear of failure is that most people don't understand the role of failure in achieving success. The rule is simply this: *It is impossible to succeed without failing*. Failure is a prerequisite for success. The greatest successes in human history have also been the greatest failures. In the same year that Babe Ruth became the home run king of baseball, he also struck out more than any other player.

Success is a numbers game. There is a direct relationship between the number of things you attempt and your probability of ultimately succeeding. Even if you were the worst player in baseball, if you swung with all your heart at every ball that came over the plate, you would eventually get a hit, and if you kept swinging, you would finally get a home run. The important thing is to swing with all your might and to keep swinging, and not worry about striking out occasionally.

Thomas Edison was the most successful inventor of the modern age. He received patents for 1,093 inventions, 1,052 of which were brought into commercial production during his lifetime. But as an inventor, he was also the greatest failure of his age. He failed more times, in more experiments, attempting to develop more products, than any other living scientist or businessman. It took him more than 11,000 experiments alone before he finally discovered the carbon-impregnated filament that led to the production of the first electric light bulb.

There is a story about Edison that, after he had conducted more than 5,000 experiments, a young journalist came to him and asked him why he persisted in these experiments after having failed more than 5,000 times. Edison is said to have replied, "Young man, you don't understand how the world works. I have not failed at all. I have successfully identified 5,000 ways that will not work. That just puts me 5,000 ways closer to the way that will."

Napoleon Hill said, "Within every adversity is the seed of an equal or greater opportunity or advantage." The way to deal with temporary failure is to seek within each setback for the valuable lesson that it contains. Approach every difficulty as if it were sent to you at that moment and in that way to teach you something you need to learn so you can continue moving forward.

Become an "inverse paranoid": Tell yourself that everything that is happening is moving you toward the achievement of your goals, even when temporary failures seem to be moving you away from them. Keep looking for the good. Great successes are almost always preceded by many failures. It's the lessons learned from the failures that make the ultimate successes possible.

Decide, in advance, to take every setback as a spur to greater effort, especially in business and sales, knowing that you are getting closer and closer to success with every experience.

Look upon temporary defeat as a signpost that says "STOP, go this way instead." One of the qualities of leaders is that they never use the words *failure* or *defeat*. Instead, they use words like "valuable learning experiences" or "temporary glitches."

The great football coach Vince Lombardi had the right spirit. After a game in which the Green Bay Packers were defeated, one of the reporters asked Lombardi how he felt about losing. Lombardi replied, "We didn't lose, we just ran out of time."

You can learn to overcome the fear of failure by being absolutely clear about your goals, and by accepting that temporary setbacks and obstacles are the inevitable price you pay to achieve any great success in life.

THE PRINCIPLES OF GOAL SETTING

Goal setting can be a powerful, life-changing experience, if you do it properly. There are five basic principles of goal setting that are essential for maximum achievement.

The first is the principle of *congruency*. For you to perform at your best, your goals and your values must fit together like a hand in a glove. Your values represent your deepest convictions about what is right and wrong, what is good and bad, and what is important and meaningful to you. High performance and high self-esteem only happen when your goals and your values are in complete harmony with each other.

The second principle of goal setting is your *area of excellence*. Each person has the capacity to be excellent at something, and perhaps several things. You can achieve your full potential only by finding your area of excellence and then by throwing your whole heart into developing your talents in that area.

You will never be happy or satisfied until you find your heart's desire and commit your life to it. It is the one thing that you are uniquely capable of doing in an excellent fashion. It is your job to identify it, if you haven't already.

Your area of excellence may change as your career evolves, but all truly successful men and women are those who have found it. And your area of excellence is invariably doing what you most enjoy and doing it well.

The third principle of goal setting is the *acres of diamonds* concept. *Acres of Diamonds* was the title of a talk by a minister named Russell Conwell. The talk became so popular that he was eventually asked to give it more than five thousand times, word for word.

In the story, an old African farmer became very excited one day upon hearing from a traveling merchant of men who had gone off into Africa, discovered diamond mines and become fabulously wealthy. He decided to sell off his farm, organize a caravan, and head into the vast interior of Africa to find diamonds so he could crown his life with fabulous wealth.

For many years, he searched the vast African continent for diamonds. Eventually, he ran out of money and was abandoned by everyone. Finally, alone, in a fit of despair, he threw himself into the ocean and drowned.

Meanwhile, back on the farm that he had sold, the new farmer was out watering a donkey one day in a stream that cut across the farm. He found a strange stone that threw off light in a remarkable way. He took it into the house and thought no more of it. Some months later the same merchant, traveling on business, stopped for the night at the farm. When he saw the stone, he grew very excited and asked if the old farmer had finally returned. No, he was told, the old farmer had never been seen again, but why was he so excited?

The merchant picked up the stone and said, "This is a diamond of great price and value." The new farmer was skeptical, but the merchant insisted that he show him where he had found the diamond. They went out on the farm to where the farmer had been watering the donkey, and as they looked around, they found another diamond, and another, and another. It turned out that the whole farm was covered with acres of diamonds. The old farmer had gone off into Africa seeking for diamonds without ever looking under his own feet.

The moral to this story was that the old farmer did not realize that diamonds do not look like diamonds in their rough form. They simply look like rocks to the uneducated eye. A diamond must be cut, faceted, polished and set before it looks like the kind of diamond that you see in the jewelry stores.

Likewise, your acres of diamonds probably lie right under your own feet. But they are usually disguised as hard work. "Opportunities come dressed in work clothes."

Your acres of diamonds probably lie in your own talents, your interests, your education, your background and experience, your industry, your city, your contacts. Your acres of diamonds probably lie right under your own feet if you will take the time to recognize them and then go to work on them.

Remember the words I quoted earlier from Theodore Roosevelt who said, "Do what you can, with what you have, right where you are." You don't need to move across the country or to make a major upheaval in your life. In most cases, what you are looking for is right at your fingertips. But it doesn't look like an opportunity on the surface. In many cases, your great opportunity will simply look like hard, hard work.

The fourth principle for success in goal setting is the principle of *balance*. The principle of balance states that you need a variety of goals in the six critical areas of life in order to perform at your best. Just as a wheel on an automobile must be balanced for it to go around smoothly, you must have your goals in balance for your life to go smoothly.

You need family and personal goals. You need physical and health goals. You need mental and intellectual goals, and goals for study and personal development. You need career and work goals. You need financial and material goals. Finally, you need spiritual goals, goals aimed at inner development and spiritual enlightenment.

To maintain proper balance, you need two or three goals in each area, a total of twelve to eighteen goals in all. This kind of balance will enable you to be constantly working on something important to you. When you're not working on your job, you can be pursuing family goals. When you are not working on physical fitness, you can be working on personal and professional development. When you are not practicing meditation, contemplation and other inner development work, you can be working on your material goals. Your objective is to make your life one continuous stream of progress and achievement.

The fifth principle of goal setting is the determination of your *major purpose* in life. Your major purpose is your number-one goal, the goal that is more important to you than the accomplishment of any other single goal or objective at *this* time. You may have a variety of goals but you can only have one major central purpose. The failure of a person to choose an overarching, dominating major goal is the primary reason for diffusion of effort, wasting of time and the inability to make progress.

The way you choose your overarching goal is by analyzing all your goals and asking, "Which goal, if I accomplish it, would do the most to help me achieve all my other goals?"

Usually, this is a financial or business goal, but sometimes it can be a health or relationship goal instead. The selection of your central purpose is the starting point of all great success and achievement. This goal becomes your "mission," the organizing principle for all your other activities. Your major purpose becomes the catalyst that activates the Laws of Belief, Attraction and Correspondence. When you are excited about achieving a clear major goal, you start to move forward rapidly in spite of all obstacles and limitations. All the forces of the mental universe begin to work on your behalf. You become an irresistible force of nature. You become virtually unstoppable.

GOAL-SETTING RULES

There are several important rules that accompany effective goal setting.

First of all, your goals must be in *harmony* with one another, not contradictory. You cannot have a goal to be financially successful, or to build your own successful business, and simultaneously have a goal to spend half your day at the golf course or at the beach. Your goals have to be mutually supportive and mutually reinforcing.

Second, your goals must be *challenging*. They must make you stretch without being overwhelming. When you initially set goals, they should have about a 50 percent or better probability of success. This level of probability is ideal for motivation, yet not so difficult that you can become easily discouraged. After you develop some skill in setting and achieving goals, you will quite confidently set goals that may only have a 40 percent, or 30 or 20 percent probability of success, and you will still be motivated and excited as you strive to achieve them.

Third, you should have both *tangible* and *intangible* goals, both *quantitative* and *qualitative*. You should have concrete goals that you can measure and evaluate objectively. At the same time, you should have qualitative goals, for your inner life and your relationships.

You may have a *quantitative* goal for your family of acquiring a larger home. Your *qualitative* goal for your family could be to become a more patient, loving person. The two goals fit nicely together. They balance the inner and the outer.

Fourth, you need both *short-term* goals and *long-term* goals. You need goals for today and goals for five, ten and twenty years from today.

The ideal short-term goal for business, career and personal planning is about ninety days. The ideal longer-term period for the same goals is two to three years. These time horizons seem to be the ideal for continuous motivation.

The very best major purpose or overarching goal is quantitative, challenging and aimed at two or three years out. You can then break it down to ninety-day segments, and subsequently break those down to monthly, weekly and daily subgoals with measurable benchmarks to enable you to assess your progress.

The ideal life is focused, purposeful, positive and organized so that you are moving toward goals that are important to you every hour of every day. You always know what you're doing and why. You have a continuous sense of forward motion. You feel like a "winner" most of the time.

The decision to become a goal-setting, goal-achieving, future-focused person gives you a tremendous sense of control. You feel wonderful about yourself. You feel that you are the master of your own destiny.

Your self-esteem increases as you progress toward your goals. You like and respect yourself more and more. Your personality improves and you become a more positive, confident person. You feel happy and excited about life. You open the floodgates of your potential and begin moving faster and faster toward becoming all that you were meant to be.

HOW TO IDENTIFY YOUR GOALS

Here are seven goal-setting questions for you to ask and answer over and over again. I suggest that you take a pad of paper and write out your responses.

Question number one:

What are your five most important values in life?

This question is intended to help you clarify what is really important to you, and by extension, what is less important, or unimportant.

Once you have identified the five most important things in life to you, organize them in order of priority, from number one, the most important, through number five.

Choosing and defining your values and their order of importance comes before setting your goals. Since you live from the inner to the outer, and your values are the core components of your personality, clarity concerning them makes it possible for you to select goals that are consistent with what is the very best for you.

Question number two:

What are your three most important goals in life, right now?

Write the answer to this question within thirty seconds.

This is called the "quick list" method. When you only have thirty seconds to write down your three most important goals, your subconscious mind sorts out your many goals quickly. Your top three will just pop into your conscious mind. With only thirty seconds, you will be as accurate as if you had thirty minutes.

Question number three:

What would you do, how would you spend your time, if you learned today that you only had six months to live?

This is another *value* question to help you clarify what is really important to you. When your time is limited, even if only in your imagination, you become very aware of who and what you really care about. As a doctor said recently, "I never met a businessman on his deathbed who said, 'I wish I'd spent more time at the office.' "

Someone once said that you are not ready to live until you know what you would do if you only had one hour left on earth. What would *you* do?

Question number four:

What would you do if you won a million dollars cash, tax free, in the lottery tomorrow?

How would you change your life? What would you buy? What would you start doing, or stop doing? Imagine that you only have two minutes to write your answers and you will only be able to do or acquire what you have written.

This is really a question to help you decide what you'd do if you had all the time and money you need, if you had virtually no fear of failure at all. The most revealing answers to this question are made when you realize how many things you would do differently if you felt you had the ability to choose.

Question number five:

What have you always wanted to do, but been afraid to attempt?

This question helps you see more clearly where your fears could be blocking you from doing what you really want to do.

Question number six:

What do you most enjoy doing? What gives you your greatest feeling of self-esteem and personal satisfaction?

This is another *values* question that may indicate where you should explore to find your "heart's desire." You will always be most happy doing what you most love to do, and what you most love to do is invariably the activity that makes you feel the most alive and fulfilled. The most successful men and women in America are invariably doing what they really enjoy, most of the time.

Question number seven, and perhaps this is the most important:

What one great thing would you dare to dream if you knew *you could not fail?*

Imagine that a genie appears and grants you one wish. The genie guarantees that you will be absolutely, completely successful in any one thing that you attempt to do, big or small, short- or long-term. If you were absolutely guaranteed of success in any one thing, big or small, what one exciting goal would you set for yourself?

Whatever you wrote as an answer to any of these questions, including the question, *"What one great thing would you dare to dream if you* knew *you could not fail?"* you can be, have, or do. The very fact that you could write it means that you can achieve it. Once you've identified what it is you want, the only question you have to answer is, "Do I want it badly enough, and am I willing to pay the price?"

Take a few minutes and write out your answers to each of these seven questions. Once you have your answers on paper, go over them and select just one as your major definite purpose in life right now.

By this simple act of deciding what you really want, and writing it down, you will have moved yourself into the top 3 percent. You will have done something that few people ever do. You will have established a written set of goals for yourself. You are now ready to make a giant leap forward.

CONTINUOUS GOAL SETTING

The most important contribution you can make to your success and happiness is to develop the habit of continuous goal setting. The key to developing this habit is learning how to deliberately set and achieve one clear, challenging goal. When you have set a specific goal for yourself and then achieved it according to your plans, you change from having an attitude of *positive thinking* to possessing an attitude of *positive knowing*. You must reach the point in your own mind where you know beyond the shadow of a doubt that you can accomplish any goal you set for yourself. From that point on, you are a different person. You are the master of your fate.

The thrill of achievement, the feeling of having overcome adversity and won through, in spite of the odds, gives you a sense of pleasure and excitement that can come from no other source. The habit of continuous goal setting, of using all your mental powers, soon becomes a positive addiction. You reach the point where you can hardly wait to get up in the morning, and you hate to go to bed at night. You become so positive and self-confident that your friends hardly recognize you.

The most difficult mental obstacle you have to overcome is inertia, the tendency to slip back into your comfort zone and to lose your forward momentum. That is why perhaps the best definition of *character* is "the ability to carry through on a resolution after the mood in which the resolution was made is past."

Anyone can set goals and many people do. Probably half the population makes a series of resolutions every New Year's. But that is not enough. It is the way the goals are set and the way plans are made to accomplish them that determines what happens afterward. To maximize your goal-achieving ability, you need a method. You need a proven process that you can use over and over, with any goal, in any situation, to bring all the powers of your mind to bear on accomplishing whatever it is you desire.

THE TWELVE-STEP SYSTEM

The twelve-step system you are about to learn is perhaps the most effective goal-achieving process ever developed. It has been used by hundreds of thousands of men and women all over the world to revolutionize their lives. It has been used by corporations to reorganize themselves and to go on to greater sales and profitability. It is simple, as all true things are simple, but it is so astonishingly effective that it continues to amaze even the most skeptical people.

The purpose of this goal-achieving system is to enable you to create the mental equivalent of what you wish to achieve in your external world. The Law of Mind states that your thoughts objectify themselves in your reality. You become and you accomplish what you think about. If you think about something with tremendous clarity and intensity, you will bring it about much faster and more predictably than in any other way.

There is a direct relationship between how clearly you can see your goal as accomplished, on the inside, and how rapidly it appears on the outside. This twelve-step system takes you from abstract fuzziness to absolute clarity. It gives you a track to run on, a track that enables you to get from where you are to wherever you want to go.

Step one: Develop desire—intense, burning desire. This is the motivational force that enables you to overcome the fear and inertia that holds most people back. The greatest single obstacle to setting and achieving goals is fear of all kinds. Fear is the reason you sell yourself short and settle for far less than you are capable of. Every decision you make is made on the basis of emotion, either fear or desire. And a stronger emotion will always overcome a weaker emotion. The Law of Concentration states that whatever you dwell upon, grows. If you dwell upon your desires, if you think about them and write them out and make plans to accomplish them continually, your desires eventually become so strong that they override and push aside your fears. An intense, burning desire for a specific goal enables you to rise above your fears and move forward over any obstacles.

Desire is invariably *personal.* You can only want something for *yourself,* not because you feel someone else wants it for you. In setting your goals, and especially your major definite purpose, you must be perfectly selfish. It must be your own goal. You must be absolutely clear about what it is that you want to be, to have or to do.

What is your major definite purpose? What is your overarching goal? If you were guaranteed success in any one area, what would you want to accomplish? Review the seven goal-setting questions until you become perfectly clear about what would make you the very happiest. Deciding what you really want is the starting point of all great achievement.

Step two: Develop belief. In order to activate your subconscious mind and, as you will learn, your superconscious capabilities, you must absolutely believe that it is possible for you to achieve your goal. You must have complete faith that you deserve the goal and that it will come to you when you are ready for it. You must nurture your faith and belief until they deepen into an absolute conviction that your goal is attainable.

Because belief is the catalyst that activates your mental powers, it is important that your goals be realistic, especially at first. If your goal is to earn more money, you should set a goal to increase your income by 10 or 20 or 30 percent over the next twelve months. These are believable goals, goals that you can get your mind around. They are realistic and can therefore be a source of motivation for you.

If your goal is too far beyond anything you've accomplished in the past, setting it too high actually makes it a *demotivator*. Because it is so distant, you seem to be making little or no progress toward it. You become discouraged more easily and you can soon stop believing that it is possible for you.

In my own case, when I first started using this process of goal setting, I was earning about $40,000 per year. I got really excited and decided to set a goal to earn $400,000 per year within twelve months.

What happened was that instead of increasing my income, nothing seemed to happen at all. The goal of $400,000 was much more than I could believe, so my subconscious mind simply refused to accept it as a possibility. It ignored my commands because I had no real faith behind them. When I realized my mistake, I adjusted my goal down to $60,000, a 50 percent increase over the previous year. And I achieved that by changing jobs six months later.

Napoleon Hill wrote, "Whatever the mind of man can conceive and believe, it can achieve." However, completely unrealistic goals are a form of self-delusion, and you cannot delude yourself into goal attainment. It requires hard, practical, systematic effort, working in harmony with the principles we have been discussing.

If you want to lose weight, don't set a goal to lose thirty or forty or fifty pounds. Instead, set a goal to lose five pounds over the next thirty to sixty days. As you lose the first five pounds, set a new goal to lose another five pounds, and so on until you achieve your ideal weight. A five-pound weight loss is believable, whereas a thirty-pound weight loss is so much beyond your current self-concept that your subconscious mind doesn't take you seriously.

One of the kindest and most helpful things you can do for your children is to help them to set realistic and believable goals. Help them to develop the habit of setting and achieving goals, not necessarily the ability to set big goals. There's an old saying that if you save your pennies, the dollars will take care of themselves. If children develop the habit of setting and achieving small goals, they will eventually move on to medium-sized goals, and then to goals of any size.

Before you can achieve big goals, major efforts are necessary. Sometimes you will require weeks, months and even years of hard work and preparation before you will be ready to achieve really big things. In every field, you must pay your dues in advance. Unless you are extraordinarily brilliant or talented, you must be honest with yourself and accept that, if the goal is worth achieving, it is worth working for patiently and persistently.

Many people set goals that are far beyond their capacity to achieve, work at them for a little while, and then quit. They become discouraged and conclude that goal setting doesn't work, at least for them. The primary reason this happens is that they have tried to do too much too fast.

Your responsibility is to create and maintain a positive mental attitude by confidently expecting and believing that if you continue to do the right things in the right way, you will eventually attract to yourself the people and the resources you need to reach your goal right on schedule. You must absolutely believe that if you keep on keeping on, you will ultimately be successful.

Step three: Write it down. Goals that are not in writing are not goals at all. They are merely wishes or fantasies. A wish is a goal with no energy behind it. When you write a goal down on a piece of paper, you crystallize it. You make it something concrete and tangible. You make it something that you can pick up and look at and hold and touch and feel. You have taken it out of your imagination and put it into a form that you can do something with.

One of the most powerful of all methods for implanting a goal into your subconscious mind is to write it out clearly, vividly, in detail, exactly as you would like to see it in reality. Decide what's right before you decide what's possible. Make the description of your goal perfect and ideal in every respect. Crystallize the ideal images you created in Chapter One, Make Your Life a Masterpiece.

Don't worry, for the moment, about how the goal is going to be achieved. Your main job in the beginning is to be absolutely certain about exactly what it is that you desire, and not to worry about the process of achieving it.

Some years ago, in the middle of a recession, my wife and I had to sell our home to raise cash and pay our bills. We moved into a rented house temporarily and ended up living there for two years. During this time, we decided to get serious about our dream home. Even though we had financial problems, we subscribed to several magazines filled with pictures and descriptions of beautiful homes.

About once a week, Barbara and I would sit down and page through these magazines, discussing the various features that we would like to see in our ideal home. We put all thought of cost, location and down payment out of our minds temporarily. We eventually drew up a list of forty-two features that we wanted in our home someday. We then put the list away, put our heads down, and continued to work.

Three years passed and a thousand things happened. We bought a beautiful home and moved out of the rented house. All kinds of unexpected and unpredictable events took place. And when the dust finally settled, we had moved again and we were in a beautiful five-thousand-square-foot home in sunny San Diego, California.

While we were unpacking our belongings, we found the list we had drawn up three years before. The house we had just moved into turned out to have forty-one of the forty-two features that we had written down. The only thing it lacked was a built-in vacuum cleaner system, which was, perhaps, the least important.

We knew the house would be somewhere in California. That was on our list under the heading "Location." Barbara envisioned a house that had no fence in the backyard. She could clearly see "an unbroken view with no obstructions." I explained to her that, for security reasons, virtually all homes in California had fences. Some of them even have gated neighborhoods with security guards and barbed wire. But she was adamant. She saw a completely wide-open backyard stretching as far as the eye could see.

As it turned out, our dream house backs onto a beautiful valley containing a lovely golf course surrounding two lakes. The long slope behind our home, plus the valley, plus the lakes, gives ample security and makes a fence unnecessary. The visualization came true.

This is just one of a hundred stories that I could tell you that flow from the act of writing down your goals clearly and then thinking about them all the time. The most important reason for writing them down, aside from clarifying them in your mind, is that the very act of writing them down intensifies your desire and deepens your belief that they are achievable.

Too many people do not write their goals down on paper because, deep in their hearts, they don't think that their goals are achievable. They don't think writing them down will do any good. They attempt to protect themselves from disappointment. And in so doing, they only assure themselves disappointment and under-achievement on their journeys through life. But when you discipline yourself to write your goals down, the very act overrides your failure mechanism and turns your success mechanism on to full power.

Step four: Make a list of all the ways that you will benefit from achieving your goal. Just as goals are the fuel in the furnace of achievement, reasons "why" are the forces that intensify your desire and drive you forward. Your motivation depends upon your motives, your reasons for acting in the first place, and the more reasons you have, the more motivated you will be.

The German philosopher Nietzsche wrote, "A man can bear any *what* if he has a big enough *why*." You can only motivate yourself to accomplish great things if you have a big exciting dream of some kind. Your reasons "why" must be uplifting and inspiring. They must be big enough to drive you onward.

It is when you have big reasons for achieving your major goal that you develop the "intensity of purpose" that makes you irresistible. If your reasons are big enough, your belief solid enough and your desire intense enough, nothing can stop you.

YOUR REASONS WILL PROPEL YOU

A young man once went to Socrates and asked him how he could gain wisdom. Socrates replied by asking the young man to come with him while they walked together into a nearby lake. When the water got to be about four feet deep, Socrates suddenly grabbed the young man and pushed his head under the water. Then he held it there. The young man thought it was a joke at first and did not resist. But as he was held under the water longer and longer, he became frantic. He struggled desperately to get free as his lungs burned for lack of oxygen. Finally Socrates let him up, coughing and spluttering and gasping for air. Socrates then said, "When you desire wisdom with the same intensity that you desired to breathe, then nothing will stop you from getting it." It's the same with your goals.

One of your jobs is to keep your desire burning brightly by continually thinking of all of the benefits, satisfactions and rewards you will enjoy as a result of achieving your goal. Each person is excited and motivated by different things. For example, the English novelist E. M. Forster said, "I write to earn the respect of those I respect." Some people are motivated by money and the possibility of living in a big house and driving a beautiful car. Others are motivated by recognition, status and prestige, by the idea of earning the admiration of others.

Make a list of all the benefits, tangible and intangible, that you can possibly enjoy as a result of achieving your goal. You will find that, the longer the list, the more motivated and determined you will become. If you have only one or two reasons for achieving a goal, you will have a moderate level of motivation. You will be easily discouraged when the going gets rough, as it surely will. If you have twenty or thirty reasons for achieving your goal, you will become irresistible. Nothing will discourage or dissuade you from keeping on until you accomplish what you have set your mind on.

Step five: Analyze your position, your starting point. If you decide to lose weight, the very first thing you do is to weigh yourself. If you want to achieve a certain net worth, the first thing that you do is to sit down and create a personal financial statement to find out how much you are worth today.

Determining your starting point also gives you a baseline from which you can measure your progress. Again, I cannot emphasize too strongly that the clearer you are about where you are coming from and where you are going, the more likely it is that you will end up where you want to be.

Step six: Set a deadline. Set deadlines on all tangible, measurable goals, such as increases in income or net worth, or losing a certain number of pounds, or running a certain number of miles. But don't set deadlines on intangible goals, such as the development of patience, kindness, compassion, self-discipline or other personal qualities.

When you set a deadline for a tangible goal, you program it into your mind and activate your subconscious "forcing system," which ensures that you accomplish your goal by that date, at the latest. When you set a deadline for the development of a personal quality, this same forcing system ensures that your deadline will be the first day you begin to actually demonstrate the quality you've chosen.

Often people resist setting deadlines for fear that they will not achieve their goals by the time they've set for themselves. They do everything possible, including leaving the deadline vague, to avoid the feelings of discouragement that might occur.

What if you do set a goal and a deadline and you don't achieve it by your deadline? Simple: You set another deadline. It just means that you're not ready yet. You guessed wrong. You were too optimistic. And if you don't achieve your goal by your new deadline, you set still another deadline until you finally do achieve it. As my friend sales trainer Don Hutson says, "There are no unrealistic goals, only unrealistic deadlines."

But in probably 80 percent of cases, if your goals are sufficiently realistic and your plans are sufficiently detailed, and you work your plans faithfully, you will achieve your goal by your deadline.

If your major definite purpose has a two-, three- or five-year deadline, your next step is to break your goal down into ninety-day subgoals. Then break the ninety-day goals down into thirty-day goals. With your long-term goal as your Mount Olympus, you can more readily set realistic short- and medium-term goals that enable you to make steady progress day by day.

BACK-FROM-THE-FUTURE THINKING

In your thinking, start from a visualization of your goal as already accomplished and *work back* to the present. Project yourself forward in your mind to your completed goal, and then look back to where you are today. Imagine the steps that you would have taken to get from where you are now to where you want to be in the future. This process of planning backward from the actual achievement of your goal gives you a special perspective on what you will have to do to achieve it. "Project forward, look backward" is a powerful technique that enables you to see possibilities and pitfalls that you might otherwise miss. It sharpens your perceptions and gives you insights you can get in no other way.

Step seven: Make a list of all the obstacles that stand between you and the accomplishment of your goal. Wherever great success is possible, great obstacles exist. In fact, obstacles are the flipside of success and achievement. If there are no obstacles between you and your goal, it probably is not a goal at all, merely an activity.

When you have listed every obstacle you can think of, organize the list in order of importance. What is the *biggest single obstacle* that stands between you and your goal? This is your "rock." On your pathway to the accomplishment of anything worthwhile, you will experience a series of obstacles, detours and roadblocks. But almost invariably, there is one big rock or major obstacle that lies across your path and blocks your progress. It is this rock that you must focus on removing before you get sidetracked dealing with smaller obstacles and problems.

Your main obstacle, or "rock," may be internal or external. It may be within yourself or within the situation. If it is internal, it may be that you lack a particular skill, ability or attribute that you must have to achieve your goal. You must be completely honest with yourself and ask, "Is there anything about myself that I will have to change, or any ability that I will have to develop in order to achieve my goal?"

Your major obstacle may be external. You may be in the wrong job, or with the wrong company or in the wrong relationship. You may find that you need to start over, doing something else, somewhere else, if your goal is to be achieved. What is your personal "rock"?

The second question you must ask yourself in identifying what might be holding you back is, "What is my limiting step?" What part of the process of moving from where you are now to the achievement of your goal determines the speed at which you reach it? If you are in sales, and your goal is higher income, your limiting step is the size and number of the sales that you make. Your limiting step to more sales could be the number of new prospects that you generate. It might be your ability to ask for the order.

In almost every case, there is a limiting step. This bottleneck determines how rapidly you move toward your goal. Your job is to identify your limiting step and then do everything possible to relieve it. Sometimes the alleviation of one chokepoint, if it's the right one, can do more to move you forward than any other single thing you could do.

Step eight: Identify the additional information you will need to achieve your goal.

We live in a knowledge-based society, and the most successful people are those who have more essential information than others. Almost all mistakes that you make in your financial life and your career will be the result of having insufficient or incorrect information. One of your responsibilities is to learn what you need to know, so you can accomplish what you want to accomplish.

If you do not have the knowledge or information yourself, where can you get it? Is it a *core skill* or ability that you need to develop yourself through study and practice? Or can you hire someone else with this knowledge? Can you employ someone temporarily, such as a consultant, or a specialist, with the knowledge you require? Who else has achieved success in your particular field, and could you go to him or her for advice?

Make a list of all the information, talents, skills, abilities and experience that you will need and then make a plan to learn, buy, rent or borrow this information or skill as quickly as you can. Determine the most important information that you lack. Since 80 percent of the value of the information that you need in any area will be contained in 20 percent of the information available (the 80/20 rule), what is the most important information or ability that you will require to achieve your goal?

Step nine: Make a list of all the people whose help and cooperation you will require. This list may include your family, your boss, your customers, your bankers, your business partners or sources of capital, and even your friends. To accomplish anything worthwhile, you'll need the help and cooperation of many people. Take this list and organize it in order of priority. Whose help is the most important? Whose help or cooperation is the second most important?

THE LAW OF COMPENSATION

The law of compensation is a special variation on the Law of Sowing and Reaping. It is a restatement of the Law of Cause and Effect. It has its counterpart in physics in a law that states that for every action there is an equal and opposite reaction. It states that, for everything you do, you will be compensated in kind. You will get out what you put in.

This law also states that other people will help you achieve your goals only if they feel that they will be compensated for their efforts in some way. No one works for nothing. Everyone has his or her own personal motivation. This should be your starting point in gaining the cooperation of others. Ask yourself the question, "What are you going to do for them to get them to help you?"

THE LAW OF RECIPROCITY

You must continually tune in to each person's favorite radio station, WIIFM, "What's in it for me?" Our social and business relations in America are all based on the Law of Reciprocity. The Law of Reciprocity states that people are internally driven to be *even,* to reciprocate for anything done either to or for them. They will be willing to help you achieve your goals only when you have demonstrated a willingness to help them to achieve their goals.

The most successful people in our society, in all fields, are those who have helped the greatest number of other people to get the things they want. They build up a reservoir of goodwill and create a propensity in others to help them, to reciprocate for having been helped in the past.

The Law of Overcompensation is triggered by the habit of always doing more than you are paid for. Successful people and successful businesses are those that always exceed expectations, who always do more than is expected of them. And the only part of the equation of compensation and reciprocity that you can control is the amount that you put in. The amount you get out is determined by yourself. Because this is part of the Law of Sowing and Reaping, if you take every opportunity that you can to help others, others will eventually give you all the help you need.

Your returns in life come back to you as a result of your contributions to others. If you contribute hard work, helpfulness and honesty, you will get back riches, rewards and the respect of other people.

If you want to increase the quantity and quality of your returns, your rewards, you need but to increase the quantity and quality of your service. By always doing more than you're paid for, you'll eventually be paid more than you're getting now. By putting more in, you'll get more out. By "overcontributing" you'll end up being "overcompensated."

The principle of organized effort, working together in harmony with other people toward mutually agreed upon goals, is the basis for all great accomplishment. Your willingness and your ability to cooperate effectively with others, to help them achieve their goals so that they will help you achieve yours, is indispensable to your future success.

Step ten: Make a plan. Write out, in detail, *what* you want, *when* you want it, *why* you want it and *where* you are starting from. Make a list of the *obstacles* you must overcome, the *information* you will require, and the *people* whose help you will need. With answers to steps one through nine, you have all the ingredients of a complete master plan for the achievement of any goal.

YOUR MASTER PLAN

A plan is a list of activities organized by time and priority. A list organized on the basis of time starts with the first thing that you have to do, in order, through to the last task that must be completed before your goal is achieved. Many activities can be worked on simultaneously. Other tasks have to be done in sequence, one after the other. Certain activities have to be done continuously from the beginning of the process through until the end.

A plan organized by priority lists activities in their order of importance. What is the *most* important thing that you have to do? What is the *second* most important thing? Keep asking this question until you have listed every activity based on its value to the completed goal.

Some years ago, the chairman of a large company for which I was working offered me an opportunity. He had been approached by a Japanese automobile company and offered the distributorship for their vehicles for a large geographical area. He asked me if I would like to do a market study with a view toward taking on the distributorship. This would involve setting up several dealerships, and then importing and distributing the vehicles through them.

Not really thinking about it too much, I accepted immediately. But there was just one problem. I did not have the slightest idea of where to start or what to do. So I immediately went out and did two solid months of research on the importation and distribution of Japanese automobiles. I visited every dealership selling similar cars. I asked everybody I could find for help and advice. And I got lucky. One of the consultants I spoke to had been hired four years earlier by a large corporation to do a complete feasibility study on automobile importation from Japan. Nothing had come of his study, but he still had all his notes.

I asked him if I could take a look at his notes and he showed them to me. Among his notes, I found a list of forty-five things that a company had to do to import and distribute Japanese vehicles through a network of dealerships. It was a blueprint for the business.

I took a copy of the list and used it as my road map. I carried it with me day and night. I began with item number one. Within three months, I had completed every item on the list and the first vehicles rolled off the ship from Japan. We went on to set up sixty-five dealerships and sell $25 million worth of vehicles. The division earned millions of dollars in profits for the company.

It was not easy. There was a tremendous amount of effort and ability involved in sales, service, parts, promotion, people, financing and administration. But the starting point was a detailed list of what needed to be done from beginning through to completion.

A good list gives you a track to run on and dramatically increases the likelihood of your achieving your goal. It is the essence of all personal planning and individual effectiveness. And all it takes to start is a pad of paper, a pen, a goal and *you*.

IMPROVE THE PLAN AS YOU GO

Once you have a detailed plan of action, get started. Accept that your plan will have flaws in it. It will not be perfect the first time out. Don't worry about it. Avoid the temptation of "perfectionitis."

If every possible obstacle must first be overcome, nothing will ever get done.

One of the characteristics of superior men and women is that they can accept feedback and make course corrections. They're more concerned with what's right than with who's right. Keep working on your plan until you have all the bugs out. Each time you hit a roadblock or an obstacle, go back and review your plan and make the necessary changes. Eventually you will have a plan that will work for you like a well-oiled machine.

The more detailed and the better organized your plans, the more likely you are to achieve your goals on schedule, and exactly as you have defined them.

Inc. magazine recently reported on interviews with the presidents of more than fifty corporations. They found that there was a direct relationship between the amount of detail that had gone into preparing their business plans and the level of success that the businesses had achieved.

But, in almost every case, the business that developed was different from the original plan. According to the study, it was the process of planning itself, of thinking through every single detail in advance, that led to ultimate success. It was having a well-designed plan to which modifications could be made, as they got feedback from the market, that ensured their sales and profitability.

The development of a detailed, constantly revised and finely honed personal plan is essential to the achievement of your major goals, as well.

Step eleven: Use visualization. Create a clear mental picture of your goal as it would appear if it were already achieved. Replay this picture over and over again on the screen of your mind. Each time you visualize your goal as accomplished, you increase your desire and intensify your belief that the goal is achievable for you. And what you *see* is what you *get*.

Your subconscious mind is activated by pictures. All your goal setting and planning up to this point has given you the details of an absolutely clear picture that you can feed repeatedly into your subconscious mind. These clear mental pictures concentrate your mental powers and activate the Law of Attraction. You immediately begin attracting to you, like iron filings to a magnet, the people, ideas and opportunities you need to attain your objectives.

Step twelve: Make the decision, in advance, that you will never, never, give up. Back your goals and plans with persistence and determination. Never consider the possibility of failure. Never think about quitting. Decide to hold on, no matter what happens. And as long as you refuse to quit, you must eventually be successful.

Develop the ability to persevere in the face of the inevitable obstacles and difficulties you will face. Sometimes, your ability to persist is what it takes to overcome the most difficult obstacles. Goal-setting begins with desire and comes full circle to persistence. The longer you persist, the more convinced and determined you become. You finally reach the point where nothing can stop you. And nothing will.

There are many poems on persistence and determination, and here is one of the most helpful that I've ever come across:

DON'T QUIT

When things go wrong, as they sometimes will,
When the road you're trudging seems all uphill,
When the funds are low and the debts are high,
And you want to smile but you have to sigh,
When care is pressing you down a bit
Rest if you must, but don't you quit.
For life is queer with its twists and turns,
As every one of us sometimes learns,
And many a failure turns about,
When he might have won if he'd stuck it out.
Success is just failure turned inside out,
The silver tint of the clouds of doubt.
And you never can tell how close you are,
It may be near when it seems so far.
So stick to the fight when you're hardest hit,
It's when things seem worst that *you must not quit!*

—ANONYMOUS*

* For a free copy of this poem, suitable for framing, see Appendix C.

CONTINUOUS ACTION TECHNIQUE

Once you have clearly established your goals and plans, and you have made the decision that you will never give up until you achieve them, you begin to use the continuous action technique to maintain your momentum toward your objectives.

The continuous action technique keeps you on track toward your goal. It is based on Isaac Newton's physical principles of inertia and momentum. These principles state that a body in motion tends to remain in motion unless acted upon by an outside force. They also state that while it may take a large amount of energy to get a body from a resting position to a state of forward motion, it takes a smaller amount of energy to keep it in motion at the same speed. This is one of the most important of all principles underlying great success.

The principle of momentum also has emotional and spiritual dimensions. You feel it in the sensations of motivation and excitement you experience as you move toward the achievement of something you care about. You have more energy and enthusiasm. You move faster toward your goal and it seems to move faster toward you.

Many people launch themselves toward a goal and then allow themselves to slow and stop. Once they stop, they often find that getting themselves going again is so difficult that they can't do it. Don't let this happen to you. The maintenance of momentum, once you've begun, is essential to great success and achievement.

You maintain your forward momentum by taking continuous action toward goal attainment. You keep up the pressure. You define your goals in terms of the activities necessary to accomplish them, and then you discipline yourself to perform the activities. You do something every day to move you toward the achievement of your major goals.

"Nothing succeeds like success." You must develop the *success habit* by doing something every single day to move you toward your goals. Review them every morning and think about them every day. Always be looking for something you can do to contribute to their achievement.

It may be major or minor, but for you to maintain momentum

and keep yourself positive and motivated, you must be continually taking actions consistent with what you hope to achieve.

Use the continuous action technique every day until you become a perpetual-motion, goal-setting and goal-achieving individual. Make sure that you mark each day with an accomplishment of some kind, the earlier in the day, the better. Remember, fast tempo is essential to success. The more things you do and try, and the faster you do and try them, the more energy and enthusiasm you will have and the more you will achieve.

A TRUE STORY

Here is an example of how effective this goal-achieving system can be. I was giving a lecture on the importance of goal setting to a public audience of about eight hundred people when a man I recognized from a previous seminar came up out of the audience and asked if he could have the microphone. He said he had a story to tell about what had happened to him after he began implementing this system in his life.

He told the audience that he had attended our seminar about six weeks before with his girlfriend. He was an insurance executive, and he explained that he had been through many personal and professional development seminars in his fourteen years in the insurance industry. He and his girlfriend had planned to come for the first morning of the two-day seminar and then leave and go shopping. He was convinced that there was nothing new for him to learn after all the courses he had already attended.

He said that they ended up staying for the entire two days. When they left, they were excited about what they had learned and eager to put it into practice, especially the system for goal setting. He went on to tell the audience that he had taken the following day off so that he and his girlfriend could spend the entire day planning the next few years of their lives with this goal-setting methodology. It took them ten full hours to complete their plan.

They had been dating for two years and had discussed marriage, but had made no decisions or commitments. They decided that one of their goals was to get married, and in accordance with what they had learned, they wrote it down and set a specific *deadline* for the wedding to take place.

They then set three subgoals associated with their wedding.

The first goal was that they would buy and pay for their dream house before they got married. This was the end of October and they had been through the seminar in the middle of September. The wedding date was set for February fourth of the coming year. That date therefore became their deadline for their house, as well.

Their second goal was to be married by Dr. Robert Schuller in the Crystal Cathedral in Garden Grove, California.

Their third goal was to hold their wedding reception aboard the "Love Boat" in Long Beach, California.

After writing out these goals in detail, they immediately took action. They went out for the next few evenings looking at houses and finally found exactly the one they wanted. The asking price was $220,000, but they learned that they could get it for $180,000 if they could come up with the money. The problem was that they had almost no savings at all. They needed to find or earn the entire amount, so they set a new goal, to earn $180,000 within ninety days.

They phoned Dr. Schuller's office at the Crystal Cathedral to arrange for their wedding on February fourth. They were told, however, that Dr. Schuller no longer did weddings. It was impossible, out of the question. But they were persistent. They asked if there was any way that he would change his mind. The secretary explained that he was far too busy and there was nothing that could be done.

Again, they persisted. Was there any way that they could appeal to him personally? Finally, the secretary, to conclude the conversation, told them that they could write to him personally, but that they shouldn't hold out much hope.

They immediately sat down and wrote Dr. Schuller a letter. They explained how much they believed in "possibility thinking," how important being married by him was to them, and how much difference it would make in their lives. They sent off the letter and went on to their second goal, the Love Boat and their reception.

Again, they ran into an obstacle. When they phoned the booking agent for the Love Boat, they were told that the ship would be at sea that day, arriving back at 4:00 P.M. and departing at 8:00 P.M. It would not be possible for them to have their reception on the ship that day.

But they were determined and incredibly optimistic. They had the attitude that they had nothing to lose. They called a friend in the travel business and asked her if she could pull a few strings. She got the same answer back through her channels. It wouldn't be possible.

Their experience wasn't unusual. They had set three big goals for themselves and had run into roadblocks on every one. So will you. Remember, if there are no obstacles, it's probably not a goal at all; it's just a task.

Whenever you set any goal for yourself that is above and beyond anything you've ever done before, you will immediately meet with frustrations and difficulties you had never anticipated. Especially, you will hear a thousand variations on the word "no."

But again, don't worry and don't be disheartened. The negatives you experience are part of the "persistence test." They go with the territory. They will determine how badly you really want it, whatever it is. And if it's not worth fighting for, it's probably not worth having in the first place.

This couple was not about to be stopped. They sat down and wrote another letter, this time to the shipping agent for the Love Boat. They explained their situation and repeated their request to book a stateroom for their reception on the afternoon of February fourth.

Their biggest single obstacle was getting enough money to buy their dream house before it was sold to someone else. But, acting in faith, they put down a one-thousand-dollar deposit with a closing date two months away.

Then, amazing things started to happen. A large corporate insurance policy he had been working on for six months, involving health, pensions, life and property covering every aspect of the company, finally came through. The president of the company called him and told him it had been approved by the board and they wanted to get it all set up and paid for by the end of the year. When the transaction was complete, his commission on the multiyear policy was just over $90,000, the largest commission he had ever made.

But it didn't end there. A week later, the president of the client company called him and told him that he had been describing his insurance coverage to a friend of his who owned a similarly sized company. His friend was interested in installing the same policy in his own organization. Could he help?

Could he help? You bet he could! Within two weeks, he had put together an almost identical package for the new client. When the sale day closed, his commission on the second policy was another $90,000!

That was just the beginning. A few days later, they got a phone call from Dr. Schuller's office, from the same secretary they had spoken to two weeks before.

"I don't know what you said in your letter," she said, "but Dr. Schuller came out of his office a few minutes ago with your letter in his hand and said, 'I'm going to do this wedding.' If you can be here on February fourth, he can marry you at 2:00 P.M."

Then, if that wasn't enough, a week later they got a call from the shipping company. They had just worked out the sailing schedule for the Love Boat for the new year. The ship would be docking at noon rather than 4:00 P.M. on February fourth and departing at 8:00 P.M. If they still wanted to have their reception aboard the ship, it would be available for them from 4:00 P.M. to 6:00 P.M.

He concluded this story from the stage with these words: "I feel I've accomplished more in the past six weeks using these ideas than I have in the last five years. I thought I understood goal setting before, but I had no idea how powerful it could be until I actually sat down and approached it in an organized fashion."

THE TWELVE STEPS REVISITED

Notice the incredible power these two people put behind their goals by following the twelve steps. They activated all the mental laws and got them working in harmony behind a major definite purpose.

Step one: Desire. They knew exactly what they wanted. It was intensely personal. They felt very strongly about it.

Step two: Belief. They were absolutely convinced that they could have their wedding exactly as they dreamed it could be. They remained confident and optimistic in the face of adversity. They had complete faith that everything would work out for them.

Perhaps most important, they demonstrated their faith by taking specific actions to achieve their goals, even when they had been told that nothing could be done.

Step three: Write it down. They crystallized their hopes and dreams on paper, thereby committing themselves to them. And by writing them out in detail, they reinforced their desires and deepened their beliefs in their ultimate ability to attain them.

Step four: Determine how you will benefit from achieving your goal. They were very clear how every part of their planned wedding, and their dream home, would contribute to laying the foundation for their happiness in the years ahead.

Step five: Analyze your starting point. They sat down and took a serious look at their lives. They assessed where they were relative to where they really wanted to be. Then they made some clear decisions. Everything followed from that.

Step six: Set a deadline. They picked a specific date for their wedding and then worked back from that. When they ran into difficulties, they refused to change the date. They dug in, as soldiers do when they come under fire. They refused to be put off by the initial resistance they encountered.

Step seven: Identify the obstacles that stand in your way. They first determined that they wanted to buy a home in which to start their married life. Their main obstacle was that they did not have the money to purchase it. They began with that. The money for the home was their "rock," their limiting step.

Step eight: Identify the additional knowledge or information you will require. They got busy and began finding out what they needed to know. They asked questions. They wrote letters. They took action.

Step nine: Identify the people whose cooperation you will require. They made a list of all the people they would need to work with to achieve their goals on the schedule they had set. He went to work with his prospective clients and they jointly went to work on the details of the wedding.

Step ten: Make a plan. Once they had worked through the first nine steps, they had all the ingredients of the plan worked out, like the ingredients in a recipe. It was then a relatively simple matter to put the plan together. With a complete list to work from, they had a unifying force for the next four months that brought them together and brought their goals to fruition.

Step eleven: Visualization. They got a clear mental picture of what they wanted. They walked through every room of their dream house. They got brochures with pictures of the Crystal Cathedral. They watched services conducted there on Sunday television. They looked at photos of the Love Boat and saw it on television as well. Throughout the day, and whenever they were together, they imagined and fantasized about their perfect wedding and their ideal home.

Step twelve: Persistence. They never considered the possibility of failure. They held to their dreams. They looked for ways over or around their obstacles. If one thing didn't work, they tried something else. They persevered until they finally succeeded.

And then, when all was done, everyone stood around and told them how lucky they were!*

GOING FOR THE GOLD

There are very few limitations on what you can accomplish. Most of them are self-imposed. They are the result of fears and doubts that stop you from trying. And you can overcome these self-limiting beliefs by taking actions consistent with your major purpose. The success and happiness you dream of begins with this system of goal setting, with you deciding exactly what you want and then doing what it takes to accomplish it.

The process and the system described in this chapter are far more than simply a mechanical means to make achievement more organized. They contain within them the combination to open the lock of your unlimited potential. These steps not only activate your positive mind and release your creativity, but they also cause all the mental laws to converge harmoniously toward the achievement of your dominant goals.

Most important, practicing these principles and rules for goal attainment unlocks the powers of your *superconscious mind.* This methodology makes available to you resources that you can use to change your life in ways you cannot yet imagine.

The proper activation and use of your superconscious mind is the most important discovery you can ever make. It is the key to happiness, health, prosperity and complete self-expression. The superconscious mind is the foundation of all personal greatness and high achievement, as you'll see in the next chapter.

* For a complete goal-setting guide and workbook that enables you to create a master plan for your life, write to me at 462 Stevens Ave., Suite 202, Solana Beach, CA 92075, or phone 619-481-2977. (See Appendix C for details.)

The Master Power

There is a story told by the ancient Greeks about when the world was young. The gods on Mount Olympus, having created the earth and man, the birds and animals, the creatures of the sea, the plants and flowers, and all living things, had one thing left to do, and that was to hide the secret of life where it would not be found until man had grown and evolved in consciousness to the point where he was ready for it.

The gods argued back and forth over where the secret of life should be hidden. One said, "Let us hide it on the highest mountain. Man will never find it there." But another god replied, "We have created man with insatiable curiosity and ambition, and he will eventually climb even the highest mountain."

Then one suggested they should hide the secret of life at the bottom of the deepest ocean. To this, another replied, "We have created man with boundless imagination and a burning desire to explore his world. Sooner or later, man will reach even the greatest ocean depths."

Finally, one of the gods came up with a solution. "Let us hide the secret of life in the last place that man will ever look, a place that he will only come to when he has exhausted all other possibilities and is finally ready."

"And where is that?" asked the other gods. To which the first god replied, "We will hide it deep in the human heart." And so they did.

For five thousand years of recorded history, some of the wisest men and women of each civilization have occupied themselves searching for the secret of the ages, the key that would enable them to unlock the vast treasure trove of potential that lies deep within each person. They have established brotherhoods and sisterhoods, secret societies and private communities dedicated to exploring the last frontier, and the first: the inner powers of the human mind.

Many men and women spent their entire lives in religious communities, monasteries and secret orders proceeding through elaborate rituals and initiations, during which glimpses of this great secret would be revealed to them.

THE MARCH OF PROGRESS

More progress has been made in finding this secret in the last one hundred years than in all the previous centuries that man has been on the earth. The secret of the ages, the key to health, happiness and prosperity for you and me, has been found in what is called *the superconscious mind*.

When you use your superconscious mind correctly, you will be able to solve any problem, overcome any obstacle and achieve any goal you sincerely desire. All personal greatness and individual achievement is based on it. In fact, everything we have discussed up to this point has been preparing you to use the powers of your superconscious mind to transform the quality of your life.

Many of the greatest thinkers who have ever lived have stood in awe before this power and have written about it, calling it many different names. Madame Blavatsky, the Russian theosophist, called it "the secret doctrine." Poet and philosopher Ralph Waldo Emerson called it "the oversoul," and he said, "We lie in the lap of an immense intelligence that responds to our every need." Emerson compared this intelligence to an ocean and said that when we receive insights from it, we recognize them as coming from far beyond ourselves and our own limited minds.

Napoleon Hill referred to this power as "infinite intelligence," calling it the universal storehouse of knowledge and the source of all imagination and creativity. He claimed that the ability to access this intelligence was a central part of the great success enjoyed by the hundreds of wealthy men and women he interviewed over the years.

Carl Jung, the Swiss psychoanalyst, called it the "supra-conscious mind," and said that it contained within it all the wisdom of the human race, past, present and future. It has also been called the "universal subconscious mind," the "collective unconscious" and the "universal mind," and many people refer to it as the "God-mind," or the "creative subconscious."

Whatever you choose to call it, there is almost no limit to what you can accomplish when you tap it, use it and let it use you on a regular basis.

It would be very difficult to explain to you how your superconscious mind works if you were not already familiar with it. Throughout your life, you have used it in a random and haphazard fashion many times. In fact, much of what you have already accomplished can be attributed to your accidental use of this power. My purpose in this chapter is to show you how to use it in a systematic way so you can dramatically increase the amount of health, happiness and prosperity that is possible for you.

THE SOURCE OF CREATIVITY

The superconscious mind is the source of all pure creativity. All truly classical art, music and literature come from the superconscious mind. Emerson confessed that his essays seemed to "write themselves." He would sit down at his desk and the words would simply pour through him and onto the paper. His essays remain as some of the most beautiful and inspiring writing in the English language.

Mozart was composing music at a young age. He could actually see and hear the music in his mind and was able to write it down, note perfect, the first time he put pen to paper. So clear were his music manuscripts that in the movie *Amadeus,* the court composer Salieri says of Mozart, "He writes the most beautiful music in the world as though he were taking dictation."

Beethoven, Bach, Brahms and Stravinsky all accessed this mind when composing their greatest pieces of music. Whenever you hear a piece of music, or see a work of art or read a piece of writing that seems timeless and which somehow touches something deep inside you, you are experiencing a superconscious creation.

INVENTIONS

The superconscious mind is responsible for new inventions and scientific breakthroughs. Edison regularly tapped his superconscious mind to find the solutions that led to his hundreds of successful inventions. Nikola Tesla, perhaps the greatest electrical genius of his age, was able to construct models of electric motors in his mind, disassemble them mentally, reassemble them, and repair them until they were perfect. He could then go into a workshop and build a totally new machine or motor that would work perfectly the very first time.

INSPIRATION

The superconscious mind is the source of all inspiration, all motivation, and the excitement that you feel when aroused by a new idea or possibility. It is the source of hunches, of intuition, and of flashes of insight—the "still small voice" within. Whenever you have been wrestling with a problem and have suddenly come up with a great idea that turned out to be the perfect solution, you were tapping your superconscious mind. Every time you experienced a new insight into a challenge you were facing, your superconscious mind was working.

ACCESS TO ALL STORED INFORMATION

When your superconscious mind computes on a problem or works on a goal, it has access to all the information stored in your subconscious mind. It can draw upon everything you have ever learned or experienced.

It also has the ability to discriminate between what is true and what is false. Each person has stored in his or her memory an enormous amount of information that is simply not true. Some of it is unimportant, like the actual height of Mount Everest, or the number of pecks in a bushel. Some of it is very important, such as critical facts that affect your personal fortunes. But in all cases, the superconscious mind uses only stored information that is *true*. It thus brings you answers and solutions that are correct and appropriate to your situation.

Sometimes you will get an idea that seems inconsistent with what you *know* to be true. It will then turn out that your knowledge was incomplete or based on erroneous information. Your seemingly contradictory idea or solution turns out to be the correct one. It is exactly the answer you need.

ACCESS TO INFORMATION OUTSIDE YOUR BRAIN

The superconscious mind also has access to knowledge and information from outside and beyond your personal knowledge and experience. It actually lies *outside* your brain, outside your conscious and subconscious minds.

The Englishman Michael Faraday, who was not trained as a scientist, awoke once in the middle of the night with his mind teeming with scientific formulations. He sat down and wrote several pages of mathematical formulas and scientific calculations that seemed to flow through him like a river of energy. Once he had finished writing, he fell back asleep, exhausted.

When he later took his notes to one of the most learned scientists in England, it was determined that he had produced knowledge that had never before existed. That work of Michael Faraday laid the foundation for the development of the vacuum tube by Lee De Forest, and for the entire electronic age in which we now live.

THE UNIVERSAL MIND

You are surrounded by a universal mind that contains all the intelligence, ideas and knowledge that has ever existed, or that will ever exist. Because of this, different people in different parts of the world will often tap this energy and come up with the same ideas at the same time.

One of our seminar graduates had worked with a team at the Atomic Energy Research Council of Canada to develop what he called a Gamma Ray Backflash Measuring Device. It took them two years to perfect the device, but the key was an insight that he had while working on the project.

Some months later, at an international symposium that included scientists from the Soviet Union, they found that a Soviet scientist had had exactly the same insight at almost exactly the same time, which led to the Soviets' developing almost exactly the same device. Since both of these projects were top secret before being shared publicly, there was no way that the creative insights could have been exchanged through any medium except the superconscious mind.

IDEAS BEYOND YOUR CURRENT EXPERIENCE

Once you begin using your superconscious capabilities in a systematic way, you will get ideas from *out of the blue*. Almost everyone has had the experience of thinking of a good idea for a new product or service, dismissing it because it was in a field in which they had no experience, and then seeing some other company come out with the same product or service a couple of years later and make a fortune. This is an example of superconscious functioning.

The difference between the person who had the idea and ignored it, and the person who came up with the idea and ran with it, was that the person who did something with the idea had a higher level of trust and confidence in himself and his ability to turn the idea into reality. Because of childhood conditioning, we tend to ignore our own ideas, assuming that they could not be worth very much, when, in fact, they could change our whole lives. When you begin accepting the value of your superconscious insights, you will be amazed at the kind of ideas that come to you, and the next time you have an idea, you'll do something with it.

CONTINUOUS FUNCTIONING

Your superconscious mind functions on a nonconscious level twenty-four hours per day, 365 days per year. Once you have programmed a goal or problem into your subconscious mind, and then released it, it is transferred to your superconscious mind and your superconscious goes to work on it. You can then go about your daily life, with your conscious and subconscious energies focused on the work at hand, while your superconscious mind is busily working to bring you whatever you need to achieve your goal.

Remember, the functions of the conscious mind are to identify, compare, analyze and decide. The subconscious mind stores and retrieves information and obeys the commands of the conscious mind. The superconscious mind functions outside and beyond both of them, but is accessed through them.

GOAL-ORIENTED MOTIVATION

Your superconscious mind is capable of goal-oriented motivation. It is the source of the enthusiasm and the excitement you feel when you begin setting goals and moving progressively toward their accomplishment. However, to generate this motivation, your superconscious mind requires *clear, specific goals* to which you are completely committed. It then releases ideas and energy for goal attainment.

The superconscious mind is a source of "free energy." This is a phenomenon you've experienced many times before. It is the mental and physical energy that surges through you during periods of great excitement, intense desire or even extreme danger. When you are working toward something that is important to you, you often experience a boundless flow of energy that enables you to work day and night with very little sleep. Usually this is called "nervous energy," but of course, we know that nerves have no energy of their own.

Have you ever had the experience of having to get up in the middle of the night because of an emergency? In no time, you find yourself wide awake, alert and functioning effectively, whereas a short while before you were tired and sound asleep. This is an example of tapping the "free energy" of your superconscious mind.

Another example of this "free energy" is the phenomenon of men and women performing superhuman feats in life-threatening situations. In Florida a few years ago, a frail, sixty-eight-year-old grandmother, Mrs. Laura Schulz, was working in her kitchen while her forty-year-old son was working under a car in the driveway. Suddenly, the jack slipped and the car fell on his chest, crushing him and threatening to kill him.

When he cried out in pain, his elderly mother rushed out of the house, saw what had happened and immediately acted. She rushed forward, grabbed the bumper, and lifted the two-thousand-pound automobile off her son's chest, saving his life.

Two neighbors saw her do it. But afterward, when she was interviewed by reporters, she denied that it had ever taken place. She completely blotted the experience out of her mind because it was so far beyond what she "knew" to be true about her own strength.

When you become fully attuned to your superconscious mind, you will experience a continuous stream of health, energy, and strength that will enable you to produce more in a few hours than the average person produces in a week. You will enter into the state of "flow," where the world seems to slow down while your mind speeds up. During this time you seem to have an easy ability to produce large quantities of high-quality work. You have a wonderful sense of well-being. Your mind sparkles with a stream of ideas that flow to you exactly as you need them.

CLEAR COMMANDS

Your superconscious mind responds best to clear, authoritative commands, or what are called "positive affirmations." Every time that you affirm a goal or a desire from your conscious mind to your subconscious mind, you activate your superconscious mind to release the ideas and energy that you need to bring your desire into reality.

This is why *decisiveness* is such an important trait of successful men and women. Because they know exactly what they want, their superconscious powers are working for them continuously. You will also find that when you stop vacillating and make a firm, clear decision that you are going to do something, no matter what the cost, everything suddenly starts to work in your favor.

When you affirm "I like myself," or "I can do it," or "I earn $XXX per year," you are throwing the master switch on all your mental powers. You are "turning on" in the most powerful way possible.

I mentioned earlier that the primary reason that people do not achieve their potential is that they are simply *not serious*. By "not serious," I mean that they simply refuse to make the decisions that they must make if their lives are going to change for the better.

You will be amazed at how much more effective you become when you make firm decisions and burn your mental bridges behind you. Cut off all thought of quitting or retreating, or doing something else. Make the decision that you are going to do whatever it takes to achieve your goal, and that nothing is going to stop you. At that point, even a person with average abilities becomes an extraordinary agent of accomplishment.

THE SOLUTION TO EVERY PROBLEM

Your superconscious mind automatically and continuously solves every problem on the way to your goal, as long as your goal is *clear*. If your goal is to make a lot of money and you are absolutely clear about the amount that you want to earn and keep, you must, you will eventually achieve it.

The history of the human race is written in the stories of men and women who have set big exciting goals for themselves, and who have then persisted indomitably, sometimes for many years, before finally reaching them. Peter Drucker, the well-known management expert and author of *The Effective Executive,* says, "Whenever you find something getting done, anywhere, you will find a monomaniac with a mission." Whenever you find great achievement, you find an individual who is absolutely clear about what he or she wants to do, and who is willing to do whatever it takes, for however long it takes, to achieve it.

Your main job is to keep your thoughts on your goal. Your superconscious mind will automatically and continuously solve each problem on the way to your goal as and when the problem arises. You can trust absolutely in this superconscious power to function for you as long as your goal is clear.

THE PROPER MENTAL CLIMATE

Your superconscious mind operates best in a mental climate of *faith* and *acceptance*. The attitude of confidently expecting that your problems will be solved, obstacles removed, and your goals achieved is the mental state that intensifies the rate of the vibration of thought and causes your superconscious mind to function at its best.

Although it is difficult initially, it is only when you are completely relaxed about the outcome of any situation that the situation seems to resolve itself, sometimes in the most unexpected way. The outcome, however, will always be everything that you could ask, and sometimes much more. It seems that the harder you "don't try," the better your superconscious mind works in bringing you the things you want.

All great men and women have been people of faith. They have been able to "take no thought." They developed the almost childlike ability to entrust themselves to the goodness of the universe, with the simple faith that everything was unfolding as it should, in its own time. They have had an attitude of calmness and confidence and a belief that there was a power greater than themselves that was helping them.

Any kind of negativity, anger, worry or impatience shuts down your superconscious mind. It diminishes your powers. It clouds your thinking. It confuses the messages you are sending from your conscious to your subconscious mind. Destructive emotions of any kind interfere with the calm, positive attitude your superconscious requires for optimal functioning.

IT BRINGS YOU THE EXPERIENCES YOU NEED

Your superconscious mind brings you the experiences you need to be successful. Because you can never permanently achieve anything on the outside that you are not fully prepared for on the inside, whenever you set a goal of any kind, you will have to grow and develop to the point that you are ready to achieve it. Your superconscious mind will guide you through the experiences you need to teach you the lessons you have to learn, in order, so that when you finally arrive at your destination, it will almost seem like an anticlimax. You will by then have developed the mental equivalent of the corresponding outer reality that you desire.

This is a very important point: If you achieve anything without having prepared yourself for it in your thinking, you will not be able to hold on to it. If you make a lot of money unexpectedly, and your self-concept is not equal to it, you will be subconsciously driven to engage in behavior to get rid of the money. That is why it is said, "easy come, easy go."

However, if you achieve your successes gradually, growing as a person on the inside as you increase in your productive capacity on the outside, when you finally reach the position in life that you desire, you will be ready to hold on to it indefinitely.

If you look back over your life, you will find that almost everything worthwhile that you have accomplished was preceded by what appeared to be difficulties, disappointments and temporary failures. Often, you had to ride an emotional roller coaster of fear, anxiety and worry. However, in retrospect, you can see that every one of those difficult experiences was essential to your becoming the kind of person you are today, and to achieving your ultimate goal.

This is a very important point. Your superconscious mind sets up a series of hurdles, or learning experiences, to train you in exactly what you need to learn. Your superconscious mind is also very patient. If you do not learn the lesson, whether it's in relationships, in business, with money or with your health, your superconscious mind will send you back through the learning experiences over and over until you finally *get it,* until you learn what you are meant to learn. Then and only then will you be allowed to proceed to the next step in your development.

Napoleon Hill found that almost every one of the wealthy men he interviewed had achieved their great successes one step beyond what appeared to be their greatest failure. It was when every outward indication suggested that it was time to quit and to give up that they were the very closest to breaking through to their goals.

It is almost as if your superconscious mind gives you a final test just before you arrive at your destination. It is when you are going through your most difficult learning experiences that you must draw on your ability to control your mind and have faith that the difficulty you face is simply part of the process that will inevitably bring you through to your goal.

A characteristic of successful men and women is that they never use the word "failure." They look upon temporary defeats and setbacks as simply another way of learning how to succeed. They seek within every obstacle or disappointment the seed of an equal or greater benefit or opportunity. They learn from every experience. They refuse to get upset. They keep their minds calm, positive and focused on their goals. As a result, they keep their superconscious capabilities switched on.

USE IT OR LOSE IT

Your superconscious mind grows in capability as you use it and trust it. Men and women begin to achieve great things only when they begin trusting completely in this mysterious power or force surrounding them. The "Law of Use" states, "If you don't use it, you lose it." It also states that whatever mental or physical capabilities you *do* use become stronger and more responsive to your demands. When you develop the habit of continually turning to your superconscious mind to guide and direct you, to inspire and illuminate you and to solve every problem on your path, it will work faster and more efficiently every day.

IT GIVES YOU UNERRING GUIDANCE

Your superconscious mind makes all of your words and actions, *and their effects,* fit a pattern consistent with your self-concept and your dominant goals. You will always be inspired to say and do exactly the right thing, in every situation, when you are tuned in to your superconscious.

Sometimes words will seem to fall out of your mouth that will turn out later to have been exactly the right thing to say at the time. Sometimes, you will get an urge to buy a book or a tape, to telephone or visit someone, to write a letter or make a decision that later turns out to be exactly the thing for you to do at that moment. You will pick up a book or magazine or open it to the exact page that has the answer you need. And this will start happening repeatedly, the more you trust yourself to this great power.

SYNCHRONICITY EXPLAINED

Synchronicity is a common phenomenon that occurs when two seemingly unrelated events happen at the same time and, somehow, both these events help you to move toward one of your goals. For example, you could think about taking a vacation to Hawaii in the morning before you go to work, and later on that day, receive a special offer for a week in Hawaii at a cut-rate price. You might decide over the weekend that you need to be earning more money, and Monday your boss could offer you a promotion with greater responsibilities and higher pay. The only connecting link between these synchronous events is the meaning imposed upon the events by your thoughts and your goal. This is another example of super-conscious activity.

Another word that is often used to describe this kind of coincidence is "serendipity." Serendipity is the facility of making happy discoveries. People who experience serendipity all seem to have one thing in common: They are actively *seeking* something. They all seem to have very clear goals and the remarkable things they find are all associated with something they want to accomplish.

People are always telling me, after they have started using their superconscious minds, "You won't believe what happened to me!" I have heard this exclamation a thousand times: "You won't believe what happened to me!" Other people, even when remarkably coincidental things happen to them, will tend to dismiss these seemingly inexplicable events by calling them "luck," or by saying that they just happened by accident. But now you will know better.

We live in a universe that is governed by *law*. Nothing happens by chance. Everything happens as the result of definite laws and principles, even if you don't know what they are.

In England during the darkest days of World War II, in the fall of 1941, Prime Minister Winston Churchill was urged by members of his cabinet to make peace, to seek some kind of accommodation with Hitler. Churchill refused. He said that something would happen to bring America into the war, and that would change the entire equation. When he was pressed on this point, and asked how he could be so confident, he replied, "Because I study history and history shows that if you hold on long enough, something always happens."

On December 7, 1941, only a few weeks after this conversation took place, the Japanese bombed Pearl Harbor. When Hitler heard of this, he immediately declared war on the United States. Over-night, everything changed, and the industrial might of America was thrown onto the scales on the side of Britain. The unilateral action of Japan on the other side of the world triggered the chain of events that enabled Churchill to achieve his goal of saving England from being overrun by Nazi Germany.

The more you can hold this mental state of calm, confident

expectation, even when buffeted by the storms of life, the more likely it is that you will experience synchronicity and serendipity. They are delightful experiences that always fill you with a feeling of happiness and excitement.

TWO OPERATING CONDITIONS

Your superconscious mind operates best under two conditions. The first is when your conscious mind is concentrating 100 percent on a specific problem or goal. The second is when your conscious mind is busy with something else altogether. You should try both methods on anything you want to accomplish.

Here is a simple, five-step process you can use to bring all the powers of your superconscious mind to bear on a single issue.

Step one: Define the problem or goal clearly, preferably in writing. What is it exactly that you want to achieve, or exactly what is the problem you wish to solve?

Step two: Gather as much information as you can. Read, research, ask questions and actively seek the answer that you need.

Step three: Consciously try to solve the problem by reviewing all the information you have gathered.

Step four: If you still have not been able to solve the problem *consciously,* turn it over to your superconscious mind. Release it confidently, the way you would release a balloon, and let it float away.

Step five: Get your conscious mind busy elsewhere. Turn your attention away and let your superconscious mind take care of it for you!

Take any problem you are wrestling with right now and try this method on it. You will be amazed at the results.

IT BRINGS YOU THE ANSWERS YOU NEED

Your superconscious mind will bring you exactly the right answer at exactly the right time. When the answer comes, you must act on it immediately. It is "time-dated" material. If you get the urge to telephone someone, or to say something or do something, and it feels exactly right, act in faith and follow your instincts. It will always turn out to be the right thing to do.

If you are having a problem with another person and you get a clear idea of what you should do or say, even if it involves some confrontation or unpleasantness, follow your hunch and carry through with it. The outcome will always be equal to or better than what you could have expected.

As a professional speaker, I will sometimes be unsure about exactly how to structure and begin a talk or a seminar. When I turn it over to my superconscious mind, at a certain point, often as I am walking to the podium, the entire talk will crystallize in my mind and it will turn out to be exactly the right thing to say.

Recently, I was asked to address a corporate audience on the challenges of professional selling in the 1990s. I had prepared for this talk and I was ready to speak on the subject. But as I was introduced, I had this irresistible urge to talk instead about the importance of long-term goals and strategies and having the courage to give up the old and embark in new directions. At the end of the talk, I got a standing ovation.

Later, the president of the company told me that, before my talk, they had had two full days of meetings at which they discussed and debated the future direction of the company. My talk had clarified the issues they were wrestling with and had given them the keys to solving some of their most pressing problems. It turned out that my superconscious mind was guiding me to say the things that their superconscious minds were directing them to learn.

YOUR MENTAL ALARM CLOCK

Your superconscious mind enables you to program yourself so you remember to do things at certain times in the future. For example, you can program your mind to wake you up at any hour, day or night. There are many people, including myself, who never use alarm clocks, and who never oversleep. All you need to do is to decide at what time you want to wake up tomorrow morning. Then forget it. At exactly that time, or a few minutes before, you will come wide awake.

I travel back and forth over several time zones, going to bed and getting up at all hours. And my superconscious mind always wakes me up at exactly the right time. I never oversleep. It's better than an alarm clock.

You can remind yourself to call someone at a certain time, or to stop off and pick up something on the way home. At exactly the right time or place, the thought you programmed will leap into your mind. And you can use this power by simply deciding to do so.

You can eventually reach the point where you won't need to carry a watch. You will always know within a few minutes exactly what time it is.

FINDING PARKING SPACES

Among other things, you can use your superconscious mind to find parking spaces. If you can clearly visualize a parking space, even on a crowded street or a parking lot, when you arrive, the parking space will be waiting for you. If it is especially busy, someone will be holding the space until you arrive. Just as you drive up, no sooner and no later, the other car will pull out to make way for you. My wife, Barbara, has developed this capability to the point where she can plan a whole series of errands and get a parking spot right next to the door of every store or office that she is going to.

Technical people, like engineers and accountants, find this very hard to believe. But I run into people all over the country who tell me they've never had a problem finding a parking space since they went through the seminar.

In a recent seminar that we conducted in San Diego, we gave the participants Saturday afternoon off. Two groups of people decided to visit the San Diego Zoo for the afternoon. The first group was made up of four young entrepreneurs. They were positive, optimistic, and fully confident that this method of finding parking spaces would work. The other group was made up of three engineers. They were quite clear that there was no way that you could find parking spaces using visualization and their superconscious minds.

Both groups went separately to the San Diego Zoo. The car full of young entrepreneurs drove straight up to the parking spaces by the front entrance, even though the parking lot was jammed as far as the eye could see. Just as they arrived at the front entrance, the very first parking stall opened up. The car that was in it backed out. They drove right in, laughing, and went on into the zoo.

The engineers, on the other hand, did not believe that it would work. They drove around for a while and then parked on the far side of the parking lot and walked about two blocks to the entrance.

Although this is a simple way to use a powerful force, try it for yourself and see. Remember, the key is your attitude. If you confidently believe that you will find a parking space, you most certainly will. But any trace of doubt or skepticism will short-circuit the process and cause it to fail.

THE LAW OF SUPERCONSCIOUS ACTIVITY

This is the most important of all the laws in this book. It is the summary law that binds them all together. The Law of Superconscious Activity states, "Any thought, plan, goal or idea held continuously in your conscious mind must be brought into reality by your superconscious mind, whether positive or negative."

Any thought, plan, goal or idea that you can hold continuously and confidently in your conscious mind, whether positive or negative, will eventually be brought into your reality by your superconscious mind. This law explains how you create your world by the thoughts that you allow to dominate your thinking. If you keep your mind on the things that you want, and keep them off the things that you fear, your goals, whatever they are, will eventually materialize and become your realities.

Like all laws, this law is neutral. It is no respecter of persons. It is the highest manifestation of the principle of cause and effect. If you use this power for good, then only good will come into your life. If you use this power negatively, it will bring you illness, unhappiness and financial frustration. The choice is always yours. You are always free to choose the kind of world that you wish to live in. And you choose it every day by the thoughts you think.

A successful life is merely a series of successful days, hours and minutes, minutes during which you think about your goals and your desires, about health and happiness and prosperity, and refuse to dwell on anything that you do not want to see manifested around you.

STIMULATING SUPERCONSCIOUS ACTIVITY

There are several ways to stimulate superconscious activity. The first and most dependable is simply to *think about your goals* all the time. This alone will keep you happy and focused. It will cause superconscious energies to flow through you in the form of ideas and motivation toward goal attainment.

The second way to stimulate your superconscious mind is through the practice of *solitude,* "going into the silence." Men and women begin to become great when they start taking time to be alone with themselves. Solitude is a wonderful tonic that gives balance and clarity to thought. It provides an opportunity for you to reflect on who you are and what is important to you. Most of all, solitude provides the mental medium of calmness and serenity that causes superconscious solutions to spring into your mind full-blown and complete in every detail.

If you have never tried it, the simplest way to practice solitude is to go and sit somewhere, perfectly silently, without moving, for an entire hour. Do not drink coffee, take notes, smoke cigarettes, listen to music or do anything else. Just sit perfectly still for an entire hour.

Most people have never deliberately sat down alone with themselves for any period of time. If this is your first experience with solitude, you will find it excruciatingly difficult. For the first twenty-five to thirty minutes you will have an almost irresistible urge to get up and move around. You will find it almost impossible to sit still. But if you have the self-control to sit without moving for thirty minutes, something remarkable will happen. You will start to feel calm, relaxed and at peace with yourself. You will feel happy and at one with the world.

Then, at a certain point, you will feel a river of creative energy flowing through you. You will start to have ideas and insights you can apply immediately to be happier and more effective. At exactly the right moment for you, the answer that you need to your most pressing problem will emerge in your mind. You will recognize it immediately. When you get up from your period of solitude and go out and implement the solution that came to you, you will find that it was exactly the right thing to do. It is almost as if this ideal answer had been brought to you by a force from far beyond, which, of course, it has.

The third way to trigger superconscious activity is to *visualize* your goal as realized. Create a clear mental picture of exactly the goal or outcome you want. Dwell on this picture repeatedly until it is accepted as a command by your subconscious mind and is passed on to your superconscious mind for realization.

Superconscious activity usually happens when you are making as little effort as possible. Releasing your problem or goal completely often stimulates ideas of tremendous value. Letting it go with complete confidence and getting your mind busy elsewhere is often the trigger that unlocks your hidden powers.

Many people find that daydreaming or relaxing on a park bench triggers superconscious activity. Listening to classical music, alone or in the company of people you enjoy, will often cause wonderful ideas to spring into your mind.

Perhaps one of the most enjoyable ways to turn on your superconscious powers is to go for a walk or to commune with nature in some way. The sounds of the ocean on the seashore seem to have a powerful impact on the superconscious, as do those of any running water or natural environment. Any form of deep relaxation or meditation also stimulates your superconscious mind.

One good superconscious insight or idea can save you months, even years, of hard work. You must resist the temptation to procrastinate on trying one or more of these methods on the most pressing issues facing you. It is exactly when you are too busy that you most urgently need to listen to your inner voice.

THE SUPERCONSCIOUS SOLUTION

A superconscious solution will come to you from one of three sources. The first and most frequent source is from *intuition*. Sometimes this *inner* voice will be so loud you will be unable to think of anything else. The answer will be so clear and obvious that you will know this is exactly the right thing for you to do. It will not only be right, it will feel right as well.

Always trust your intuition; never go against it. Your intuition is your direct pipeline to your superconscious mind and to infinite intelligence. All successful and happy men and women listen closely to their intuitions and to the *feel* of a situation. Most of the problems you've had and mistakes you've made in life have been the result of ignoring your "gut feelings."

The second source of superconscious solutions is *chance encounters* with other people or information. Once you have a clear goal, or a problem to solve on the way to your goal, you will unexpectedly run into people who can help you. Often they will be strangers you meet traveling or in social situations. You will come across books, magazines and articles that contain exactly the information you need. You will hear the solution you're looking for on an audiotape. The information will seem to be drawn to you in exactly the form you require it at the time.

A friend of mine, a famous photographer, was wrestling with a personal problem one evening at home when he had the urge to walk across his living room and get a book from the shelf. As he moved toward the book, it fell off the shelf onto the floor, face down and open. When he bent over and picked up the book, the first paragraph contained exactly the answer he was looking for. He had just been through our seminar, and he recognized immediately that he had experienced a superconscious solution. He implemented it the next morning and it turned out to be exactly the right thing to do.

Earlier I encouraged you to start off each morning by saying, *"I believe something wonderful is going to happen to me today."* If you go through your day believing that something wonderful is about to happen to you, you will meet people and come across information that will make your expectation a reality. You will get superconscious solutions to your problems in the most surprising ways.

The third source of superconscious solutions is *unpredictable events.* Peter Drucker writes in his book *Innovation and Entrepreneurship* that the primary source of innovation in business is the unexpected success or the unexpected failure. It is often the completely unanticipated event that contains the superconscious solution that you are seeking. And the unexpected event that contains the answer you need can often appear to be a major setback or failure.

Sir Alexander Fleming was conducting experiments on bacteria in his laboratory in London when some mold flew onto his culture dishes and killed the bacteria, thereby ruining the experiment. As he was about to throw away the culture medium and begin again, he noticed the mold that had killed the bacteria. He began to study the mold very carefully, and the result was the discovery of penicillin, which won him a Nobel prize in medicine and saved the lives of millions during World War II.

Norman Vincent Peale says that whenever God wants to send you a gift, he wraps it up in a problem. The bigger the problem, the bigger the gift. Is the glass half empty or is the glass half full? Successful, happy people make a habit of looking into even the most difficult situation for something positive, something they can learn or some way they can benefit. And this very attitude often triggers a superconscious insight or solution to their problem.

CHARACTERISTICS OF A SUPERCONSCIOUS SOLUTION

A superconscious solution has three characteristics. First of all, when it comes, it is *100 percent complete,* and deals with every aspect of the problem. It is always within your resources and capabilities at the time. It is always simple and fairly easy to implement.

Second, it appears to be a *blinding flash of the obvious.* It seems to be so simple and so evident that you often have the "Aha!" experience. You wonder why you hadn't thought of it before. Of course, the reason you hadn't thought of it before was either that you weren't ready or that the timing was not right.

The third way that you can tell a superconscious solution is that it always comes accompanied by a *burst of joy and energy,* a feeling of elation that makes you want to take action immediately.

If you get a superconscious solution in the middle of the night, you will be unable to sleep until you get up and write it down or do something about it.

There is the famous story of Archimedes taking a bath and suddenly having the superconscious solution that enabled him to determine the proportions of gold and silver in a wreath made for the king. He became so excited that he ran through the streets of Syracuse naked, shouting, "Eureka! Eureka!" ("I have found it, I have found it!")

When a superconscious solution comes to you, even after a long period of mental and physical effort, you will get a feeling of excitement, joy and enthusiasm. You will have a burst of "free energy." You will want to implement the solution immediately. You will feel happy and confident and sure that it will work.

When you have clearly defined goals and detailed plans, backed by a positive mental attitude and a calm, confident expectation of success, you activate your superconscious mind into bringing you virtually anything you could ever want in life. When you affirm positively, visualize clearly and believe absolutely, you will be led irresistibly to do and say the right thing at the right time in every situation. You unlock your full potential for health, happiness and prosperity. You bring yourself into complete alignment with the greatest power of the universe.

ACTION EXERCISE

Schedule *one solid hour* of solitude during which you sit perfectly still for the entire sixty minutes. Discipline yourself to do this as soon as possible. During this period of silence, shut everything else out of your mind. Just push your problems aside for the moment. Let your mind wander. Daydream. Don't try to think of anything specific. Temporarily step outside of your work and personal life. Turn everything over to your superconscious mind and release all your cares and worries.

Sometime during this hour, your mind will go calm and clear. You will feel relaxed and happy. And with no effort at all on your part, exactly the answer you need at that moment will come to you.

At the end of the hour get up and follow your intuition. Do what your superconscious has guided you to do. Don't worry about whether someone else will approve or agree. The answer will be exactly right, and you'll probably never make another mistake.

CHAPTER 7

The Master Decision

Everything we've talked about in this book up to now will succeed or fail for you depending upon your ability to apply it to your life. The master decision is the key to personal liberation, happiness and high achievement.

The starting point of personal liberation is for you to accept complete responsibility for who you are and for everything that you become. You must accept, without reservation, that you are where you are and what you are because of yourself. If you want things to change, then you must change first. Your thinking determines your attitude, your conduct and your behavior, and they in turn largely determine your success or failure in life. Because you are always free to choose the content of your conscious mind, you are always fully responsible for the consequences of what you think.

You can dream big dreams, learn how to control both your conscious and subconscious minds and improve your self-concept and performance. But none of these efforts will give you any lasting benefit until you embrace personal responsibility.

When I was twenty years old, having failed high school, I was living in a tiny one-room apartment and working as a construction laborer in the middle of a very cold winter. I had almost no money. I was far from whatever home I'd had and I wasn't planning to go back. One night, as I sat alone at my little kitchen table, it suddenly dawned on me that everything that I would ever become was completely up to me. No one else was going to do it for me. Someone once said, "True maturity only comes when you finally realize that no one is coming to the rescue." That revelation suddenly opened my eyes. I was never completely the same again.

You are programmed from infancy to believe that someone or something else is responsible for much of your life. When you are a child, if you are fortunate, your parents take care of everything. They provide you with food, clothing, shelter, educational opportunities, recreation, money, medical attention and whatever else you need. You are entirely provided for by other people. You are a passive player in the process.

It is normal and natural that our parents provide for us during our formative years. The problems begin when people come into adulthood with the unconscious expectation that somewhere, somehow, someone else is still responsible for them and for their situation. But from the age of eighteen onward, and sometimes earlier, you are in the driver's seat. You are the architect of your own destiny. Whether or not your parents have succeeded in raising you as a totally self-reliant individual, from that moment forward there is no looking back. Everything you are, everything you become from then on, is up to you.

In one of Tolstoy's short stories, he writes about a group of children who are told that the secret of happiness is hidden in the backyard of their home. They will be able to find it and possess it forever as long as they refrain from doing one thing. They must not think about a white rabbit while they are searching for the secret. Each time the children go out to search for the secret they try not to think about it. But the harder they try, the more they think about a white rabbit, and of course, they never do find the secret of happiness.

RABBIT HUNTING

Everyone has a "white rabbit," and sometimes, many white rabbits. These are the excuses that you use to avoid setting clear goals and making total commitments to the things you really want. Since the quality of your thinking determines the quality of your life, you need to become a skilled thinker if you sincerely desire to fulfill your potential. Part of being a skilled thinker is to objectively analyze any mental blocks, or excuses, that you have that you may be using as reasons for not moving ahead.

Some of the most popular "white rabbits" that people use as excuses are self-limiting ideas, such as "I'm too young," or "I'm too old," or "I don't have any money," or "I don't have enough education," or "I have too many bills," or "I'm not ready yet," or "I can't do it because of my boss, my children, my parents" or some other reason.

What are your personal "white rabbits"? What are your favorite excuses for not making the changes that you know are necessary if you are going to achieve your goals and fulfill your dreams? Go "rabbit hunting" in your own life. Root them out and run them down. Carefully analyze them to see if they have any validity.

Here's a simple way to test your excuses. Ask yourself: "Is there anyone, anywhere with my problem or limitation who has succeeded in spite of it?"

If the answer is "yes," you know that your excuse is not valid. It is not a legitimate reason for your failure to make progress. What one person has done, someone else can do as well. The disease of "excusitis," the inflammation of the excuse-making gland, is invariably fatal to success. If you have it, resolve to get over it right away before it sabotages all your hopes for great success.

THE WAY OUT

The acceptance of complete responsibility, the giving up of all your excuses, is not easy. It's one of the hardest things you ever attempt. That's why most people never do it. It is like making a parachute jump for the first time: It is both scary and exhilarating. When you cast free from your excuses, as when you leap out of the plane, you suddenly feel completely alone, completely vulnerable. However, in a few moments, you start to feel a rush of excitement, your heart starts pounding faster and you feel remarkably happy and free.

You can never give responsibility away. The only thing that you can give away is control. And you know, from the Law of Control, that you only feel good about yourself to the degree to which you feel you are in control of your own life. If you try to make someone or something else responsible, you end up giving them control over your emotions. You are still completely responsible, but by giving up control, you lose your peace of mind.

Self-responsibility is the core quality of the fully mature, fully functioning, self-actualizing individual. Superior men and women take both the credit and the blame for everything that happens to them. People who are failures take credit for their successes, but they blame their problems on bad luck, other people or circumstances beyond their control. Successful men and women have a strong sense of internal accountability, which extends to their work and to all of their relationships. Failures try to evade accountability at every turn.

Sometimes I ask my seminar audiences the question, "How many of you are self-employed?" Usually, fewer than 20 percent of the audience raise their hands. Then I point out to them that this is a trick question. I tell them that the biggest mistake one can ever make is to think that one works for anyone but oneself. *We are all self-employed,* no matter who signs our paycheck. You are the president of your own personal services corporation. *You are in charge.*

The top 3 percent in every field treat their company as if it belonged to them. They see themselves as self-employed. They act as if they own the place. When they refer to their company, they use words like "we" and "our" and "my" and "us." The average employee, on the other hand, always refers to the company as if it were something separate and apart from him or her, as if it were just a job, with no other meaning or significance.

There is a direct relationship between how much responsibility you are willing to accept for results and how high you rise in any organization of value. There is a direct relationship between your income, your status, your position, your level of prestige and the recognition you receive, on the one hand, and the amount of responsibility you are willing to accept, without excuses, for achieving the goals and objectives of your organization, on the other.

Here's an easy question: If you were an employer and you had two people working for you, one who treated the company as if it belonged to him, and another who treated it as just a job, a place to come from nine to five each day, which one of these two would you be most likely to promote? Which one would you want to invest in? To which of these would you give additional training? For which of the two would you create opportunities for advancement? I think the answer is obvious.

YOUR STATEMENT ABOUT YOURSELF

Your attitude toward self-responsibility is one of the most important statements you can make about yourself and the kind of person you are. Everyone can be located somewhere on a scale, from high acceptance of responsibility, all the way down to low acceptance of responsibility, or *irresponsibility*.

A highly responsible person tends to be positive, optimistic, self-confident, self-reliant and self-controlled. A person at the lower end of the scale, with an attitude of irresponsibility, will be negative, pessimistic, defeatist and cynical, as well as aimless, fearful, unsure and often neurotic or mentally unstable.

Thomas Szasz, the controversial psychiatrist, says, "There is no such thing as mental illness; there are merely varying degrees of irresponsibility."

Self-responsible individuals tend to be positive and mentally healthy. Irresponsible individuals tend to be negative and mentally ill. This observation brings us to one of the most important discoveries in the history of human psychology and personal performance.

There is a direct relationship between how much responsibility you accept in any area of your life and how much control you feel in that area. In turn, there is a direct relationship between how much control you feel in any given area and how much freedom you feel you have in that area. Responsibility, control and a sense of freedom, or autonomy, go hand in hand. The equation looks like this:

RESPONSIBILITY = CONTROL = FREEDOM

There is also a direct relationship between responsibility, control and freedom, on the one side, and the number of positive emotions you enjoy, on the other. In other words, there is a direct relationship between the level of responsibility you accept and how positive and happy you are overall. Self-responsibility and mental health go hand in hand. They are always in balance. Here is the equation in its shortened form:

RESPONSIBILITY = POSITIVE EMOTIONS

At the lower end of the scale, people with attitudes of irresponsibility, who feel that they are not responsible for their life or what happens to them, also feel they have little control, or feel out of control entirely. They feel that they have little or no ability to make a difference in their life. Nonresponsible people feel that they are controlled by external forces and by other people.

This feeling of not being in control causes them to feel a lack of freedom, to feel trapped. An attitude of irresponsibility, feeling out of control and feeling trapped triggers negative emotions, such as unhappiness, anger and frustration. Here then is the opposite equation from the above:

IRRESPONSIBILITY = LACK OF CONTROL = LACK OF FREEDOM

In its shortened form, the equation looks like this:

IRRESPONSIBILITY = NEGATIVE EMOTIONS

THE "ROBBER" EMOTIONS

Negative emotions are the "robber" emotions of life. They are the primary causes of underachievement and failure. They make people physically and mentally ill, ruin relationships and destroy careers. They cast a shadow over everything a person tries to do. Negative emotions strip out any joy a person might get from any achievement. They are totally harmful and are the great enemies of human happiness.

The elimination of negative emotions is job one for the person who aspires to great success and achievement. Nothing is more important. Peace of mind is the highest human good, and peace of mind only exists in the absence of negative emotions. You can't be negative and at peace at the same time. One cancels out the other.

When I began studying this subject some years ago, I was astonished to discover that virtually all the problems that we have in life are rooted in negative emotions of one kind or another. It became clear to me that if you could find a way to eliminate negative emotions, your life would be wonderful. All the mental laws described earlier would begin to work in your favor. You would accomplish more in a short period of time than the average person accomplishes in years.

On the other hand, the failure to eliminate negative emotions would undermine all your efforts and take much of the joy and pleasure from anything you managed to accomplish. Negative feelings would cause the mental laws to work against you. Destructive emotions could cause you more grief and heartache in a shorter period of time than any other factor in your life.

I saw clearly that the elimination of negative emotions was central to the achievement of all lasting health, happiness, freedom and prosperity.

The insight that changed my life was the discovery that negative emotions are completely unnecessary and unnatural in the life of man. There is no need for them. They serve no good purpose. They are only destructive. They are the major reason men and women fail to grow and evolve to higher levels of consciousness and character. And you do not have to suffer them at all if you consciously choose to get rid of them.

Up to that time, I had always thought that negative emotions were a normal and natural part of being a human being. I thought that, just as you have positive emotions, you have negative emotions. They were a part of human nature, to be accepted as inevitable, just like the rain or the sunshine.

Then I learned that no one is born with negative emotions. Have you ever seen a negative baby? Every negative emotion that we experience as adults, we had to learn, starting in childhood, through a process of imitation, practice, repetition and reinforcement. And since negative emotions are learned, like most things, they can be unlearned, and you can be free of them.

Many people have a hard time with this subject. They have been negative for so long that they find it difficult to accept that negative emotions are completely unnecessary. They resist the idea that they can be eliminated. Of course, the Law of Belief states that whatever you believe, with feeling, becomes your reality. If you absolutely believe that negative emotions are a necessary part of your life, then they certainly will be, and they will remain so. However, it is easy to prove that negative emotions serve no useful purpose. Realizing this is the first step to getting rid of them.

THE MOST COMMON NEGATIVE EMOTIONS

The most common and easily identifiable negative emotions are *doubt* and *fear*. There are also *guilt* and *resentment,* which usually go around together, like twins. Then there is *envy,* the root negative emotion of socialism, communism and much political demagoguery. This is followed closely by *jealousy,* that great destroyer of happiness and relationships.

More than fifty negative emotions have been identified. But they all eventually boil down to and are expressed in the core negative emotion of *anger*. Anger is perhaps the worst of all the negative emotions, the most powerful and the most destructive. Anger, once generated, is always expressed, either inwardly or outwardly.

If it is expressed inwardly, as when you suppress or repress your angry feelings, you make yourself sick. If you express your anger outwardly, you harm your relationships with others. You make them unhappy, and in extreme cases, physically ill.

How do you feel when you are angry? How do you think or reason? How do you get along with others? How do you sleep or digest your food? When you're angry, docsn't it feel as if there was a dark cloud over your mind? Don't you find that you cannot concentrate or think straight? Doesn't your mind become totally preoccupied with the object of your anger? Don't you talk furiously to yourself as you rehash what happened, how you were wronged, and what you'd likc to do to even the score?

The longer your anger continues, the more all-consuming it becomes, like a brush fire burning out of control. It can rob you of sleep, of friends and of employment. It can cause you to behave irrationally and to act in ways that make you feel ashamed and embarrassed.

Does anything good ever come from anger, or any other negative emotion? The answer is a definite *no*. Negative emotions, rooted in irresponsibility, serve no useful purpose at all. Why, then, do people experience so many negative emotions? Let's answer that by starting off with the main causes of negative emotions in the first place.

WHAT CAUSES NEGATIVE EMOTIONS

There are four main causes of negative emotions. The first cause is *justification*. Justification occurs when you attempt to justify and explain, to yourself and others, why you should feel this negative emotion, why you are entitled to feel angry or upset for some reason. Justification and self-righteousness feed on each other, and are flip sides of the same reasoning process.

Whenever you feel badly used for any reason, your first reaction is to flare up in anger. Your second reaction will be to marshal all the reasons anger is a justifiable reaction. You need to be able to say, "I have every right to be angry." You look for people who will agree with your reasoning and your feelings. You lay out the situation for them in great detail so they will see clearly that you are obviously the wronged party in this situation. In fact, without being able to justify yourself and your anger, you can't keep your anger going.

You can begin the process of eliminating negative emotions by simply refusing to justify them. Refuse to allow yourself to create all kinds of reasons you are entitled to feel as bad as you do. Refuse to pass judgment on the other person. You will find that all judging of others eventually leads to some form of condemnation, and the negative emotions of intolerance and anger that go with that condemnation. But when you withhold judgment, which is an act of mental control, it is often sufficient to stop the negative emotion from starting in the first place.

When someone does or says something that causes you to react, neutralize your tendency to flare up by excusing the other person for some reason. What I say to control my emotions is something like, "God bless him; he's probably having a bad day."

Have you ever been driving along in traffic and been cut off by another driver? Did you notice how you instantly became angry? Even though you had never seen the other driver before, and the other driver has never seen you, you reacted exactly as if that driver had carefully plotted and planned, and then waited to ambush you as you came driving innocently along. But, the instant you stop telling yourself what a terrible driver he or she is and just laugh it off, your anger quickly dissipates and disappears. Refusing to set yourself up as a judge and jury removes the trigger that starts the anger and allows you to calm down and take control of your emotions.

The second main cause of negative emotions is *identification,* or taking things personally. You can only become angry about something to the degree to which you can personally identify with it and see it as affecting or harming you in some way.

The minute you stop taking things personally, you get your emotions back under your own control. The way to do this is to practice detachment, standing back from the situation and forcing yourself to look at it objectively. Be philosophical; try to see it from the other person's point of view. Your ability to "disidentify" with what has happened gives you greater calmness and clarity and makes you much more effective in dealing with the problem, whatever it is.

This need for detachment and objectivity in dealing with difficulties is why it is said that "a man who acts as his own lawyer has a fool for a client." Perhaps the most valuable quality of a senior executive is his or her ability to function well in a crisis. This ability is solely a result of refusing to get caught up in the emotionality of the moment.

The third major cause of negative emotions is *lack of consideration.* You become angry when you feel that people are not giving you your just due, that people are not respecting you the way you feel you deserve to be. If someone is rude to you, or slights you, or does not acknowledge you properly in a social situation, your ego becomes involved and you feel hurt, angry and defensive. This is why a wise man once said, "You should not worry so much about what other people think of you, because if you knew how seldom they did, you would probably be insulted."

You must starve your negative emotions. You must withdraw the energy from them by refusing to justify them, by refusing to identify with them and by refusing to let the behavior of others toward you get under your skin. But the very fastest way to eliminate negative emotions, virtually in an instant, is to go right to the root of them and cut them off.

Blaming is the fourth and final cause of negative emotions and it lies at the root of almost all of them. Probably 99 percent of your negative emotions depend for their very existence on your ability to blame someone or something else for something that is making you unhappy. The instant you stop blaming, the instant you refuse to blame anyone or anything else for anything, your negative emotions cease, just as if the power to them was suddenly cut off, just as unplugging the Christmas tree lights causes all the lights to go off at once.

THE LAW OF SUBSTITUTION REVISITED

The simple switch you can throw to short-circuit any negative emotion is explained by the Law of Substitution. This law states that the conscious mind can only hold one thought at a time, positive or negative, and you can deliberately choose that thought. You can substitute a positive, constructive thought for a negative, destructive thought, and in so doing, you can push the negative thought out of your mind.

Whenever you feel negative or angry for any reason, you can immediately cancel the thought that is causing the negative emotion by saying, very firmly, *"I am responsible."*

This is the most powerful of all affirmations for mental control. These words put you back in the emotional driver's seat. The words "I am responsible!" switch your mind immediately from negative to positive. They enable you to assert complete control over your emotions. They make you feel calm and relaxed, and enable you to see the situation with greater clarity. The words "I am responsible" put you in charge of yourself and enable you to deal with the situation more effectively.

You can develop no further than you have up to this moment with your negative emotions intact. It is not possible for you to grow and evolve to higher levels of understanding and effectiveness except to the degree to which you free yourself from them. Your negative emotions are like forces of mental gravity that are holding you in your current reality. You must leave them behind.

MANDATORY, NOT OPTIONAL

This acceptance of responsibility, and the accompanying elimination of negative emotions, is not optional. It is mandatory. It is central to your health, happiness and personal effectiveness. The development of a positive mental attitude toward yourself and your life, characterized by the elimination of negative emotions, is essential if you want to develop your higher mental powers. Positive, constructive emotions are the foundations of all happiness, achievement and long life.

To begin the process of clearing your mind, pause for a moment and think over your entire life, past and present. Analyze each memory or situation that makes you feel negative in any way, as if you were holding it up to the light. Then neutralize any negativity associated with it by simply saying, "I am responsible," over and over.

The fact is that you are responsible. Whatever your difficulty or problem, you probably got yourself into it. You were free to choose. And you are still free. You probably knew at the time that you should not be doing it, but you went ahead anyway. So you are absolutely, completely, 100 percent responsible for your situation, for the consequences of your decisions.

Often people ask, "Isn't accepting responsibility the same as accepting blame?" The answer to that is that responsibility always looks forward, always to the future. Blame always looks backward, to the past, for someone who is guilty.

Responsibility says "next time" or "in the future" or "what do I do from here?" Blame always says "he did" or "she did" or "if only." Responsibility gives you a sense of control, of self-reliance, of proactivity. Blame makes you feel angry and frustrated and vengeful.

Someone runs into your car at a stoplight. Legally, you are not at fault. But you are responsible for the way you react to the situation. You are responsible for your conduct and your behavior. You can respond either by becoming angry, upset and emotional, or by being mature, calm and controlled. The choice is yours. And how you feel is determined by how you decide to respond, not by the situation. Responsibility or irresponsibility; the choice is yours. It always has been.

RELEASE YOUR BRAKES

Usually when you think about responsibility in these terms, you decide that, from this point forward, you are going to accept complete responsibility for your life. However, almost every person is still carrying around at least one negative experience for which there is no way that he or she is going to accept responsibility. Each person has a favorite negative emotion that he or she is not going to part with by accepting responsibility for his or her emotions, or for what happened.

You say, "If you only knew what that other person did to me, you could not ask me to accept responsibility." But here is a key point. The continued existence of even one negative emotion in your conscious or subconscious mind is in itself enough to sabotage all your chances for happiness. A single negative emotion of blame or anger can interfere with your peace of mind indefinitely.

To illustrate this critical point, imagine that you have just purchased a brand new Mercedes 600 SEL, from the factory, beautifully engineered and mechanically perfect in every detail. There is only one problem with this car. A mistake was made in assembling the braking system and one front wheel brake is locked. The wheel will not turn. Now, let us say that you decide to take your beautifully engineered car for a drive. You get in, you start the engine, you shift it into gear and you step on the gas. If everything in this car is perfect except for that one front wheel brake which is locked on, what would happen when you stepped on the gas?

The answer is that you would spin around that locked wheel. The car would go around and around. No matter how hard you stepped on the gas or how much you twisted the wheel, you would simply go in a circle.

Your world is full of people who are just like that new car. You may be one of them. They may be intelligent, good-looking and well-educated, and may seem to have everything going for them, but their lives just seem to go around in circles. Almost invariably this is because they are holding on to at least one key experience from their past for which they are refusing to accept responsibility. They are still blaming someone or something for a hurt they have suffered.

I have spoken to men and women fifty years old who are still angry and resentful over something that happened to them in childhood. This unresolved bitterness affects their relationships with their spouses, their children, their coworkers and their friends. It manifests itself in psychosomatic illnesses, and in extreme cases, it can even lead to early death.

The field of psychotherapy is built around helping people to deal with these unresolved feelings of anger, guilt and resentment. The patient is cured when he or she can identify what is holding him or her back, face it honestly and let go of it. You can accomplish very much the same thing by identifying any feelings of negativity you have toward anyone, accepting responsibility for the situation and then letting it go. You will discover that you are cured as soon as you do.

PASS IT ON

You become what you teach. Once you have begun accepting responsibility for every part of your life, encourage your friends and associates to do the same thing. When people tell you about their problems and their frustrations, empathize with them and then remind them, "You are responsible."

Perhaps one of the kindest things that you can do for a true friend is to put that person back in touch with his or her own good sense by reminding him or her that he or she is responsible. When a person complains, respond by saying, "You are responsible, what are you going to do about it?" Don't try to give advice. It's probably not wanted and will be ignored anyway. Just listen. Be sympathetic. Then encourage the person to accept responsibility and get busy doing something about the situation.

At one time, my wife, Barbara, wanted to be a guidance counselor and eventually a psychologist or psychotherapist. She wanted to help people through their problems. She would practice by spending many hours listening to her friends and counseling them the very best way that she could. She would give them her very best guidance and advice to help them deal with their difficulties.

Whenever I was involved in one of these "counseling sessions," especially with her friends and coworkers, I would avoid all the hours of going back and forth dissecting the problem and simply cut to the core of the matter by saying "You are responsible, what are you going to do about it?"

Barbara felt this was too simplistic. She told me that I was not giving sufficient consideration to the complexities of the various situations these people were facing. She was then astonished to see how many of her friends, after endless counseling sessions, actually went out and got themselves together. They took action shortly after they had been told, in no uncertain terms, that they were responsible, and that it was up to them to do something about their situations.

Barbara and I now have a standing joke around the house. When Barbara has lunch with a friend who has a problem, or some kind of personal difficulty, I will ask her what she told the person to do. She replies by saying, "I just gave her 'the advice.' "

It is much simpler, it works much better, and it is much easier on everyone involved. The advice is, "You are responsible, what are you going to do about it?"

Become your own psychotherapist by repeating to yourself over and over, "I am responsible, I am responsible, I am responsible." Then, give "the advice" to others who have problems. Just say, "You are responsible, what are you going to do about it?" Let them get on with the rest of their lives so you can get on with yours.

ACTION EXERCISE

Take a pad of paper and draw a line down the center. On the left side, make a list of every person or situation about which you harbor any negative feelings at all. Number each one.

On the right side of the page, write out a series of sentences that begin with "I am responsible for this because . . ." and complete this sentence. Do this for each item and be as hard on yourself as you possibly can. Be brutally frank and honest. Write out every reason why you might be responsible for what happened. Do the same for every negative situation in your past or present.

When you have completed this exercise, you will be amazed at how much more positive and in control you feel. You will be free from the mental burdens you've been carrying for so long.

GETTING OUT OF YOUR OWN WAY

The golden key to inner peace and outer success, especially in your relationships with other people, is contained within yourself and your responses to the world around you. There is a principle that is indispensable for the development of higher consciousness and for the full use of all your mental powers. It will enable you to largely eliminate negative emotions of all kinds and to take full responsibility in everything you do. This principle will liberate you from the burden of countless problems in your past, going back to your earliest childhood. It will develop in you a fine and noble character and make you the kind of person that people want to be around and be like. Thousands of our graduates have reported to us that the practice of this principle has revolutionized their lives, as it will yours. You will learn this principle in this chapter.

Everything that you are today is a result of your habitual ways of thinking. As the Law of Correspondence states, your outer world is a physical manifestation of your inner world. Everything you see around you—your health, your relationships, your career, your family and your worldly accomplishments—is an expression of the workings of your mind.

Your behavior, attitudes, values and habits of thought are learned. You did not have them when you came into the world. You have learned them as the result of input and repetition, over many years. And because they have been learned, they can be un-learned. You can unlearn the habits of thought you have acquired that are not consistent with the person you want to be or the goals you want to achieve.

A feeling of optimism is a prerequisite for success and happi-ness. Yet most of us are plagued by negative emotions of all kinds, especially anger, fear, doubt, envy, resentment, irritability, impa-tience, intolerance and jealousy. In spite of our best intentions, these negative emotions tend to arise unexpectedly, often at the worst possible moments, and cause us to act in ways that we later regret.

Negative emotions are feelings and responses that have been learned like any habits. They can be unlearned as well, if you have the key to the lock that holds them in place. To unlearn them, however, you must understand the psychological factors that create a fertile breeding ground for negative emotions in the first place.

Fortunately, there is no permanent place for negative emotions in your subconscious mind. If negative emotions could become permanent, there would be no hope for you to improve your tem-perament or your personality through your own efforts. They are *vagabond* emotions, which can be chased away with the correct procedure.

THE BREEDING GROUND

Just as you are born with no self-concept, you are born without negative emotions. You have to be taught negative emotions as you are growing up. You usually learn the negative emotions that are the most popular in your family. You imitate the negative emotions and reactions of your mother or your father, or both. You imitate the negative emotions of the people with whom you identify. If someone suggests to you that your way of acting is inappropriate, you dismiss their input by saying, "That's just the way I am."

Often, you've had certain negative ideas for so long that you're not even aware of them, or where they came from originally. But one thing you can be sure of: You weren't born with them. They are not permanent. You can be free of them if you want to be.

THE ROOTS OF NEGATIVITY

You develop a propensity for negative emotions as a result of two experiences that happen to you early in life. The first of these experiences is destructive criticism. More damage has been caused and more people destroyed by destructive criticism than by all the wars in history. The difference is that wars kill the physical bodies of people while destructive criticism destroys the inner person and leaves the bodies walking around. Virtually every problem you have with yourself and with other people can be traced back to some incident in which your value and worth were challenged or attacked by some sort of criticism.

Children up to the age of six are open and vulnerable to the influences of the important people in their lives. They have no capacity to discriminate between true and false evaluations and criticisms. The child's mind is like wet clay upon which their parents and siblings write and leave marks. And the more intense the emotion, the deeper the groove.

When you grow older and develop the powers of discrimination, you can "consider the source" of negative input. If someone criticizes you, or disagrees with you, you can stand back and judge whether the assessment is valid. You can choose to accept what you consider to be helpful and reject the rest.

When you're a child, however, you have no such ability. Because you are still in the process of learning who you are, you are like a little sponge. You absorb the evaluations of the important people around you as if they were telling the absolute truth, as if they were actually in a position to know your true character and capabilities. The more you value their love and respect, the more likely you are to accept what they say about you as a valid assessment of your character and worth. And once you accept something as true about yourself, you begin to see yourself by the light of that belief.

Your mind attempts to serve you by validating what you've decided is correct about you. It sorts and winnows your perceptions. It causes you to see examples that "prove" your beliefs while simultaneously causing you to ignore experiences that contradict it.

If you're told that "you're a bad boy," or "you can't be trusted," or "you're a liar" (all children tell lies; it's part of their learning how to interact with other people), you start to believe that these criticisms are indelible facts about your basic personality. If you accept them consciously, they are then accepted by your subconscious mind where they are recorded as instructions for future behavior.

When I was growing up, I was told that I would never amount to much, that I was a big disappointment to my parents. Not meaning to, they judged me by impossibly high standards. Not understanding that children are little learning organisms who make mistakes continually, they demanded behavior of me, their first child, that I wasn't capable of delivering.

When I had my own children, I resolved not to do to them what was done to me. Instead, I tell them every day that I love them and that I think they are the best kids in the world. When we are driving together, I talk to Barbara as if they weren't in the backseat and tell her how lucky we are to have such wonderful children. Privately, I whisper to each of them, "You're the best in the West!"

Even when I have to reprimand them, I start by saying, "I love you very much, but you mustn't do that because you could get hurt," or whatever is necessary.

Parents criticize with the intention of helping the child, of improving the child's performance. But because destructive criticism lowers the child's self-esteem and weakens the self-concept, the child's overall performance actually declines. The child's self-confidence diminishes. The likelihood of the child's making mistakes increases. If the child is criticized too often, or if the criticisms are taken too emotionally, the child will become anxious and afraid and will begin to avoid doing those things altogether.

In the worst case, the child will become *hypersensitive* and will be insecure and afraid of trying anything new. When the child grows up, he or she will be extremely emotional about criticism of any kind and will react angrily and defensively to any suggestion of disapproval from a spouse, boss, friend or coworker.

Everyone has areas where they are hypersensitive, usually in the parts of their lives where they have the greatest emotional investment, such as their families or careers. One of the most important things you can do for yourself is to develop a certain objectivity or detachment about criticism in these key areas. Learn to stand back and evaluate the opinions of others unemotionally. It's not easy, but it saves a lot of wear and tear on your system. This ability to avoid being overly affected by the criticism of others is a key quality of the self-actualizing person.

THE DESTROYER OF HAPPINESS

The second factor that predisposes you to negative emotions is a lack of love. The most traumatic experience a child can endure is the withdrawal of love by one or both of his parents. When parents react to the child with anger and disapproval, the child is terrified. He or she feels anxious and fearful and flails around emotionally. Because the child needs his or her parents' love so much, when it's withheld for any reason, he or she begins to wither inside. If the love is withheld indefinitely, or given unpredictably, it causes severe personality problems that erupt in anger and negativity in adult life.

If you did not receive a sufficient quality and quantity of love during your formative years (and most people did not), you seek it all your life. You will continually feel an emotional deficiency, a longing, an insecurity, that you will strive to satisfy or compensate for. You will look for unconditional love in your relationships and you'll feel tense and uneasy if love is interrupted or withheld. Just as early calcium deficiency causes rickets in children, which shows up as bowed legs in the adult, a deficiency of love in childhood is manifested in negative emotions when you grow up.

THREE CONDITIONS

For you, or anyone, to feel completely loved as a child, three conditions must exist. An absence of any one of these three will appear in adolescence and adulthood in the form of insecurity, negative emotions and destructive behavior.

The first condition for healthy emotional development is that your *parents must love themselves*. Your parents cannot give you more love than they have for themselves. If your mother or father doesn't like himself or herself very much, he or she will have little love to give to you. The rule is that high self-concept parents raise high self-concept children, while low-concept parents raise low self-concept children. As within, so without. The self-concepts of the children become mirrors of the self-concepts of their parents.

Your parents gave you all the love they had to give. They didn't withhold any. They just didn't have any more to give in the first place. There wasn't anything you could have done to get any more than you got. You got all there was.

The second condition that must be fulfilled for a child to feel fully loved is that his or her *parents must love each other*. Children learn about love by experiencing it directly and by observing it taking place in their families. It has been said that the kindest thing that a man can do for his children is to love their mother, and the reverse is also true. When children grow up in a household in which the mother and father love each other in a way the children can see and experience, they are far more likely to grow up with feelings of security and self-confidence.

You learn how to have your own adult relationship with a member of the opposite sex by observing such a relationship in your own family. If you grew up in a household in which you didn't experience it, you can spend the first few years of your adulthood learning how to get along with another person by trial and error. Many first marriages today are "practice marriages," in which individuals learn how to be married. They learn what it is they want or don't want in a marriage partner and how to make a relationship work.

The third condition that must exist for a child to feel fully loved is that the *parents must love the child*. This is one of the most sensitive subjects that an adult ever has to deal with. The fact is that many of our parents did not love us. They wanted to, and they intended to, and they planned to, but they never really got around to it. Perhaps they didn't have the time, or the emotional energy, or the interest, or perhaps they had unresolved conflicts with their parents or with their spouses that made loving us impossible.

Many parents do not like their children very much. Sometimes this is because they start off with the idea that the role of the child is to fulfill their expectations. If the child has a personality of his or her own, the parents often take this as a personal affront. They respond by criticizing the child or withdrawing their love. If they do this for long enough, it eventually becomes a habit. Parents then get into the habit of criticizing and tolerating their children instead of loving and cherishing them.

It is important for you to know that whether or not your parents loved you, you are still a valuable and worthwhile person. Your parents' love or lack of love says nothing about your inherent possibilities. Parents are what they are. They do the best they can. At the very least, they got you here and gave you a chance at life. Accepting that one or both of your parents may not have loved you, or may not have loved you enough, is an important step to full maturity.

Most adults were brought up in homes in which they were the victims of destructive criticism, and they suffered a lack of love in some way. If this was your experience, you were too young to know why this was happening. You merely internalized the message that "for some reason, my mommy and daddy criticize me and don't love me. Since they know me better than anyone else, it must be because of something I've done."

Destructive criticism and lack of love, in combination, create the negative emotion of *guilt*. Guilt is the major emotional problem of the twentieth century. It is the root cause of most mental illness, unhappiness and almost all other negative emotions. A child who feels guilty feels that he or she is not worth very much, that he or she is, in fact, *worthless*. Destructive criticism and lack of love instill in the child's subconscious mind the feeling of *worthlessness*.

Guilt is used on people deliberately for two reasons: *punishment* and *control*. Using guilt on another person as a form of emotional punishment is extremely effective. It is an essential part of negative religious teachings. It is used by many parents to make their children feel bad, to make them feel worthless and insignificant.

Guilt is also used as a tool of control or manipulation. If you can make a person feel guilty, you can control their emotions and their behavior. If you can make them feel guilty enough, you can get them to do things for you that they might not do in the absence of those guilty feelings.

Mothers are often skilled at the use of guilt. I used to say that my mother had a black belt in guilt and gave courses at the local YMCA. My mother learned to use guilt as a tool of interaction from her mother, who learned it from her mother, and so on back through the generations. Fathers are often skillful at using guilt as well.

ADULT MANIFESTATIONS OF GUILT

If you were raised under the influences that produce feelings of guilt, you will experience this guilt in several different ways.

The first and most common manifestation of guilt is feelings of *inferiority, inadequacy,* and *undeservingness.* You feel that you do not deserve good things to happen to you. In fact, if several good things happen to you in a row, you will become extremely uncomfortable. You will feel out of your comfort zone of deservingness, and you will probably start engaging in self-sabotaging behavior to stop the good things from happening.

The truth is that you deserve all the good things that come to you when you keep your mind focused on what you want and keep it off what you don't want.

These feelings of inferiority, inadequacy and undeservingness are often expressed in the words, *"I'm not good enough."* Some psychologists refer to this as the "fear of success." The fear of success is simply another way of saying that, because of your deep down feelings of unworthiness, any achievement that contradicts your self-limiting beliefs makes you feel uncomfortable.

Very often, people will work extremely hard for the success they desire. They will put in long hours and make great sacrifices. However, just as they almost reach their goal, something will go wrong. They will act consciously or unconsciously to kick the chair out from under themselves.

The salesman on his way to close the deal of a lifetime gets into an automobile accident. The lawyer on the way to the signing of a big contract leaves his briefcase in the taxi with the only copy of the contract locked inside. Many people turn to alcohol, drugs or extramarital affairs in an attempt to escape from the discomfort of succeeding in spite of their inner feelings of unworthiness.

The second adult manifestation of guilt is destructive self-criticism and self-defeating behavior. If one is criticized while one is growing up, one soon learns to criticize oneself, and continues it through life. You often hear people say things like, "I'm always late," or "I'm terrible with numbers," or "I'm not very good at this." They are continually reinforcing negative ideas that may have little or no basis in fact. They are repeating what they've been told about themselves, and in so doing, making it their reality.

Your subconscious mind accepts whatever you say about yourself as true. When you constantly criticize yourself, your subconscious mind accepts your words as commands. Your subsequent words and actions will then fit a pattern consistent with your self-criticism. You will behave on the outside the way you talk to yourself on the inside.

The third way you demonstrate that you've been raised with feelings of guilt is that you are easily manipulated by guilt. You are an easy mark for the irritation or impatience that others use to manipulate your behavior. Even people you don't know can pull your "guilt-strings" and make you feel uncomfortable or even acquiesce to their demands. You become like a puppet, and the guilt-thrower becomes the puppeteer.

Virtually all charitable solicitations are based on the skillful use of guilt to manipulate your emotions, to make you feel that you are undeserving of your standard of living and your accomplishments.

Taxi drivers, waitresses and flight attendants use guilt on you to control your behavior. I know, for example, that you lose a pint of water per hour through dehydration when you fly. I therefore drink a lot of water in the air. I continually ask for refills to my water glass.

Most stewardesses resent this. They know all about dehydration and they are schooled to drink fluids continually when they fly. But they don't want the extra work of refilling your water glass. So instead of asking, "Can I get you anything else," they ask, "Will that be all?"

If you ask for more water, they sigh heavily, as if you just asked them to carry a hundred-pound suitcase, and go off to get it for you. When they bring it back, they tend to be abrupt and disapproving, as if this will cow you into submission so they can go back to the galley and continue reading their magazines.

You need to be aware of how commonly guilt is used as a tool to influence you. You will see it everywhere.

The poet W. H. Auden wrote, "Those to whom evil is done, do evil in return."

The fourth manifestation of guilt is using guilt and blame with others. If you were raised as a victim of guilt, being constantly criticized and blamed, you will grow up and use guilt as a way of communicating with others. Many parents use guilt exclusively to get their children to do what they want. Many bosses rely on guilt as their primary method of control.

The fifth manifestation of guilt, and perhaps the most common, is the development of the "victim complex." The individual feels like a victim and talks like a victim. The person with deep feelings of guilt is always making excuses or apologizing. He or she is always saying, in effect, "I'm sorry." In addition, he or she uses "victim language," ways of speaking that are really pleas of "not guilty."

Perhaps the most common forms of victim language you hear are phrases like "I can't" or "I have to," or combination phrases such as "I have to, but I can't; I can't, but I have to."

Another form of victim language is the word "trying." Whenever people say "I'll try," they are apologizing for failure in advance. They are telegraphing their belief that they are going to fail in whatever it is they are saying they will try to do. And you intuitively know that these words are signals for upcoming failure.

If you went to a lawyer and you asked him to defend you in a lawsuit, and he examined your case and replied by saying, "Well, I'll sure try," how would you feel?

If you went to a doctor with a life-threatening condition, and you said to the doctor, "I sure hope you can help me," and the doctor said, "Well, I'll try," it would be time for you to get a second opinion.

The words "I'll try" mean "I'm going to fail at this, and I want you to know in advance so that you can't come back to me later and say that I didn't give you any warning. If you do come back I can remind you that I only said that I would *try*."

In our business, whenever a supplier says that he or she will *try* to get something done by the end of the week, or will *try* to complete a project on a certain schedule, all our alarm bells go off. We immediately recognize that the individual is probably planning to fail. We go back and insist that he or she give us a firm commitment rather than saying that he or she will "try." You only accept "I'll try" when the schedule or outcome is not that important to you.

Another form of victim language is contained in the words "I wish." Whenever you say "I wish" before a goal or ambition, you are signaling to your subconscious mind that you don't really believe it. If you say, "I wish I could quit smoking," or "I wish I could lose weight," or "I wish I could save money," what you are really saying is, "But I don't believe that it is possible for me."

Every time you use victim language—"I can't," or "I have to," or "I'll try," or "I wish," or "I'm sorry," or "Don't blame me," or "That's not my fault"—you are reinforcing the negative emotion of guilt and driving it deeper into your subconscious mind.

Make the decision, right now, to eliminate victim language from your conversation. Speak with definiteness and conviction instead. Say "I will" or "I won't." Say "I want to," rather than "I have to." Especially say "I can" or "I will" rather than "I can't" or "I wish."

FREE YOURSELF FROM GUILT

How do you rid yourself of the feelings of guilt that interfere with your happiness? There are five things you can do.

First: Eliminate destructive self-criticism from your thoughts and your conversation. Refuse to say anything self-deprecating. Refuse to say anything about yourself that you do not sincerely desire to be true. At the same time, refuse to allow anyone else to speak to you in a negative way. If someone criticizes you, simply say, "I would appreciate it if you not speak to me like that because it's not true."

Remember, your subconscious mind is absorbing information constantly and internalizing it as part of your self-concept development. If you allow someone to say something negative about you without responding, your subconscious accepts it as a valid description of you and files it away to reinforce your feelings of guilt and inferiority. Negative statements by yourself or from others, if not canceled out or challenged, set you up for failure in the future.

Second: Refuse to blame anyone for anything. Accept complete responsibility for your life and everything in it that you can do something about. Most people do what they think is right most of the time. There is nothing to be gained by criticizing, condemning or complaining. Criticizing and blaming others actually lowers your own self-esteem and reinforces your own feelings of guilt and inferiority. When you start to feel angry with someone, use the Law of Substitution and simply say, "No one is guilty; I am responsible."

Third, refuse to be manipulated by the guilt-throwing behavior of others. Each time anyone says or does anything to make you feel guilty, and you acquiesce to their demands, you reinforce the guilty feeling and make it easier for people to manipulate you in the future. You should have a decent respect for the feelings and needs of others, but this doesn't mean you should sacrifice your emotional integrity to them.

There is probably at least one person in your life, perhaps more, who is accustomed to interacting with you on the basis of making you feel guilty. It can be a mother, a spouse, a boss or a coworker. You may be in a relationship in which guilt is the basic operating principle. In any case, you are responsible for changing this dynamic.

There are two techniques you can use to break another person of the habit of using guilt to manipulate or control you. The first and easiest is simply the use of *silence*. It takes two to tango. If you refuse to respond, the game comes to a halt.

The next time someone attempts to use guilt on you, go completely silent. Say nothing. Refuse to answer. Don't allow yourself to be provoked. Remember, you are conditioned to respond automatically to guilt by defending or apologizing. When you exert your mental control and refuse to react, you become stronger and more capable of dealing with the person and the situation.

When the other person asks you what you have to say, you reply, "I'm not going to respond to that."

Be polite, friendly and courteous. Smile gently, even if you're talking on the phone. Resist the temptation to explain yourself. You don't have to say anything, and you don't have to explain yourself to anyone. You're in charge. Even the feeling that you have to respond is based in the reaction pattern of guilt that has been set up in the past.

Guilt throwing and guilt catching is like tennis. It only works as long as you are willing to hit the ball back across the net. You stop the game of guilt by being silent, and by sticking to it.

People who are used to getting the things they want by using guilt will react quickly and angrily to any attempt by you to change the game. They will become more demanding and adamant. They will sense immediately that they are in danger of losing control and will pull out all stops, using every tool in their repertoire to bring you to heel. They will vehemently resist their loss of power over you. Be prepared for this and don't give in.

What you want is either a healthy relationship with the other person or none at all. To achieve this, be willing to change the dynamic. Be willing to undergo the negative reactions of the other person until he or she realizes that guilt throwing and manipulation is no longer effective. He or she will be forced to try something else, and that something else will almost invariably be an improvement.

The second method you can use to break someone of the habit of using guilt is an assertiveness technique called "broken record." It's both simple and effective. It requires courage and willpower at first, but then it works better and better.

When the other person attempts to manipulate you using guilt, you respond by saying, "Are you trying to make me feel guilty?" You ask this question in a low-keyed, nonthreatening way, even with a tone of genuine wonder and curiosity, as if you're amazed at such a possibility.

When Barbara and I were first married, we found ourselves using guilt on each other as a regular tool of interaction. We had come by our skills honestly, both of us having been brought up in homes in which guilt was the common language of control. And we had learned well. We could slip into an aggrieved tone of voice at the slightest suggestion that we were not going to get exactly what we wanted, exactly when we wanted it.

Fortunately, we recognized this dynamic forming and we decided to use "broken record" to break ourselves of it and abolish it from our marriage.

The way it worked was simple. Whenever one of us felt that the other was starting to use guilt for any reason, he or she would stop and say, "Are you trying to make me feel guilty?"

There is something in the human psyche that knows that guilt is a bad thing. No one consciously sets out to use guilt on another. It is a habit that we learn as children and slip into as adults. We learn to do whatever works in our relationships with others, and as long as the other person buys in, guilt works as well as or better than any other behavior to enable us to get others to do what we want them to.

If I asked Barbara, "Are you trying to make me feel guilty?" she would immediately respond by saying, "No, of course not."

I would say, "That's good, because for a moment there I thought you were using guilt on me, and that's not a good thing."

A little while later, she would try to use guilt again. And again I would ask, "Are you trying to make me feel guilty?"

Again she would deny it. Again I would say, "That's good, because guilt is no way to run a relationship."

This exchange would continue until, in exasperation, she would reply to the question by saying, "Yes, I am!"

Then I would say triumphantly, "Well, it's not going to work!" And that would be our moment of recognition. It would be our signal to stop trying to use guilt, and get back to open, honest discussion of the issue. Discontinuing the use of guilt would give us no choice but to settle down and talk like mature adults.

You're not trying to make the other person feel guilty for using guilt. You're not trying to punish him or her for making you feel bad. Your sole aim in using silence or broken record is to bring his or her behavior to a higher level of awareness. At that level, you can deal with guilt, and begin eliminating it from your relationship. You can both be free of an emotion that is as destructive to the user as it is to the victim.

The fourth way to rid yourself of guilt is to refuse to discuss the guilt of others. Refuse to gossip or exchange "dirt" about other people. Refuse to get into "ain't it awful" conversations. Eliminate badmouthing and backbiting from your discussions. Remember, everything you talk about and think about is having an influence on your subconscious mind and on your personality. Make sure that what you're saying about others is what you would want to be true for yourself. Talk about others as if they were present and you wanted to make them feel good about themselves.

THE LAW OF FORGIVENESS

The fifth way to eliminate guilty feelings and reactions is the most effective method of all. It is perhaps the most powerful and practical principle ever taught to build happiness, health, prosperity and wonderful relationships with others. It is what I referred to earlier and it is the Law of Forgiveness.

The Law of Forgiveness states that you are mentally healthy to the exact degree to which you can freely forgive and forget offenses against you.

The inability to forgive lies at the root of guilt, resentment and most other negative emotions. Holding grudges and remaining angry toward people who you feel have hurt you is the major cause of psychosomatic illness. The inability to forgive causes diseases that run the entire gamut from simple headaches to heart attacks, cancer and strokes.

To fulfill your potential, to develop your full mental capacities and to liberate your emotional and spiritual energies, you absolutely must forgive everyone who has ever hurt you in any way. You must "let go" and walk away from your anger and your resentment. You must refuse to continue paying, over and over, for the same unfortunate experience. You must put your desire to live a great life, to develop a fine character, and to become an outstanding person *higher* than any negative emotion that you might still be holding toward any other person.

Because your outer world reflects your true inner world, because you attract people and circumstances that harmonize with your dominant thoughts, because you become what you think about, your ability to forgive is the one indispensable quality you have to develop, through practice, if you sincerely want to be happy, healthy and completely free.

THE PRACTICE OF FORGIVENESS

There are *three* people in your life who you need to forgive to free yourself from negative feelings of guilt, inferiority, inadequacy, undeservingness, resentment and anger. When you let these people go, you will experience a feeling of release and joy and your life will begin to open up for you in wonderful ways.

The first people you have to forgive are your *parents*. Whether or not they are living, you must decide today to freely forgive them for every single thing that they ever did that hurt you. You must forgive them for every injustice and for every act of unkindness or cruelty you feel they inflicted upon you. You must rise above the hurts of childhood and let them go, accepting that your parents did the very best they could with what they had.

Almost everyone is still upset and angry over something that one or both of his or her parents did when he or she was growing up. Many men and women in their forties and fifties are still in a state of emotional distress because they have not yet forgiven their parents. A lifetime of resentment is a terrible price to pay for something about which nothing could have been done anyway.

In many cases, your parents are not even aware of what it is they did that you are still upset about. Usually, they have no memory of it at all. If you tell them why you are still angry, they will often be astonished because they have no recollection of the event ever taking place.

There are three ways that you can forgive your parents. The first is the most important, and that is to forgive them in your heart. Each time you think of the thing that he or she did that hurt you, use the Law of Substitution and replace the thought by saying, "I forgive him (her) for everything, I forgive him (her) for everything."

Each time you recall the hurtful experience, you quickly cancel it by saying, "I forgive him (her) for everything." If you continue forgiving them every time you recall the incident, before very long you will be able to think back on the experience unemotionally, with no negativity attached to it. Eventually you will forget it completely. You will be free.

The second way to forgive your parents is simply to go and see them personally, or telephone them. Many of the people who take our seminars go and sit down with their parents and discuss *what* they did and *why* they are still angry. Then they say, "I just want you to know that I forgive you for every mistake that you ever made bringing me up, and I love you." By forgiving them, you set them free, and you free yourself.

The third way to forgive your parents is simply to write them a letter, in as much detail as you desire, forgiving them for every mistake they ever made. Many parents with low self-esteem hope that someday their children will forgive them for the mistakes they made in bringing them up, which they are not strong enough to admit.

It is only when you forgive your parents completely that you become a fully functioning adult. Until then, you are still a child inside. You are still dependent on them emotionally. It is only when you let go of the unhappy experiences of growing up that you can have a mature relationship with your mother and father. For most people, the very best years of their lives with their parents begin on the day that they forgive their parents and put all the negatives of growing up behind them both.

The second person that you have to forgive is *everyone else*. You have to unconditionally forgive every single person in your life who has ever hurt you in any way. You have to forgive every wicked, senseless, brainless, cruel thing that anybody has ever said or done or spoken about you, without exception. The refusal to forgive just one person can be in itself enough to undermine or even destroy your future happiness.

You don't have to *like* the person. You just have to forgive him or her. Forgiveness is a perfectly selfish act: It has nothing to do with the other person, it has only to do with your own peace of mind, your own happiness, your own success and your own future. Perhaps the dumbest thing in the world is for you to still be angry or resentful toward a person who doesn't care about you at all. As someone put it, "I never hold grudges; while you're holding a grudge, they're out dancing."

Whatever the situation, you probably got yourself into it anyway. Whether it was a business deal, an investment, a job or a relationship, you made the choices and decisions that made it possible in the first place. It probably couldn't have happened without your active participation, which you could have withheld. You were responsible. You were free to choose and, unfortunately, you chose inappropriately. Now, let it go.

Even if you had nothing whatever to do with it, even if you were a completely innocent third party, you are still responsible for how you respond. You are in charge of yourself and your emotions.

You are free to decide what you do from this moment onward, and the best policy of all is to forgive.

THE LETTER

If you have been through a bad relationship or a bad marriage and you're still not over it, there is a technique that you can use to get yourself free. It is called simply "the letter." It is taught in several places now and is incredibly powerful and liberating.

The first thing you do is to sit down and write the person a letter. This letter consists of three parts, which you may make as long or as short as you want. In the first part, you say, "I accept complete responsibility for our relationship. I got myself into it and I have no excuses to offer." You refuse to mention how innocent and aggrieved you are, as you may have done in the past.

In the second part of the letter, you write, "I forgive you for everything you ever did that hurt me in any way." Sometimes it is a good idea to spell out all the things that you forgive the other person for. A woman I know who used this technique wrote eight pages of things that she forgave her ex-husband for.

In the last part of the letter, you end by saying, "I wish you well." Then you take the letter, address it properly, put sufficient postage on it, take it down to the mailbox and send it off.

The instant you let go of the letter and let it fall irretrievably into the mailbox, you will feel a sense of freedom and exhilaration that you cannot now imagine. At that moment, the relationship will be over and you will be ready to get on with the rest of your emotional life. Up to that moment, however, you remain trapped in the quicksand of the unresolved anger and resentment that attaches to any romantic relationship that doesn't work out.

A businessman who came through our seminar told me a remarkable story with regard to "the letter" and forgiveness. He had been married and had four children. He and his partner worked together for ten years to build a successful business. One day, his partner wasn't in the office and when he got home that night, his wife was gone. He learned later that his wife and his partner had been conspiring together for some time to strip the business of its assets, several hundred thousand dollars, and then go off together. And they were now gone. His whole life collapsed around him. He was left with four children and an incredible sense of anger and betrayal.

For four years, he was consumed with bitterness and resentment. His wife and partner had moved to another country and the cost of going after them legally was prohibitive. He turned all his attention to keeping himself from going into personal bankruptcy. His relationships with his children suffered terribly. Day and night, he was preoccupied with how badly, how unfairly, how unjustly he had been treated.

Throughout the first day of our seminar, during which we explained the concept of forgiveness, he sat silently. He got up and left that evening without saying a word. The next day, however, when he came back into the room, he was a different man. He was relaxed and smiling. He greeted other people and introduced himself. He told me privately that he had sat up for three hours the night before writing the letter. He then got up and walked several blocks to mail it. He said that it had worked exactly as I had described in the seminar. From the minute he dropped the letter in the mailbox, he felt like a totally different person.

After the seminar, he went out on his first date in four years, with a woman he met in the class. Later, he told me that his relationships with his children had been transformed. They all forgave the mother for leaving, and then resolved to get on with the rest of their lives, together. They were happy again for the first time in years.

The third person that you have to forgive is *yourself*. You have to forgive yourself for every foolish or hurtful thing you have ever said or done.

Remember, you are not perfect. You make mistakes. You say and do a lot of foolish things in the course of growing and maturing. If you had them to do over, you would have done them differently. But remorse and regret over previous mistakes serves no purpose. It is a sign of weak character. Remorse is often used as an excuse for not moving ahead. All wise and mature men and women have made silly, foolish mistakes. That's how they became wise and mature. And now you must forgive yourself for everything.

Forgiveness is the key to the kingdom of mental and spiritual development. When you practice being a totally forgiving person, you are emulating the character traits of the greatest men and women who have ever walked the earth. You are putting yourself on the side of the angels. The act of forgiveness begins the process of washing away all the accumulated residue of guilt, anger and resentment that breed negative emotions in your subconscious. The regular practice of freely forgiving everyone for everything makes you a calmer, kinder, more compassionate and optimistic human being.

GOOD FOR THE SOUL

Finally, if you have done anything to hurt someone else and you still feel badly about it, go to him or her and apologize. Say, "I'm sorry." Repentance is good for the soul. It frees you from the feelings of guilt and unworthiness that go with the knowledge that you have done something that is not consistent with your highest ideals.

It doesn't matter how the other person reacts or responds. All that matters is that you have had the courage and character to accept responsibility for your actions, to apologize and say that you're sorry. You can then get on with the rest of your life, and let the other person get on with his or hers.

PUTTING THE PRINCIPLE INTO PRACTICE

Here is an exercise: First, take a sheet of paper and make a list of everybody you can think of who has hurt you in any way. Second, go down the list, read the name, think of what happened, and say, "I forgive him or her for everything; I now let it go." Repeat these words two or three times for each person on your list. Then put the list away. From now on, whenever you think of that person or that situation, immediately cancel the negative emotion associated with it by saying, "I forgive him (her) for everything, I forgive him (her) for everything," and then get your mind busy elsewhere.

Your whole life begins to open up for you when you finally forgive and let go. Forgiveness is the key to the kingdom of inner peace, the hardest thing you ever do, and the most important.

The Master Goal

Your ability to manage the day-to-day stresses of your life is essential to your happiness and success. Performing at your best requires calmness, clarity and an ability to maintain a certain amount of objectivity about yourself and your work. In this chapter you will learn how to be your own psychotherapist. You will learn how to control your thinking processes so you can minimize your stress and maximize your energy and optimism. You will learn how to be happy and effective no matter what is going on around you. The master goal is the achievement of peace of mind, the ultimate aim of all your efforts.

THE HIGHEST HUMAN GOOD

The highest human good is peace of mind. Your ability to achieve and maintain your own peace of mind is perhaps the best single measure of how well you are doing as a person. Peace of mind is the essential precondition for happiness and for getting the maximum amount of enjoyment and pleasure out of your work and your personal life. When you make inner peace your highest goal and organize all your activities, decisions and behavior around it, you will be happier and more effective in your life and career than under any other circumstances.

The opposite of inner peace is negativity. Negative emotions are the main cause of unhappiness in life. Negative emotions are the "robber" emotions. They rob you of peace, happiness and enjoyment. They make you sick. They shorten your life. All stress, tension and anxiety is ultimately manifested in negative emotions of some kind. Negative emotions, once aroused, are always expressed, either inwardly or outwardly. You either make yourself sick or you poison your relationships with others.

One of your major goals in planning your life must be to eliminate negative emotions and become a truly happy, healthy person. And the way you eliminate negative emotions is, first, by understanding the root causes of negative emotions, and, second, by learning how to neutralize them at will.

COURAGE AND HONESTY

You need courage to be your own psychotherapist. You require tremendous honesty. You must be willing to look deep into yourself for the real cause of any stress or negativity that you may be experiencing. You must accept complete responsibility for both your inner and your outer life, and for how you feel about them. This requires tremendous strength of character but it pays off in terms of the best kind of life you could want for yourself.

Hans Selye, the pioneer in stress management, defined stress as "any nonspecific response to internal or external stimuli." The key word in this definition is "response." Stress is not contained in external events; there is no such thing as an inherently stressful situation. There are only stressful responses. Stress is not contained in what happens to you. It is the way you respond to what happens to you. You can choose to respond in a stressful way or you can choose to respond in a nonstressful way. The choice is yours.

The starting point of stress management and the achievement of inner peace is for you to accept responsibility for your responses. It is not what happens to you but how you think about what happens to you that causes your response, positive or negative, stressful or unstressful. And this is your decision, your choice, your responsibility.

For example, on any given day, two people may be stuck in traffic on the way to work. One person will be impatient and angry, while the other person will remain calm and relaxed.

Here you have the same situation but two ways of responding to it. The response, not the situation, causes the stress.

Or the same person may be upset and angry if he is stuck in traffic on the way to work on Monday, and be quite calm if he is stuck in traffic on the way to work on Wednesday. Here you have the same person and two different responses to the same situation. The choice is always up to the individual.

A HIGH PRICE

You pay a high price for poor stress management and the loss of inner peace. Easily 80 percent, and perhaps as many as 95 percent, of physical illnesses are psychological in origin. Modern medicine has almost eliminated most of the major diseases—typhoid, typhus, cholera, smallpox, yellow fever, polio and many others that used to shorten the natural life span. Yet in spite of this, we have more sick people and more of our gross national product being spent on health care than at any other time in our history. And a large part of the reason for this is the inability of the average person to manage the rigors and stresses of daily life in our dynamic and fast-paced modern society.

The leading cause of death in America is heart disease, killing more than five hundred thousand men and women each year. Yet experts such as Dr. Kenneth Cooper, of the Cooper Clinic in Dallas, have concluded that there is little incidence of death from heart disease before age seventy in the absence of the high-stress, or Type A, personality. High stress has also been closely linked to cancer, strokes, ulcers, colitis, hyperthyroidism, skin diseases and break-outs, migraine headaches, arthritis and a variety of other life-threatening and degenerative ailments.

STRESS CAN BE UNLEARNED

If there is anything good about stress it is the fact that no one is born with any. Have you ever seen a stressed-out baby? All stressful responses are learned over the course of our lifetimes as the result of experience and conditioning. And if you have learned to respond to certain situations in a stressful way, you can also learn to respond to them in a more positive and constructive way.

In any case, stress is not all bad. The only people who are completely free from stress are those in the cemetery. Stress is an unavoidable part of being alive. But there is both good stress, or what Dr. Abraham Maslow called "eustress," and bad stress, the kind that is harmful to your health. Good stress gives you energy, enthusiasm and excitement about what you are doing. Bad stress makes you tired, irritable and unhappy. It often makes you feel overwhelmed by your work.

A MATTER OF CONTROL

The key issue in stress management is the subject of control, or what is called the "locus of control." You feel *positive* about yourself and your life to the degree to which you feel you are in control of what is happening. You feel *negative* about yourself and your life to the degree to which you feel you are not in control, or that you are controlled by external factors, such as your boss, your bills, your relationships, your health or your other problems. (We discussed this key idea in Chapter Two.)

If you think about your personal and work life, you will find that the areas in which you experience the greatest peace of mind and satisfaction are the areas in which you feel you have the greatest amount of control, or ability to exert influence, over what is going on. You will also find that the areas in which you are most unhappy, or experience the most stress, are those in which you feel you are not in control, or in which you feel there is little that you can do to solve the problem or remove the irritation.

The most effective method of stress management that I know of is called the "cognitive control method." In a way, we have been talking indirectly about this method throughout this book. "Cognitive control" means that you use your mind, your ability to think, choose and decide, to exert control over your emotions and over your responses to difficult situations. It is in using the cognitive control method that you become your own psychotherapist and assure yourself life-long enjoyment of inner peace and happy relationships.

SEVEN SOURCES OF STRESS

There are seven major causes of stress and negative emotions. These seven stressors cause probably 95 percent, perhaps even 99 percent, of all of the unhappiness you will ever experience. Once you learn how to identify them, and deal with them, you will feel more positive, more optimistic and more cheerful in everything you do. You will feel that you are back in control of your inner and outer lives.

WORRY WEARS YOU DOWN

The first major source of stress is worry. Worry is a sustained form of fear caused by indecision. Often people learn to worry from one of their parents and, by worrying repeatedly, they become chronic worriers. They worry about almost anything, almost all the time. And worry of any kind tends to depress your body's immune system and make you susceptible to all kinds of illnesses, from colds and flu all the way up to life-threatening diseases and infections. Your ability to eliminate worry is your starting point for the happy, healthy, well-balanced mental attitude you need to get the most joy from everything you do.

When people are asked what they worry about, they usually give the following percentages: 40 percent are things that never happen; 30 percent are in the past and can't be changed in any case; 12 percent are needless worries about health; and 10 percent are petty worries about unimportant matters.

That only leaves 8 percent, of which half, or 4 percent, are things about which nothing can be done. Only 4 percent of the things that most people worry about can be changed. How do your worries measure up against these percentages?

LIVE ONE DAY AT A TIME

One of the best ways to stop worrying is to live in "day-tight compartments." Live one day at a time. In the Bible it says, "Sufficient unto the day are the cares thereof." Much of your stress is a result of worrying about things in the future, most of which never happen anyway. Cross the bridge, whenever possible, when you come to it, not before. And not repeatedly.

THE "WORRY BUSTER"

Perhaps the best method for dealing with worry is the "Worry Buster." This simple four-step process has helped more people to gain control and eliminate worrying than any other method.

First, clearly define your worry situation in writing. Sometimes when you write out a clear definition of the problem, you see an obvious solution.

Second, determine the worst possible thing that could happen as a result of this situation. Often you will find that the worst possible outcome is not that bad. Just defining it clearly and considering it as a possibility often reduces the stress and worry associated with the problem.

Third, once you have determined the worst possible thing that could happen, resolve to accept it, should it occur. Once you have determined that you are "willing to have it so" you then have nothing left to worry about.

And fourth, begin immediately to improve upon the worst. Begin to do everything you possibly can to minimize the worst possible outcome. In business, this is called the "minimax" solution. It requires that you minimize the maximum worst possible consequences of any decision.

John Paul Getty, at one time the world's richest man, gave one of his secrets of success as this: In every business deal or transaction, identify the worst thing that can possibly go wrong, and then *make sure it doesn't happen*.

The only real antidote for worry is purposeful action. Once you have made a decision about what you can do to resolve your situation, get so busy working on the *solution* that you no longer have time to think about the *problem*.

The Law of Substitution states that you can substitute thoughts of positive action for thoughts of worry and drive the worry thoughts out of your mind. The key is to get busy. "Take arms against a sea of troubles, and by opposing end them," as Shakespeare said in *Hamlet*. "I must lose myself in action lest I wither in despair," said Tennyson after the death of his best friend, Arthur Hallam.

MEANING AND PURPOSE

The second major cause of stress and negativity is having no clear meaning and purpose in life. It is having no clear goals to which you are committed. In business, a major source of stress is poor time management, which is almost invariably caused by a lack of clarity concerning goals and priorities. You can't plan and organize your time efficiently and effectively if you are unsure about what it is you are trying to accomplish.

Perhaps 80 percent of all the problems and unhappiness that you experience occur because you are unclear about where you're going and what you want to accomplish. The very act of selecting a major definite purpose, and making a plan for its accomplishment, is often enough in itself to snap you out of the feeling of negativity that you experience in the absence of a goal.

There is an old saying that is corny but true: "Feeling listless? Make a list!" The very act of sitting down and making a list of ten things you would like to accomplish over the next twelve months will get you excited. Your blood pressure and your heart rate will go up. You will become more alert and aware. You'll be happier. Your mind is structured in such a way that you feel good about yourself only when you're working toward achieving something that is important to you.

THE "INCOMPLETE ACTION"

The third major source of stress and negativity is the "incomplete action." Each of us has within us a "compulsion to closure" or an "urge to completion." We feel happy and contented when we finish a job, or achieve a goal. We feel unhappy and stressed when we leave something undone or incomplete. Engaging in an incomplete act, or doing a job only partially, can cause you enormous stress. Even watching someone engage in an incomplete action is stressful.

A famous courtroom lawyer, when it appeared that his client was going to be found guilty, would arrive in court on the final day with a big cigar. As the district attorney began his summation to the jury, the lawyer would begin to puff on his cigar, and the ash would begin to grow. As the ash grew longer and longer, without falling off, the attention of the members of the jury would begin to focus on the ash. The lawyer would continually make motions and objections with the hand that contained the cigar so that it kept moving back and forth in the air.

In no time at all, the eyes of the entire jury would be fixed on the growing ash and they would stop paying attention to what the district attorney was saying. When the district attorney was finished, the lawyer would put his cigar down in the ashtray and then get up and give his final closing defense arguments to the jury. In many cases, the jury would bring back a verdict of not guilty.

After the jury had left the courtroom, the lawyer would remove a long, thin wire that he had placed down the center of the cigar. The wire had been holding the three inches of ash. There was no doubt that this wire had saved his clients in many marginal cases. The tension of watching the ash was so great for the jury members that they were unable to listen to the summation of the case by the district attorney.

Similarly, the stress of being in the middle of an incomplete action can be extremely distracting to you and can make you incapable of concentrating on anything for very long. You think about the task or situation continually.

Procrastination is the most common example of the incomplete action. Whenever you procrastinate, especially on important tasks, you experience stress. And the more important the task or responsibility, the greater the stress, the greater the disruption of your peace of mind. This stress eventually appears physically in such reactions as insomnia, negativity and irritation.

The solution to any incomplete action is to begin the task and stay with it until it is complete, which requires tremendous self-discipline. The payoff for completing a task is an immediate increase of energy, enthusiasm and self-esteem. Task completion makes you feel better and more positive. It immediately relieves the stress you experience when the incomplete task is hanging over your head.

UNFINISHED BUSINESS

A variation of the incomplete action is "unfinished business." Unfinished business refers to a relationship, personal or business, that is still hanging on. It is something you have not let go of or ended. It is not yet complete or finished. Unfinished business is often caused when you hold on to a relationship long after it is over, rather than going on to something else.

Unfinished business sometimes lingers because of an unwillingness to forgive and forget. It can be caused by a desire to get even. Often it is accompanied by bitterness and anger. Money can be involved, or a desire to get what you feel you are entitled to. Unfinished business lingers if you still want another person's love or respect. You are still emotionally attached and you feel your own self-worth is tied up in his or her estimate of you. Unfinished business ties you to the past and negatively affects your business and personal relationships.

A woman who had been summarily fired from her executive position after several years was furious. She told me she had seen her lawyer and was going to sue for wrongful termination. She was both bitter and determined to get what she felt was the justice she was entitled to.

I asked her how long the process would take. She replied that it could take up to two years to get to court.

What were her chances of winning her suit? According to her lawyer, they were better than 50 percent.

What would she do in the interim? She told me that, in all honesty, if she took another position, it would weaken her case, her claim for remuneration.

We concluded that, if she pursued legal action, she could be tied up professionally and emotionally for as long as two years, and at the end of that time, she might lose her case in court and end up having gained nothing. But she would have lost two years of her life preoccupied with her lawsuit, not to mention the expenses involved.

What advice would you give her? What advice would you give yourself in this situation? What would you do in your own life if you felt you had been treated unfairly by someone?

I suggested to her that she drop the whole matter and get on with her career and her life. Her happiness and peace of mind were far too important to be held to ransom for up to two years. She would be living in a state of "suspended animation" emotionally, and there was no payoff or settlement worth trading all that time for.

She was both smart and perceptive. She told me she would think about it. Later, I heard that she had dropped the legal action. Shortly afterward, I read in the paper that she had been appointed to a senior position with another company. When I saw her briefly some weeks later, she was radiant and happy.

At Christmas, I received a card from her with a handwritten note saying, "Thank you for the best advice I've ever received."

No one can have any control over your emotions unless there is still something that you want from that person. No one can make you feel unhappy or angry unless there is something that you still want, whether it is love, respect or money, or even custody of the children. The minute that you decide that you no longer want anything from the other person, you complete the "business." You are free again.

FEAR OF FAILURE

The fourth major cause of stress and negativity is the fear of failure. This fear is usually manifested in indecisiveness, anxiety and worry. It accompanies the feeling of "I can't," which settles in the solar plexus, ruining your digestion, making you feel afraid and insecure. It can destroy your ambition and undermine your resolve. Instead of striving toward the fulfillment of your potential, you become preoccupied with not failing. You think only about playing it safe.

Fear of failure is a conditioned response learned in childhood. Everyone has a certain amount of this fear. It causes you to be prudent, which in moderation is a good thing. But when fear of failure is carried too far, it can be a major obstacle to your success and happiness.

Everyone experiences fear of some kind. The brave person is not the person without fear, but the person who acts in spite of his or her fear. When you face your fears and move toward them, they diminish and grow smaller. But when you back away from the person or situation you fear, it grows until it can actually dominate your whole life.

Here is a simple but effective way of dealing with fear: First, affirm to yourself with energy and conviction, "I can do it! I can do it! I can do it!" This affirmation short-circuits and cancels out the feeling of "I can't! I can't! I can't!" It is a powerful and fast-acting application of the Law of Substitution.

Then, do the thing you fear. Confront your fear. Move toward your fear. Use your specific fear as a challenge and instead of backing away from it or avoiding it, confront it and face it head on.

In her wonderful book *Wake Up and Live,* Dorothea Brande wrote about the technique that turned her life around. She spent the rest of her career speaking and sharing this secret with thousands of others, many of whose lives also turned around as a result. And her secret was simply this: "Decide exactly what you want to do, and then, *act as if it were impossible to fail.*"

Act as if the fear did not exist. Pretend. Ask yourself, "If I were totally unafraid in this situation, if I had no fears at all, how would I behave?"

And then *behave that way*. You can act your way into feeling courageous and unafraid. If you pretend that you are brave and courageous, you will begin to feel brave and courageous. You take control of your emotions by taking control of your actions.

Always ask yourself, "What's the *worst* possible thing that can happen if I go ahead?" Then ask, "What is the *best* possible thing that can happen if I am successful?" You will often find that the worst possible thing that can happen is quite small, and the best possible thing that can happen is quite significant. This exercise alone can often motivate you to take the all-important first step that leads onward to success.

FAILURE IS A GREAT TEACHER

Thomas J. Watson, Sr., the founder of IBM, put it this way: "Do you want to succeed? Then, *double your rate of failure*. Success lies on the far side of failure."

Remember, failure is never final. Failure is simply a way of learning the lessons you need to succeed. The only thing of which the fear of failure can assure you is ultimate failure in life. All great men and women developed the habit of confronting their fear of failure, and acting in spite of their fear, until the habit of courage became a part of their characters.

You overcome the fear of failure by moving confidently in the direction of your dreams and acting as if it were impossible to fail. As Henry Ford said, "Failure is just another opportunity to more intelligently begin again."

THE FEAR OF REJECTION

The fifth major cause of stress and negativity is the fear of rejection. The fear of rejection manifests itself in an *overconcern* for the approval of others. The fear of rejection is typically learned in early childhood as a result of a parent giving the child "conditional love."

Many parents make the mistake of giving love and approval to their children only when their children do something that they want them to do. A child who has grown up with this kind of "conditional love" tends to seek for *un*conditional approval from others all his or her life. When the child becomes an adult, this need for approval is often transferred to the workplace and onto the boss. The boss becomes, in effect, a surrogate father. The adult employee then becomes preoccupied with the opinion of the boss.

TYPE A BEHAVIOR

Drs. Rosenman and Friedman, two San Francisco heart specialists, have defined this obsession for performance as "Type A behavior." They estimate that probably 60 percent of men and 10 percent (and growing) of women are Type A's. This behavior can vary from mild to extreme cases. People who are what they call "true Type A's" put so much pressure on themselves to perform that they burn themselves out and often die of heart attacks before age fifty-five. This is perhaps the most serious stress-related phenomenon in the American workplace.

The true Type A has several attitudes and behaviors in common with other Type A's. Compare your behavior with these symptoms and see if any of them apply to you.

The most obvious sign of the true Type A is a "harrying sense of time urgency." The Type A feels that he is in a "rat race." He feels he is on a treadmill and can't get off. He feels that he has to do more and more in less and less time. He always feels in a hurry and under pressure. This "time urgency" usually occurs because he is always volunteering for more and more work in order to win the approval from the boss that he never got from his father.

It's not uncommon for companies to deliberately hire people with the Type A profile. They know that these people will work with tremendous intensity and produce far more than the average —at least until they burn out. Then, the companies fire or demote them and hire new Type A's for their jobs.

Type A personalities have an obsession with performance, with achievement, to some *un*determined high standard. No matter how much they accomplish, it's never enough. Because they have never set themselves a measurable standard at which they can relax and enjoy their accomplishments, they keep on pushing themselves harder and harder.

No matter how successful Type A's become, they feel a tremendous *insecurity of status*. They never feel they've done enough. If they win awards for the best salesman or best manager of the year on December 31, they feel they have to start all over again on January 1. They can never relax or rest on their laurels.

Type A's are more concerned with *things* than people. They work harder and harder to rack up numbers of accomplishments—higher incomes, greater numbers of sales, more and bigger possessions, greater numbers of papers published. They believe that "the one who dies with the most toys wins!"

True Type A's measure how well they are doing by what they can count. Type A's talk about their possessions, number of achievements, or level of income all the time. They continually compare themselves with others, especially those who appear to be doing better than they are, and are determined to surpass them.

Type A's bring work home. They are always talking about the *boss*. They are preoccupied with what the boss said, what the boss did, or what the boss meant. They have an obsession with the opinions and views of their employer. Nothing makes Type A's happier than to get approval from the boss. Nothing makes Type A's more upset than to be out of favor with the boss, for any reason.

Perhaps the most important distinguishing characteristic of the Type A is a feeling of *aggression and hostility,* especially toward coworkers with whom the Type A feels in constant competition.

Type A's are typically *angry, impatient and irritated.* They work harder and harder but get little satisfaction from their work or accomplishments. They feel a sense of hopelessness, that there is nothing they can do. They feel out of control. They constantly say, "I have to do this" or "I have to do that." They feel there's no point where they can relax and take it easy. They finally send a message to their subconscious mind: "Get me out of here!" And the first signs of heart disease or other illnesses appear not long afterward.

TAKING CONTROL

If you recognize Type A behavior in yourself, especially the attitude of hostility and a harrying sense of time urgency, or time pressure, there are specific things that you can do to get over it.

The first step is simple. *Admit it!* Admit that you are a Type A personality. Many Type A's are reluctant to admit that their work controls them completely, rather than their controlling their work.

If you accuse them of demonstrating Type A behavior they will turn their hostility and aggression on you and vigorously deny it. They will lash out when their wives or husbands try to get them to slow down. They become defensive and angry when their behavior is brought to their attention.

To get over Type A behavior (which is usually fatal) you must realize that you can never find peace or happiness in your accomplishments. You can only find peace within yourself. If your father never gave you the unconditional approval you needed, you must accept that he did the best he could with what he had.

There is no point in your striving incessantly to earn the approval of your boss in order to make up for the love and approval your father never had to give you in the first place. It can only shorten your life.

The second step you must take to get over Type A behavior is for you to *make the decision to change*. Make the decision that you do not want to live like this any more. Make the decision that you want to become a more relaxed, more productive and more enjoyable person, parent or spouse.

Many people will admit that they are Type A's, but then they go on to say that they are proud of it. Don't fall into this trap. Killing yourself twenty years early with hard work is nothing to be proud of. In fact, it's just plain stupid.

The third step to overcoming Type A behavior is to *learn to relax*. And the very best way to relax is to just stop. Practice complete relaxation or meditation, even solitude, for twenty minutes, twice each day.

Going for a walk in the park at lunchtime is a wonderful antidote to stress. And it's when you are convinced that you have no time at all to take a break that it is most necessary for you to discipline yourself to do it. It is when you feel you have the least amount of time to take care of yourself that you are closest to the breaking point.

DISTINGUISHING BETWEEN TYPE A
AND THE WORKAHOLIC

There is a basic difference between the Type A personality and the "workaholic." The two are distinctly different. True Type A's cannot take time off without thinking or talking about work. True Type A's brag that they have not taken a vacation for years. True Type A's take a briefcase full of work home on the weekends, and even if they go away on family vacations, they take a load of work with them and are on the telephone back to the office all the time. One of the hallmarks of the true Type A is this inability to take time off.

Another hallmark of Type A's is that they have an *external* locus of control. You will hear them use the words repeatedly, "I have to, I have to, I have to." They don't feel that they have any control over what they do. They are always doing something because someone else wants it or someone expects it.

Workaholics are quite different. They have an *internal* locus of control. Workaholics are working toward self-determined goals and objectives. They get a tremendous feeling of satisfaction and pleasure from their work. Workaholics can work hard for ten, twelve or fourteen hours a day, five, six or seven days a week, but unlike Type A's, workaholics can take a day or a week off, or go away on vacation and not think or worry about work at all.

Workaholics tend to be positive personalities, fulfilling their potential by doing something that is important to them. Workaholics have no hostility, anger or resentment. They are full of enthusiasm and excitement about their work. Workaholics are usually doing what they love to do, what they really enjoy.

This is the key difference between the workaholic and the Type A personality: the amount of *enjoyment* each gets from his or her work. Now, honestly, which one are you? Type A or the workaholic? Your life may depend upon how accurately you answer this question.

FACING THE FACTS

The sixth major cause of stress, negativity and lost inner peace is "denial." Denial lies at the core of most stress, unhappiness and psychosomatic illness.

Denial is the behavior of a person who *refuses to face an unpleasant reality*. It occurs with all its unpleasantness when you do not want to admit that there is some part of your life that is not going well. You slip into denial and pretend there's nothing wrong. However, what the mind harbors, the body expresses. When you engage in denial for any period of time, it begins to manifest itself physically. Denial triggers insomnia, headaches, digestive problems, depression, angry outbursts and often frantic activity.

Denial takes place when some part of your life is not working and you don't want to admit it. Denial is always accompanied by a fear of embarrassment or loss of face. Denial occurs when you refuse to admit to yourself or someone else that you are not the person you appear to be. You engage in denial when you don't want to admit that you have changed your mind. You slip into denial when you no longer feel the way you did in the past. You use denial to cover up when you know you've made a mistake.

CONFRONTERS AND EVADERS

There are two personality profiles, healthy and unhealthy, that illustrate different responses to stress and denial. The first is the "Confronter" and the second is the "Evader." At a leading university, students were tested for these distinctly different personality profiles and then divided into two groups, based on whether they were predominantly Evaders or predominantly Confronters.

The first group, the Evaders, were put into a room where each person was hooked up to an electrode that gave him or her a mild electric shock every sixty seconds. There was a clock on the wall located where the students could see it. Every time the second hand passed the number twelve, the students received a shock to their fingertips.

When the Evaders were hooked up to the electrode, they engaged in a variety of behaviors to distract themselves as the second hand moved toward the twelve. The researchers had put a video camera in the clock so they could observe the faces and eyes of the students from that viewpoint. As the second hand came up to the twelve, the most noteworthy behavior of the Evaders was that they *refused* to look at the clock when it signaled that the shock was coming. Instead, they looked away. They evaded facing the symbol of their stress and discomfort.

At the end of the experiment, the Evaders were tested. Their heart rates, their respiratory rates and their blood pressures, all good indicators of stress, were 30 to 40 percent above their rates as measured before the test.

Then the students identified as Confronters were brought into the room. They were also hooked up to the electrodes and told that they would receive a mild electric shock each time the second hand crossed the twelve.

The researchers watched the Confronters through the hidden camera. The most noticeable difference between the Confronters and the Evaders was that, although the Confronters engaged in the same behavior to distract themselves and to take their minds off the coming shock, when the second hand came up to the twelve, all of the Confronters were looking straight at the clock and were mentally prepared to take the shock on the ends of their fingers.

At the end of the experiment, the Confronters' blood pressure and heart rates were almost exactly the same as they had been before the test.

Men and women who squarely confront their problems and difficulties are far healthier than those who evade them. They are far happier than those who hope that they will go away or take care of themselves. The more willing you are to honestly confront the difficulties and challenges facing you, the happier and healthier you will be.

THE KEY TO INNER STRENGTH

By continually facing your problems honestly and objectively, you become a more confident and competent person. You become stronger and more self-reliant. You stop being afraid of unpleasant situations in your work or personal life. You deal with life as it is, not as you wish it were.

To be your own psychotherapist, to achieve inner peace and outer effectiveness, there is a simple question you can ask yourself whenever you feel unhappy or "out of sorts" for any reason. Assume first of all that your discontent is caused from within. Then turn into yourself and ask this key question, "What is it in my life that I am not facing?"

This is a tough question that forces you to be totally honest with yourself. It forces you to stop fooling yourself by pretending that all is well. "What is it in my life that I'm not facing?"

You could be in the wrong job. You could be in the wrong relationship. You may feel that someone else is better than you are at your chosen profession. With men, denial is usually associated with their work. With women, denial is most often associated with problems in their relationships. Each person is especially sensitive in areas in which his or her self-esteem is most involved. You often practice denial in parts of your life in which change is seen as both inevitable and threatening.

No matter what the reason might be for your unhappiness, you must be willing to ask yourself, "What is it in my life that I'm not facing?"

Then you ask, "What is the *worst* thing it could possibly be?"

When I first started using this technique, I identified the worst possible thing it could be in my life as something being wrong with my marriage. That would involve the greatest amount of embarrassment and emotional upset for me. So I would ask myself, "Am I happy in my marriage?"

I would force myself to answer the question honestly. As it happened, my answer was always, "Yes."

Once that particular possibility was out of the way, I would then go on to ask myself if it could possibly have to do with my work. If not that, what other area of my life could it be? Eventually, I would find the cause of the stress and then take action to deal with it.

Usually, because confrontation is so painful, people try to fool themselves. They will say that the reason they are unhappy is that they got a parking ticket or that they had lost something. This is just a way of avoiding the real issue.

Whenever you begin to suffer physical or mental pain of any kind it usually means that what you are refusing to face is tied up with your *ego*. You need to search it out, whatever it is, like a detective, so that you can face it squarely. Go through the rooms of your mind, as if you were going through a darkened house with a flashlight, and shine the glare of honest confrontation on each of your problems.

There is always a price you can pay to be free from any unhappiness. There is always something that you can start doing or stop doing. And you always know what the price is. The only question you must answer is, "Are you willing to pay the price?"

PAY THE PRICE

The rule is: Whatever the price is, *pay it!* You are going to have to pay it sooner or later, and the sooner you pay it the sooner you will be free from whatever it is that is bothering you.

Never compromise your peace of mind for anything. Set peace of mind as your highest goal and organize every part of your life around it. If you ever trade your peace of mind for something else, you will end up with *neither*. If you trade your peace of mind for a job, you will end up with neither your peace of mind nor the job. If you trade your peace of mind for a relationship, you will end up with neither the relationship nor your peace of mind.

There seems to be something in nature that demands that you be true to your sense of inner peace. If you are ever false to your internal standards you will always suffer the consequences. You will always end up paying, and the price will always outweigh any temporary benefit or advantage you obtained.

THE DESTROYER OF HAPPINESS

The seventh source of stress and negativity is the phenomenon of *anger*. Anger is perhaps the most destructive of all negative emotions. Outbursts of anger can cause heart attacks, strokes, burst blood vessels, ulcers, migraine headaches, asthma and skin diseases of all kinds. Uncontrolled anger ruins marriages and relationships, destroys the personalities of growing children, loses jobs and careers and causes more unhappiness than any other emotion.

The remarkable thing about anger is that it is largely unnecessary. Nothing good ever comes from it. It is a purely destructive negative emotion that you can largely eliminate if you decide to.

Anger comes from within you, not from without. It comes from the person you are, not from what people say or do. No one makes you angry. Nothing causes you to feel anger. Anger is a response that you *choose* to a particular situation. You can decide to respond to difficulties in a calm, positive manner, or you can decide to respond with anger. You are always free to choose.

WHAT SETS YOU OFF?

Anger is triggered by pain, or by a perception that someone is attacking you, or that you are being taken advantage of. Often anger is caused by frustrated expectations. It is a reaction you have when things don't work out, or when people do not behave the way you expected. Anger can be set off by a fear of loss of some kind. Often you become angry if you feel you are being victimized, or being dealt with unfairly.

In every case, it is your *perception* that triggers the feeling of anger. It is the way you interpret the event to yourself. When you see yourself as a victim, your natural response will be to become angry. You may even strike back verbally or physically to protect yourself or to get even.

When you perceive that you are a victim of some kind of aggression, you send a signal to your autonomic nervous system that you are in danger. Immediately, your autonomic nervous system sends a message to your adrenal cortex, and adrenaline is secreted into your bloodstream. The adrenaline causes your heart and respiratory rates to increase rapidly. Your blood pressure goes up and your system goes on to "Red Alert," ready to protect, defend and counterattack.

Your entire body prepares for either *fight or flight*. If you become angry repeatedly, your resistance to anger becomes weaker and weaker. You become angry faster and faster. Eventually you have no resistance left. Anger then becomes your automatic response to any perceived problem in your environment. Some people are angry all the time. Everything and everyone makes them angry because of their perception that they are victims and under attack from a hostile world.

FIGHT OR FLIGHT?

High blood pressure is caused primarily by a pattern of angry responses. You become angry. Your blood pressure goes up. Your body prepares for fight or flight, but in a short while the situation passes and your blood pressure goes back down. Each time you become angry, your blood pressure goes up, and then down again. Eventually your blood pressure simply *stays* up.

The solution to high blood pressure is usually not a change of medication, but a change of attitude toward the inevitable ups and downs of day-to-day life.

Angry outbursts are a mark of weakness. They demonstrate immaturity and a lack of control. Someone who gets angry all the time is responding like a child, with no self-discipline or self-restraint.

Make two decisions: first, get your anger under control; and second, stop using anger as a response to things you don't like. Resolve to be more patient, and to withhold judgment until you've studied the situation and asked a few questions to slow yourself down.

WHY ANGER ACCUMULATES

Once you become angry, your entire body prepares for retaliation. However, in a civilized society this retaliation is usually frustrated, for one of three reasons.

First, retaliation or counterattack may not be possible. If someone cuts you off in traffic, or leaves a dent in your car while you're shopping, you may become angry but there is little you can do about it. The other person is long gone. The anger builds up inside you but has no outlet.

Second, retaliation is usually not acceptable. If someone is rude to you or if your boss chews you out, it is not appropriate for you to shout back or physically assault him or her. You may become angry but you end up holding the anger inside, where it accumulates.

Third, retaliation is often not advisable. If a 350-pound former football player bumps into you in a bar or a restaurant, you might become angry but you would be foolish to strike back at him. If you came back to your car and there was a gang of Hell's Angels sitting on it you would be well advised to keep your anger inside. So you suppress it.

In each case, once you become angry, if you don't do something to get it out of your system, it builds up and eventually poisons your body. Sustained anger actually changes the chemical composition of your blood. Eventually it will erupt in skin diseases, ulcers, migraine headaches or much worse. You will express the built-up anger at members of your family, or at people who can't defend themselves, such as employees or the staffs of other companies.

STOP IT AT THE OUTSET

The best way to deal with anger is refrain from becoming angry in the first place. Resolve in advance that you will not allow yourself to become upset. Take control of your tendency to blame or lash out by catching yourself and repeating, over and over, "I am responsible, I am responsible, I am responsible."

You may not be responsible for being cut off in traffic but you are definitely responsible for the way you choose to respond. You will be far more effective if you respond calmly and constructively. And you will feel much better as well.

GROSS PHYSICAL IMPACT ACTIVITY

However, if you have already become angry, you can dispel anger through contact. Dr. Hans Selye called this "gross physical impact activity." He found in his stress research that making contact of some kind relieves anger. The anger passes from your body into whatever you are making contact with.

Selye found that you can dispel anger through one of four outlets: your hands, your feet, your teeth or your voice. You can get rid of anger by hitting, kicking, biting or screaming.

Any sport that requires hitting something with your hands dispels anger. Racquetball, handball, volleyball, baseball and basketball are all excellent ways to transfer anger from the body into the ball. Hitting a bucket of golf balls on a driving range is a real tonic for the nerves. Men and women in high-stress occupations often find themselves attracted to these sports because they feel so much better after an hour of batting something around. All their anger is dispelled into the ball or object.

Much of acne in adolescents and most skin breakouts in adults is caused by repressed anger. It can be dispelled through gross physical impact activity.

One concerned father whose son was bothered by acne bought

him a huge block of wood and a big box of tenpenny nails. He then gave him a hammer and had him spend ten to twenty minutes each day hammering these large nails into the block of wood. The boy's acne cleared up in less than two weeks.

Another father bought his son a cord of wood and an axe and put him to work chopping wood every evening after school. With this gross physical impact activity, the boy's acne cleared up completely in a few days.

Any kind of sport in which *kicking* is involved, such as football or soccer, is excellent for dispelling anger. The very act of kicking something serves as an outlet. You often see angry people stamp their feet in exasperation, as an unconscious attempt to get rid of pent-up feelings of anger.

However, many forms of exercise, such as running, swimming or cycling, don't dispel anger because they involve little or no contact. They may help you reduce stress or lose weight, but they don't reduce anger.

You can dispel anger by eating something that requires a lot of chewing. Often when you're hungry for a steak, it is because you're feeling frustrated or angry and chewing the steak vigorously dispels the anger from your body into the meat. After a hearty, heavy dinner, you feel more relaxed because much of your anger is gone.

Screaming is another way in which people, both adults and children, get rid of their anger. It's a common form of release. Children develop anger as a result of feeling small and helpless. They scream to vent their frustrations. So do many adults.

There is a form of psychotherapy called "primal." In treatment, patients are encouraged to scream in the presence of trained psychotherapists. They are taught to release suppressed anger built up from childhood. It's often very effective in helping people get a grip on their emotions. It certainly beats suppression of anger on the one hand or screaming at your loved ones on the other.

In a vicious fight between two very angry people, they will *hit, kick, scream and bite*. These reactions are all ways of expelling anger. Often, after a loud disagreement or physical battle, the two combatants will become lovers or good friends. All the anger is gone; only good feelings remain.

THE COGNITIVE CONTROL METHOD

Your goal is to become a *low-stress, high-performance* personality. To achieve this, you must use the "cognitive control" method already discussed here. Performing at your best requires that you use your ability to think and to control your emotional responses. Practice the *Law of Substitution*. Deliberately think positive thoughts. Think optimistically. Think constructively. If you deliberately select a positive thought, you cannot simultaneously think a negative or stressful thought. You substitute the positive for the negative.

Repeat to yourself, "I like myself," or "I am responsible." Keep your mind fixed on your goal. Since a goal is inherently positive, when you force yourself to think continually about your goals, you keep your mind positive and optimistic most of the time.

If another person makes you angry, practice the *Law of Forgiveness*. Let go of any feelings of anger or resentment. Remember, forgiveness is a perfectly selfish act. Your job, your responsibility, is to keep yourself calm and positive rather than allowing things to make you angry and upset. If this requires letting go of negative feelings you have toward anyone else, do it! It's your key to happiness, peace of mind and long life.

SET PEACE OF MIND AS YOUR HIGHEST GOAL

You take complete charge of your inner life by deciding that you are going to set peace of mind as your highest goal. Organize your life around this goal. Become a psychological detective and carefully investigate any thoughts, opinions, attitudes or responses that cause you stress of any kind. When you deliberately set peace of mind as your organizing principle, you become a more positive person. You become more relaxed and likable. You enjoy better health and you accomplish much more than you ever could otherwise.

ACTION EXERCISE

Examine your life and identify *one* area in which you experience stress or anxiety. Write out a clear definition of the stressful situation. Then write out a list of all the things that you can do immediately to alleviate this stressful situation. Think in terms of facing it squarely and taking some positive action to address it. Be active rather than passive.

What is there in your life that you're not facing? What is the worst that it could possibly be? Go systematically through each area of your life and clear it up. Make each part of your day a source of pleasure and satisfaction rather than a cause of stress and anxiety. Set inner peace as your highest goal and you'll probably never make another mistake.

Mastering Human Relationships

The most important and the most highly paid form of intelligence in America is social intelligence, the ability to get along well with other people. Fully 85 percent of your success in life is going to be determined by your social skills, by your ability to interact positively and effectively with others and to get them to cooperate with you in helping you to achieve your goals.

Learning how to develop and maintain superior human relationships can do more for your career and for your personal life than perhaps anything else you can accomplish.

The *bad* news is that the inability to get along with others is the primary reason for failure, frustration and unhappiness in life and work. According to one study, more than 95 percent of men and women let go from their jobs over a ten-year period were fired because of *poor social skills* rather than lack of competence or technical ability.

According to psychologist Sydney Jourard, most of your joy in life comes from your happy relationships with other people, and most of your problems in life come from unhappy relationships with them. Most of your problems in life are *people problems*.

Fortunately, you can become extremely skilled at getting along with others, and in this chapter, you will learn how. You'll learn a variety of proven methods to immediately improve your relationships with virtually anyone, under almost any circumstances.

HEALTHY PERSONALITY DEFINED

All of us either *think* we have, or *feel* we have, or *want* to have a "healthy personality." There are many definitions of "healthy personality," and here are three of the most helpful.

First, your personality is healthy to the degree to which you deliberately look for the *good* in each person and each situation. Your personality is *un*healthy to the degree to which you look for the *bad* in people and circumstances. Do you look for and find good in others, or do you criticize and complain about them? That's the first measure.

Second, your personality is healthy to the degree to which you can freely *forgive* people who have hurt you in some way. Most unhappiness and psychosomatic illness is caused by the inability to forgive, the insistence on holding grudges long after an incident has passed. The very act of forgiving has a liberating influence on your personality. Truly healthy people do not hate, nor do they go around preoccupied with anger and resentment over what happened in the past. They keep their minds clear of old problems. They let them go. That's the second measure.

Third, your personality is healthy to the degree to which you can *get along easily* with many different kinds of people. Anybody can get along with a *few people*. You can always get along with people who are very much like you, positive or negative. But the truly healthy person has an easy ability to get along with a great variety of people with different temperaments, different personalities, different attitudes, different values and different opinions. That's the real measure, the real test.

There is a direct relationship between your own level of self-esteem and the health of your personality. The more you *like* and *respect* yourself, the more you like and respect others. The more you consider yourself to be a valuable and worthwhile person, the more you consider *others* to be valuable and worthwhile as well. The more you accept yourself just as you are, the more you accept others just as they are.

As your self-esteem improves, you become better and better at getting along with more different kinds of people, for longer periods of time. Your life becomes happier and more fulfilling. Men and women with high levels of self-esteem can get along with almost anyone, anywhere and in almost any situation.

Men and women with low self-esteem can only get along with a few people, and then not for very long. Their low self-regard manifests itself in anger, impatience, criticism, badmouthing and arguments with the people around them. They don't like themselves so they don't really like others. As a result, people don't like them very much either.

THE LAW OF INDIRECT EFFORT

The *Law of Indirect Effort* states that you get almost everything in your relationships with others more easily by approaching them indirectly rather than directly.

For example, if you want to *impress* people, the direct way of going about it is to try to convince them of your admirable qualities and accomplishments. But trying to impress another person by talking about yourself usually makes you feel a little foolish, and sometimes even embarrassed.

The indirect way of impressing another person, however, is simply to be impressed by the other person. The more you are impressed by the other person, by who he or she is, or what he or she has accomplished, the more likely it is that the other person will be impressed by you.

If you want to get someone *interested* in you, the direct way is to tell him or her all about yourself. But the indirect way works better. It is simply to become interested in him or her. The more interested you become in another person, the more likely it is that the other person will become interested in you.

If you want to be *happy,* the direct way is to do whatever you can think of that will make you happy. However, the most enjoyable and lasting form of happiness comes from making someone else happy. By the Law of Indirect Effort, whenever you do or say anything that makes someone else happy, you feel happy yourself. You boost your own spirits, your own self-esteem.

How do you get another person to *respect* you? The best way is to respect him or her. When you express respect or admiration for another person, he or she feels respect and admiration for you. In human relations, we call this the Principle of Reciprocity. Whenever you do something nice for someone else, the other person will want to reciprocate by doing something nice for you. Most of our romances and friendships are based on this principle.

How do you get a person to *believe* in you, given the Law of Indirect Effort? The answer is to believe in him or her. Whenever you show that you believe or have confidence in another person, he or she will tend to believe in and have confidence in you. You get what you give. What you send out, you get back.

The most important applications of this Law of Indirect Effort have to do with developing a healthy personality in *yourself*. You are structured in such a way that everything you do to another person has a reciprocal effect on yourself. Everything you do to raise the self-esteem of another person raises your own self-esteem at the same time, and in the same measure. Since self-esteem is the hallmark of the healthy personality, *you can actually improve the health of your own personality by taking every opportunity to improve the health of the personalities of others*. What you sow in the lives of others, you reap in your own life.

Everyone you meet is carrying a heavy load. This is most true in the area of self-esteem and self-confidence. Everyone grows up with a feeling of inferiority, and throughout most of our lives we need to be praised and recognized by others. No matter how successful or how elevated people may become, they still need their self-images reinforced. They still need people to say things to boost their self-esteem and make them feel more valuable and worthwhile.

There is a line that says, "I like you because of the way I feel about myself when I am with you." This line contains the key to excellent human relations. The most successful and happy men and women are those who make other people feel good about themselves when they are with them. When you go through life raising the self-esteem of others, opportunities will open up before you, and people will help you in ways you cannot now imagine.

Practice the Law of Indirect Effort. Take every opportunity to say and do things that make people feel more valuable. Each time you express a kindness toward another person, your own self-esteem improves. Your own personality becomes more positive and healthy. You impress into your own mind whatever you express toward someone else.

MAKE OTHERS FEEL IMPORTANT

The key to raising the self-esteem of others, using the Law of Indirect Effort, is simply to *make others feel important*. Everything you do or say that makes another feel more important boosts his or her self-esteem and increases your self-esteem in equal measure at the same time.

When you go throughout your day looking for ways to make others feel important you will be popular and welcome everywhere. You will be healthier and happier and get more real satisfaction from life than others do. You will have lower levels of stress and higher levels of energy. Above all, you will genuinely like and respect yourself more and experience greater peace of mind.

BUILDING SELF-ESTEEM IN OTHERS

The starting point of raising the self-esteem of others is to *stop* tearing it down. Immediately stop doing or saying anything that lowers another's self-esteem. At the very least, be neutral. Keep silent. Say nothing.

Destructive criticism of any kind lowers self-esteem faster than any other behavior. More relationships and personalities are damaged or ruined by destructive criticism than by all other negative influences put together.

Destructive criticism attacks the core of human personality, triggering feelings of guilt, inferiority and undeservingness. When a person is criticized, even with so-called "constructive criticism," he or she immediately feels angry and defensive and wants to defend and strike back. By the Law of Reciprocity, whenever you do or say something that hurts others, especially when it attacks their self-esteem, you make them want, or even need, to strike back, to get even.

We are conditioned from infancy to be very sensitive to any expression of disapproval or criticism from anyone, for any reason. When we're criticized, our reflexes take over. Our self-esteem plummets. Our feelings or attitudes toward the person criticizing us immediately turn negative.

Perhaps the best decision you can ever make is to stop criticizing other people. Eliminate destructive criticism of any kind from your vocabulary and from your conversations. Become a positive person by only saying things that build people up rather than tearing them down.

Most people you meet are doing the very best they can with what they have to work with. Very few people make mistakes deliberately or do things poorly as a matter of choice. In fact, the brain is designed in such a way that it is almost impossible for a person to deliberately do something wrong if he or she knows how to do it right. A mistake of any kind makes a person feel incompetent. Self-esteem goes down. Self-image suffers. He or she doesn't like or respect him- or herself as much. No one does this to him- or herself on purpose.

Most criticism of others comes from judging and blaming, from setting yourself up as superior to them in some way. Judging others, however, triggers the Law of Sowing and Reaping. It causes others to judge you more critically. It brings down the same negative consequences on your own head. Criticizing others causes others to criticize you.

Almost all negative emotions begin with judging and blaming others. The reason you avoid criticizing is therefore a purely selfish one. Being positive and supportive of others, or at least neutral, enables you to remain positive and cheerful yourself. Refusing to criticize allows you to remain detached rather than becoming emotionally involved.

It's easy to get into the habit of criticizing and fault-finding. Many people's entire conversation revolves around badmouthing and criticism. However, you must break this habit if you are really determined to develop the kind of personality you need to get to the top.

You must stop running people down or speaking negatively about them for any reason. No matter what a person has done, or how wrong you think it is, keep your opinions to yourself. Make a game of finding reasons not to criticize or condemn. Make up excuses for the other person, wish him or her well, and when appropriate, forgive him and let him off the hook.

Another behavior that undermines self-esteem in both the speaker and the listener is the habit of *complaining*. Many people slip into complaining, playing the game of "Ain't it awful." They say things like, "Ain't it awful what so and so did?" or "Ain't it awful that prices are so high?" or "Ain't it awful that business is so bad?" Then they try to "one-up" each other by thinking of things that are even worse.

Henry Ford said it well: "Never complain, never explain." The habit of finding things to complain about attracts other complainers into your life and your social circle. By the Law of Concentration, which states that whatever you dwell upon grows in your reality, the more you complain, the more you find to complain about, and the more people you find to complain with.

Real men and women never complain. If they have a problem and there is something they can do about it, they get busy and take action. If there is nothing they can do about it, they simply say, "What cannot be cured must be endured." They then get busy doing what they can, but they never, never complain.

The truth is that no one is really interested in your complaints anyway. People have problems of their own, and many of their problems are a lot worse than yours. Probably 80 percent of the people you talk to about your complaints don't care, and the other 20 percent are kind of glad you've got them. Ambrose Bierce defined "happiness" as "that emotion experienced upon seeing the misfortune of a friend." It's all too true.

Resolve to halt all criticizing, condemning and complaining. As the song says, "If you can't say something nice, don't speak at all, is my advice." If you simply eliminate negativity of all kinds from your conversation, that alone will have a powerful, positive impact on your relationships. You will feel better about yourself, and so will everyone else.

SEVEN KEYS TO IMPROVING RELATIONSHIPS

There are seven positive, constructive, and psychologically sound proactive behaviors you can practice to improve the way you get along with other people. Each of these appeals to the deep subconscious needs of others, to their needs to feel important, valued and respected. These subconscious needs were formed in early childhood and if you can satisfy them you will be amazed at how much more people will like you and, by the Law of Indirect Effort, how much more you will like yourself.

BE AGREEABLE

The first behavior is simply to be agreeable. People like to be around agreeable men and women, individuals with whom they can freely and easily discuss a great variety of subjects. When you nod, smile and agree with a person who is talking, he or she feels more valuable and respected, feels that what he or she has to say is important and therefore he or she is also important.

Agreeable behavior raises the self-esteem of others. Disagreement lowers it. Whenever you disagree or argue with people, you are challenging their knowledge and intelligence. You are telling them that they are wrong, that their judgment and experience are not worth very much. Therefore, by extension, they are not worth very much either.

It is a fact of human nature that we hate to be wrong and never so much as when it is obvious that we are. Being wrong on an issue makes us feel that we ourselves are somehow wrong. Our self-esteem takes a beating. We feel diminished and inadequate, and we see ourselves as deficient or incompetent.

When you tell a person that he or she is wrong, his or her immediate response will be to become defensive, to dig in and be even more adamant. Our self-esteem is usually very fragile, and when we are told that we are wrong, we react quickly to guard and protect it at all costs.

Be agreeable. Be the kind of person who agrees easily with other people. Remember the words, "Agree with thine adversary quickly." If you become an agreeable and easy person to get along with, you create far less resistance in other people to helping you or to getting along with you. Even if the other person is obviously wrong, based on your knowledge of the facts, you have to ask yourself, "How important is this?" If it's not important, rather than disagreeing, let it pass.

STOP ARGUING

When I was growing up, I became a great *arguer*. I would argue with anybody about anything at the drop of a hat. Often, I would take the time to become well informed on a subject just so that I would know more than the person I was arguing with. With my superior information, I would almost always win. Whatever he or she said, I could top it.

However, I soon found myself spending a lot of time alone. People began to deliberately avoid me. People didn't want to spend time with me at work, nor did they want to socialize with me after work. I was winning all the arguments, but I was losing all the friends.

It is said that "a man convinced against his will is of the same opinion still." I was convincing people, overwhelming them with my superior knowledge of facts, but I was losing in a much more important sense of the word. I had forgotten to ask myself, "What's important here?"

And the answer to the question was that what was important to me was that I get along with other people. The relationships were what was important, not being right or winning the arguments. You should use this same measure yourself. Always ask yourself, "Do I want to be right or do I want to be happy?" And choose happiness!

The best policy, when someone says something that you feel is incorrect, is to just let it go. But if for some reason the matter is so important that you cannot let it pass, you can still remain agreeable by using what is called "third-party disagreement."

With this method, you put the words of your argument into the mouth of an imaginary or nonpresent third person. You say, "That's a very interesting point, Bill, but if someone were to ask this question, how would you answer it?" Then, put your question into the mouth of someone else.

You could ask, "What do you think our customers would say if they knew we were doing this?" Or you could ask, "How do you think our bankers would respond to our taking this kind of action?" In each case, you can continue to be easy-going and agreeable while raising the questions that are in your own mind. Just put the words in someone else's mouth.

The advantage of this method is, that if the person has a good answer, you can go along without having been disagreeable. If the other person cannot answer the question, he or she can change his or her mind without losing face because the person who is "asking the question" is not present and his or her ego is not involved.

Your decision to become an agreeable and easy-going person will lower your stress levels and increase your ability to influence others to help you. You will raise the self-esteem of others and feel better about yourself, as well.

PRACTICE ACCEPTANCE

The second self-esteem-building behavior you can practice is "acceptance." Each of us is conditioned to seek the acceptance of other people. The infant starts off looking into the face of his or her mother or father to see if he or she is loved, respected, wanted, important, funny, intelligent and so on. As we grow up, we look into the faces of other people to see how we are doing. We have a deep need to be accepted by other people, even by people we don't know.

When two people meet, for example, either for the first time or in subsequent meetings, the very first thing that has to be established between them is a certain level of acceptance. We look into the eyes, the smile, the face and the body language of the other person, to see whether that other person accepts us and is happy with our presence. Only when we feel accepted can we relax.

Many social problems are caused by people and groups crying out to be accepted on their own terms by others. When you "step up to the plate" and express genuine, unconditional acceptance of another person, you raise that person's self-esteem, you improve that person's self-image, and you make him or her feel relaxed and safe in your company.

JUST SMILE!

And what do you have to do to express acceptance? Simple. Just smile. It takes only 13 muscles to smile and 112 muscles to frown. A genuine smile directed to another person says a lot. It says, "I accept you as you are, unconditionally." When you smile at another person, he or she feels valuable, important and worthwhile. He or she feels better about him- or herself. And all it costs you is a simple smile, an expression of genuine warmth.

A Chinese proverb says, "A man without a smile should not open a shop." Salespeople, business people, anyone whose livelihood depends on the patronage or the support of others has to learn how to practice acceptance in his or her relationships.

The Law of Reciprocity states that if you make people feel good by smiling and greeting them positively, they will want to reciprocate by treating you the same way. Willy Loman, in *Death of a Salesman,* said, "The most important thing is to be liked." When people like you, they are far more willing to cooperate with you. The starting point of being liked is to like other people. And the way that you express that you like another person is by giving that person a warm, heartfelt smile when you meet him or her.

Of course, the hardest time to smile is when you don't feel like smiling at all. But you can *act* your way into feeling. Even if you don't *feel* particularly positive, if you force yourself to smile genuinely at the people you meet for just a few minutes, you will begin to feel better again. The clouds of negativity will break up and blow away. Gradually, your smiles will become more and more genuine. You will raise your own self-esteem by making an effort to raise the self-esteem of others, and you do it by smiling.

AN ATTITUDE OF GRATITUDE

The third step you can take to raise the self-esteem of others is by expressing *appreciation.* One of the deepest cravings of human nature is the need to be appreciated. Whenever you express gratitude or appreciation toward another person for anything that the other person has done, you make him or her feel more valuable, more competent and more worthwhile.

All it takes to express appreciation are the simple words, "thank you." The words "thank you" are two of the most powerful in the English language, and the most powerful single expression in virtually any language. I have traveled and worked in more than eighty countries, and I have learned that you can get halfway across any country in the world by simply learning and saying the words "please" and "thank you" everywhere you go.

SAY "THANK YOU"

The words "thank you" have tremendous power. Each time you say them to another person, his or her self-esteem increases. Your thanks reward and reinforce his or her behavior. Your "thank you" increases the likelihood that he or she will repeat it. If you say "thank you" for small things, people will soon be doing big things for you.

Develop the habit of saying "thank you" to everybody for anything and everything they do. Say "thank you" to your spouse for everything that he or she does for you. Say "thank you" to your children for anything that they do around the house. The more you thank your spouse and your children, the more positive and happy they feel about themselves. The more eager they are to do more of the things that trigger your appreciation.

Throughout your day, say "thank you" to people who do things for you. Thank people for giving you appointments. Thank them for their time. Thank them for their comments. Thank them for their generosity. Thank them for their help. Thank people for everything you can think of.

And send "thank-you notes." Thank-you notes are some of the most powerful self-esteem and relationship builders ever invented. When you send a thank-you note to someone, even one that contains only a few words, he or she often remembers you positively for months, or even years. You can set yourself apart from the crowd by becoming known for the different ways that you express gratitude toward other people, by the number of different ways that you say "thank you."

Develop an "attitude of gratitude." The happiest and most popular people are those who go through their lives being genuinely grateful for the things that happen to them and for everyone they meet. An attitude of gratitude clears a path before you. An attitude of gratitude guarantees a healthy personality and a higher level of self-esteem. And the more thankful you are for what you have, the more things you are going to have to be thankful for.

LITTLE CHILDREN CRY FOR IT; GROWN MEN DIE FOR IT

The fourth way to raise the self-esteem of others, to make them feel more important, is to express approval of them on every possible occasion. The expression of approval, or *praise,* is one of the fastest and most predictable ways to make people feel happy and proud. Giving praise and recognition to other people is the surest way to boost their self-esteem, to reinforce their behavior and to make them want to help you and cooperate with you.

One definition of self-esteem is how much a person considers him- or herself "praiseworthy." Whenever a person receives praise from another, his or her self-esteem goes up like a thermometer on a hot day. Ken Blanchard, author of *The One Minute Manager,* recommends the use of "one minute praisings" throughout the day. He recommends that you "catch people doing something right." And the more you do, the more effective and competent they feel, and the more likely they are to repeat the behavior that earned the praise.

Tired children who are praised and approved by their parents or teachers actually perk up and recover their lost energy. When people are genuinely praised by someone they respect, their enthusiasm and alertness increase and they feel much better about themselves. There is almost nothing that has greater power to raise people's self-esteem and to make them feel good about themselves than the sincere expression of praise and approval for something that they have done or said.

THREE KEYS TO POSITIVE PRAISING

Praising is an art. Great leaders, successful business people and excellent parents are all good at praising. Here are three things you can do to achieve the maximum effect from your praising of other people.

First, the praise should be *immediate*. The sooner you praise an action or behavior, the greater the impact it has. Some companies make the mistake of giving people appraisals every three or six months or even once per year. But when you give people praise long after an incident has passed, it has very little effect on their feelings about themselves, or their future actions. So praise immediately, or as close in time to the behavior as you possibly can.

Second, praise *specifically*. When you praise a specific action or behavior, you ensure that that specific action or behavior is repeated. However, if you praise generally, as some people do, it has little effect on the recipient. For example, if you say to your secretary, "You're doing a great job," your words will have only a moderate impact. But if you say, "You did an excellent job typing and getting that report out on Thursday," you will be much more likely to see future reports completed and sent out on time.

In praising children, the same rule holds true. Instead of saying, "You're a great kid," instead say, "You did a super job of making your bed and cleaning up your bedroom this morning." Whatever specific accomplishment you praise, your child is much more likely to repeat. The rule is: Praise what you want to see repeated, praise it immediately, and praise it specifically.

Third, whenever possible, *praise in public*. If you must correct a person, correct the person in private, but praise the person in front of others. The more people that you praise someone in front of, the more it boosts that person's self-esteem and self-respect. Awards and recognition given in front of large audiences of coworkers have the greatest impact of all on a person's self-esteem and subsequent behavior.

People may work harder for more money, but they will crawl over broken glass to get more praise and recognition. All great leaders are aware of this and use their positions to dispense praise generously. It was Napoleon who said, "I have discovered a remarkable thing; men will die for ribbons." Praise is a powerful motivator when given properly.

TWO KINDS OF PRAISING

If you want a person to *develop* a habit, such as cleaning up his or her bedroom or coming to work on time, you should *praise the person every single time* he or she does it. This form of praising is called "continuous reinforcement." If you continuously praise the new behavior you want to see repeated, eventually the person will repeat it so often that he or she will make it a habit. After the person has developed the new habit, you can switch to "intermittent reinforcement." Intermittent reinforcement means that you only praise the behavior every third or fourth time it occurs.

Continuous reinforcement, once the habit has been established, may sound insincere and can actually be demotivating. Repetitive praising may even cause the person to discontinue the behavior altogether. But intermittent reinforcement, once the habit has been established, can cause the behavior to be repeated indefinitely. It is the equivalent of "keeping the plate spinning."

For example, to get your children to clean up their rooms, praise them every single time they clean up even the smallest thing. Make a big deal about it. Keep this up until the children start to clean their rooms voluntarily, or at least, with little urging. Once they've gotten into the habit of cleaning up their rooms, you only need to give them praise or approval every third or fourth time. That will be enough to keep the habit "locked in."

ADMIRATION

The fifth behavior you can practice to raise the self-esteem of others, and to make them feel important, is admiration. Whenever you admire another person for something he or she has accomplished, for some personality trait or for some possession, you raise his or her self-esteem. Admiration is a powerful tool in human relations. As Abraham Lincoln said, "Everybody likes a compliment." You can use admiration almost anywhere and in almost any situation. You can be virtually guaranteed that the other person will feel more important as a result.

You can admire personality traits or qualities. When you compliment a person for being punctual, or for being generous, or for being persistent or for being determined, you make that person feel more valuable and important. We are all proud of our positive traits. We are usually proud of what we have become. When other people recognize and admire us for these qualities, we feel better about ourselves.

You can admire people's possessions. People often invest a lot of emotion in the things they acquire. For example, most people put a lot of thought into the furniture and fixtures they purchase for their homes. You can never go wrong complimenting a person on how attractive his or her home or living room looks.

People also put a lot of thought into their clothes. You are guaranteed to make a woman feel better about herself by complimenting her on any article of her clothing or accessories.

You can achieve the same effect with a man by complimenting him on his clothes, especially his shoes or his tie. Men usually spend a lot of time thinking about the ties they wear and selecting the shoes they buy. They will be both surprised and happy when you admire them.

You can admire people's accomplishments, as well. You can compliment them on the education they've acquired or the position they've arrived at. You can admire the business they've built, or anything else that they've achieved.

Admiring people's accomplishments raises their self-esteem and makes them feel good about you. If you sincerely want to admire another person for something, you will find endless opportunities to do so. Everyone has accomplished something that is worthy of your admiration. Your job is to find it and compliment him or her on it.

Let me add one note of caution, however. Only express appreciation, approval or admiration when you genuinely feel it. Never be insincere in your attempts to raise the self-esteem of others. People are like human lie detectors. They can detect insincerity across a crowded room. Don't be guilty of it.

There is only one exception to this rule: An insincere smile is better than a sincere frown any time. But in all other cases, your compliments should be sincere. You must honestly mean what you are saying. If you don't, people will feel that you are trying to manipulate them. If they do, you will get the opposite response to the one you desired. The other person's self-esteem will go down and he or she will react to you with distrust and defensiveness.

These first five things you can do to make other people feel more important all begin with the letter A. The first is to be *agreeable*. The second is to express *acceptance,* to smile at people you meet. The third is to express *appreciation,* to say "thank you" on every occasion. The fourth is to express *approval,* to praise and recognize other people for the positive things they do. The fifth is to express *admiration,* to compliment people on their accomplishments, their traits or their possessions. This behavior on your part is the foundation of good relationships with others. Each time you practice these behaviors, you make other people feel better about themselves, and you, and you feel better about yourself.

"WHITE MAGIC"

The sixth step you can take to make others feel important also begins with an A, and it is *attention*. Life is the study of attention. You always give your attention to that which you most value, to that which most interests you, to that which is most important to you. Your attention is your life. Wherever your attention goes, your thoughts, your feelings, your life goes also.

In your relationships with others, the amount of attention you pay to them is the chief indicator of how important they are to you. You always give more of your attention to the people and things that you value the most. The opposite of attention is indifference. You ignore people and things you neither value nor appreciate.

When you pay attention to a person, you are saying, "I value you and I consider you to be important." When you ignore a person, you are saying, "I consider you to be unimportant and of little value." The very act of paying attention to a person increases his or her self-esteem. The act of ignoring a person lowers his or her self-esteem. Indifference often makes him or her feel angry and defensive.

A major cause of negative emotions is the feeling that we are being ignored by people. Being ignored, whether by a spouse, a boss or even a waiter in a restaurant, makes us feel devalued and diminished. This is why people who are effective in human relations are very sensitive to, and aware of, the need to pay proper attention to others.

How do you pay proper attention to other people? You practice the "white magic" of listening. Listening is the true measure of attention in human relations. Listening is the way you show how much you value another person and what that other person is saying. It is only when you listen, and listen well, to another person that you demonstrate to the other person that he or she is valuable and important. The best leaders and salespeople, the best managers and friends, are all excellent and skilled listeners.

There are three main benefits to becoming a good listener. The first is that *listening builds trust*. Whenever someone listens to us, we trust that other person more. The fastest way for two people to build trust between them is for each to listen attentively and appreciatively to the other person. When you listen attentively, the other person likes and trusts you far more than if you don't. He or she is then far more open to being influenced by you.

The second benefit of good listening is that *listening builds self-esteem*. When you listen carefully and attentively to a person, his or her self-esteem goes up. Whenever anyone listens to you very carefully, your self-esteem goes up as well. You feel more important. You feel that you are a more valuable person.

The third benefit of listening is that *listening builds self-discipline*. It requires tremendous personal mastery and self-control to listen attentively to another person. The average person *speaks* at about 150 words per minute, while you can *listen* at the rate of almost 600 words per minute. Active listening requires that you control your attention, and keep yourself focused on the person speaking. The more you can discipline yourself to listen without distraction, the more effective you will become in other areas of your life as well.

DON'T JUST SIT THERE!

The first part of active listening is to *listen attentively*. Face the speaker directly, rather than at an angle. Lean slightly forward, toward the speaker. If you are standing up, shift your weight onto the balls of your feet so that your energy projects forward. Watch the mouth and eyes of the other person closely. This tells the speaker that you are paying complete attention to what he or she is saying. It makes it clear to the speaker that you are fully engrossed in the conversation.

The second part of active listening is to *listen without interrupting*. Most people don't really listen when another is speaking. They are so busy thinking about what they are going to say when the other person takes a breath that they seldom hear what the other person is really saying.

Whenever a speaker senses that the listener is just waiting for a chance to jump in, or that the other person's thoughts are somewhere else, perhaps busily preparing a response, the speaker feels irritated, uncomfortable and often insulted. But when the speaker feels that the other person is tuned to him or her and to what he or she is saying, the speaker feels more valuable. So listen patiently, listen calmly, listen as if there was nothing else in the world that you would rather hear than what this person is saying, for as long as this person takes to say it.

The third part of active listening is to *pause before replying*. When a speaker finishes speaking, pause for three to five seconds before saying anything. In this pause, three things will happen.

First, you will actually hear the other person better. When you allow a few seconds for the other person's remarks to sink in, you actually understand the other person more completely.

Second, when you pause, you *avoid interrupting* the other person if he or she has just paused to collect his or her thoughts. When you pause for three to five seconds, you give the other person an opportunity to continue rather than cutting him or her off. There are few things more irritating or insulting than being interrupted in the middle of a thought or in the middle of a sentence.

Third, when you pause before replying, you make it clear, with your silence, that you consider what has just been said to be important. You are giving it careful consideration. It is a great compliment to the speaker to have the listener sit quietly and think about his or her remarks before responding, whatever the response may be.

The fourth part of good listening is to *question for clarification*. Ask questions to ensure that you fully understand what the other person has said. There is an old saying, "Errant assumptions lie at the root of every failure." When you assume you understand, without checking, you very often don't understand what the other person has said at all. This is especially true in conversations between men and women.

One of the best questions you can use to "perception check," to ensure that what you *heard* and what the person *said* are the same thing, is to ask simply, "How do you mean?" or "How do you mean, exactly?"

My experience in sales, marketing, consulting and training has been that, if you have any doubt at all about what the person really means, you have probably *not* understood. It's essential to good communications and good listening that you ask questions to ensure clarity. And you can never ask the question, "How do you mean?" without getting greater clarity.

Perhaps the best way to expand a conversation, increase your opportunities to listen and improve your understanding is by the use of open-ended questions.

An open-ended question is one that cannot be answered with a "yes" or a "no." Open-ended questions begin with, in the words of Rudyard Kipling's poem, ". . . six honest serving men/(They taught me all I knew);/Their names are What and Why and When/And How and Where and Who."

The additional benefit of asking open-ended questions is that you get more opportunity to listen, more opportunity to build trust, and more opportunity to fully understand what the other person is thinking and feeling. Remember, you never learn anything while your mouth is open. When you are speaking, all you can say is what you *already* know. But when you are listening, it's possible for you to learn something new.

The fifth part of active listening is to *feed back* the person's words to him or her. Paraphrase what he or she has said in your own words. When you paraphrase and feed it back, you compliment the speaker. You show how closely you have been paying attention. In fact, until you can feed back a speaker's meaning correctly, you haven't really understood.

Try this when another person finishes speaking. Pause for three to five seconds and then say, "Let me make sure that I understand you. What you're saying is *this*." And then go on to feed it back in your own words.

Whenever you make the effort to listen so attentively that you are able to feed a person's words back to him or her, you increase *your* ability to communicate. You build greater trust between the two of you. You build higher self-esteem in the other person, and you develop self-discipline in yourself.

EMPATHIC LISTENING

Empathic listening involves genuinely caring and acting as a sounding board for the other person, rather than trying to solve the other person's problems yourself.

Therapists use this technique of empathic listening by feeding the person's words back to him or her in a different form. If the person says, for example, "I am really frustrated with my job," you might say, "You sound as though you are feeling overwhelmed with the way things are going at work."

When you *reflect* a person's words back to him or her, you often help that person not only to come to a better understanding of the problem but also to gain insights into the solution.

There are two types of empathic listening, *simple* reflection and *interpretive* reflection. In "simple" reflection, you rephrase what the speaker has explicitly stated without adding anything to it, and without digging at hidden meanings or implied messages. You simply put into your own words what you just heard and feed it back.

If a person says, "I'm really worried," you simply say, "You seem to be really worried."

In "interpretive" reflection you go beyond simply restating what the speaker has said. Instead you reflect what appears to you to be the underlying message. "Something really seems to be bothering you about your work; could it be that your boss is putting too much pressure on you?"

With interpretive reflection, you can do one of two things. First, you can summarize what the other person has been saying and then identify *themes* in these messages. For instance, you may identify a theme such as anger, or frustration. You could say, "I sense that you are really angry or frustrated in this situation." You do not add a deeper meaning yourself.

The second type of interpretive reflection is trying to paraphrase the thoughts or feelings that the speaker hasn't stated but that you suspect are the *real* message. You attempt to deal with the core issue rather than with the symptom.

For example, one day when my son Michael was eighteen months old, my oldest child, Christina, who was almost five, came into the kitchen crying and said, "I hate my brother."

Before I understood interpretive listening, I would have said something like, "Oh, no you don't, you love your brother, and you know it." Instead, reacting to the message that was not being said, and understanding sibling rivalry, I said to her, "You feel that we are paying too much attention to your little brother and that we're not paying enough attention to you, don't you?"

At this, Christina broke into tears and said, "Yes, I sometimes feel that you love him more than you love me." She didn't really hate Michael; she simply needed to be reassured that we still loved her very much.

This form of interpretive reflection or empathic listening is very helpful. It requires you to go beneath the speaker's words and look for the real reasons the speaker feels the way he or she does.

By practicing reflective listening, you can be very helpful, not only to the members of your own family, but also to your friends and the people you work with. Sometimes, all a person requires is

an insight, reflected back by a sincere friend, to be able to understand what he or she needs to do to solve his or her own problems.
You can provide these insights by being a sensitive and skilled
listener.

THE BOOMERANG PRINCIPLE

The seventh way to raise the self-esteem of others is to use the
principle of the boomerang. This principle is that "whatever genuine emotion you express toward any other person will boomerang
back on you, sooner or later."

Shakespeare wrote, "The fragrance of the rose lingers on the
hand that casts it." Whenever you express a positive sentiment to
or about someone else, it will eventually come back to you, like a
boomerang. If you express a negative thought or idea, the same
principle holds true, so make sure that what you say about others
is what you want to have come back.

Resist the temptation to criticize, condemn or complain. Practice being agreeable and accepting. Express appreciation, approval
and admiration. Listen attentively to others when they speak, and
remember the boomerang. If you do all these things you'll make
others feel terrific about themselves and you'll be welcome wherever
you go.

THE ART OF CONVERSATION

So far, everything that we have talked about in this chapter shines
forth at its very best in the art of conversation. It is in conversing
with other people, the easy give and take, the exchange of ideas,
information and opinions, that a person demonstrates the quality
of his or her personality. Here are some ideas that will help you be
a better conversationalist in any work or social situation.

JUST FOLLOW THE RULES

The first rule of good conversation is to *cue the subject to your
listener*. Talk to people about subjects that interest them. Any subjects, including the subjects that used to be taboo in conversation,
are okay if they are of interest to the person you are speaking with.
You can discuss politics and religion if the other people you are

talking with want to do it. But if you see that you are getting no response to a particular subject, back off quickly and talk about something else.

One of the best ways to open a conversation is simply to ask the person, "What sort of work do you do?" If you know what the person does in general, the person's position or industry, ask a question like, "What exactly do you do there?" or, "How are things going at work?"

No matter what answer you get with regard to the person's specific occupation or activities, one of the most interesting questions you can ask another person is, "How did you get into that business (or line of work), anyway?"

Most people consider their personal career path to be one of the most fascinating stories ever told. Whenever the speaker stops, you can keep the conversation or momentum going by asking, "And then what did you do?"

Asking people, "How did you get into that business, anyway?" and "And then what did you do?" will enable you to keep a conversation going almost indefinitely.

Perhaps the most important part of cuing your conversation to your listener is to be sensitive to the amount of interest shown by the other person. If he or she becomes fidgety, begins looking around or off into the distance, it's a sign that you need to change the subject to something of greater interest.

When this happens, simply pause for a moment, then ask a question starting with one of the words, *What? Where? When? How? Why?* or *Who?* "How long have you lived here?" "Where did you go to school?" "When did you start at that company?"

A second rule for good conversation is to *take your turn*. This means, of course, no monologue. If ever you find that you have talked for three minutes straight, without question or comment from your listeners, you can be pretty sure that you are talking on a subject of interest only to yourself. We all make this mistake. Remember, if other people are not contributing, what you are doing is making a speech, not holding a conversation.

Taking your turn also means not interrupting when people are talking. And when you are interrupted, as when someone else joins the group, the most polite thing to do is also the hardest: *shut up*. Don't go back and finish a story unless you are asked to do so.

Good conversation has an easy ebb and flow, like the tide,

rolling in and out. Each person has an opportunity both to speak and to listen. If either party is deprived of the opportunity to speak, the conversation becomes one-sided and the person talking will be thought of as a bore.

The third rule for good conversation is to *think before you speak*. Avoid saying anything that would make someone uncomfortable, unhappy or self-conscious. Be tactful and aware of the feelings and sensitivities of other people.

The opposite of tact is just plain thoughtlessness. A good way to avoid being tactless is not to be adamant about anything. Benjamin Franklin, in his autobiography, tells about how he totally changed his personality and his effectiveness with others, by preceding each of his opinions with the words, "It seems to me that" or "Some people say that," and so on. If you present your opinions in a tentative way, to indicate that you are open to the possibility that you could be wrong, you will find it much easier for others to listen to you and to appreciate your ideas.

Be sure to indicate that you believe other viewpoints and other tastes are as valid as your own. There is nothing black or white in areas that are highly subject to individual opinions or tastes. Your views on politics, religion, sex, nutrition or any other subject on which there are many different viewpoints, are just that: *your views*. If you make it clear that you are open to other opinions and other interpretations, people will be much more open to yours.

For good conversation, *respect other people's privacy* and reserve a little privacy for yourself. Some people get into the habit of interviewing other people, and asking them a lot of questions whose answers are really none of their business. Keep your questions general and impersonal and give the other person the opportunity to decide whether or not he or she wants to open up to you.

Don't burden casual acquaintances with your troubles. There's something about social gatherings and cocktail parties that generates confessions or long discussions about all the troubles a person is having. Never criticize, condemn or complain. Be positive and cheerful. Keep your problems to yourself.

It's helpful to remember that everything you say can be used against you. Burnham's Law says "Everybody knows everything." Anything that you tell anyone under any circumstances is eventually going to be known to everyone, and especially to the worst possible person you would want to hear it. Be careful what you say; there are no secrets in social or business life. A "secret" has been well defined as "something that you only tell one person at a time." Secrets have no value unless they can be shared.

Finally, to be an excellent conversationalist, *be natural*. Be yourself. Let your personality flow. Only say what you feel comfortable saying. If, for any reason, something inside you tells you not to speak up, listen to your inner voice. Speak easily and spontaneously, without trying to impress or be impressed by anyone. Just say what comes naturally to your mind.

The very best conversationalists and the most enjoyable people to be around are those who are relaxed, positive and completely natural.

THE PLAYING FIELD IS YOURS

The art of conversation and social interaction is the playing field where you can develop all of your personality skills to their highest degree. You can practice each of the recommendations for making other people feel important that we have discussed in this chapter. You can *avoid criticizing, condemning, or complaining* when you are conversing with others. You can practice being *agreeable,* even when you disagree with the other person's point of view. You can do it as a discipline, as an exercise in personal development.

You can practice *acceptance* by smiling at the people you meet and looking into their faces and eyes. You can practice *appreciation* by saying "thank you" for everything that everyone does for you. You can practice *approval* and recognition by praising other people for their accomplishments. You can practice *admiration* by asking people about themselves and then admiring their traits, qualities and achievements.

Above all you can practice *attention,* the "white magic" of active listening. This, as much as any other habit, will make you the kind of person that other people want to be around.

There is a famous story told about Dale Carnegie. The story goes that he was once invited to a party in New York being held in honor of a wealthy woman who had just returned from a trip to Africa.

When Dale Carnegie arrived at the party, he was introduced to this woman, and the woman immediately said, "Oh, Mr. Carnegie,

I have heard that you are one of the finest conversationalists in New York. Is that true?"

Dale Carnegie replied, "Thank you very much, madam. And I have heard that you have just returned from a trip to Africa. Why did you decide to go to Africa?"

When she told him why she had gone to Africa, Carnegie then asked, "And who did you take to Africa with you?" "And when did you go to Africa?" "When did you return?" "Where did you go when you were in Africa?" "How did you get there?" "And what exactly did you do when you were there?"

The two conversed for about twenty minutes. During this time she spoke about 95 percent of the time in answer to Carnegie's questions. The next day, in the social pages of a New York newspaper, she was quoted as saying, "Mr. Dale Carnegie is surely one of the finest conversationalists in New York."

You too can become a brilliant conversationalist by learning how to speak and, especially, by learning how to listen.

Getting along well with others is perhaps the most important thing you ever learn to do. When I was growing up, I was very unpopular. I had few friends, and those I did have were, for the most part, social misfits like myself. My inability to behave so that people wanted to be around me cast a shadow over my early years. It held me back right up until I learned the great secret of relationships.

The secret is that you can become popular and likable by doing two things. First, get *out* of yourself and get *into* the lives and concerns of others. Become genuinely interested in them. Ask them questions and listen to them. Think of ways that you can help them. Practice the law of sowing and reaping. Do unto others as you would want them to do unto you.

Second, get busy working on yourself and your goals. Develop your unique talents. Get good at what you do. The better you do the things that are important to you, the more you like yourself. And the more you like and respect yourself, the more comfortable and effective you are with others. Nothing succeeds like success.

Visualize, affirm and act the part. Work on yourself as if your future depended upon it, because it does. You can become one of the most positive and effective people in your world, and you will when you put these ideas to work in all your relationships.

Mastering Personal Relationships

One of the characteristics of the fully mature, self-actualizing person is that he or she has the ability to enter into long-term, intimate relationships and maintain those relationships for long periods of time. Men and women with the healthiest personalities, those who are the most *together* as human beings, are those who seem to have the greatest capacity for these loving relationships.

The choice of a mate, and the quality of your home and family life, determines your success as a human being as much as or more than any other factor. Your relationships are a direct expression of the person you really are. The Law of Correspondence states that your outer world of relationships will correspond exactly to your inner world of thought and feeling. If your inner world is positive and loving, your outer world of relationships will be happy and satisfying.

Benjamin Disraeli, prime minister of England in the nineteenth century, once said, "No success in public life can compensate for failure in the home." Your personal relationships should take precedence over everything else. As you grow and become a better person, your relationships should grow and improve as well, and in the same proportion.

By the Law of Attraction, you will attract into your life the kind of people who are very much the way you are, the kind of people whose ways of thinking and behaving correspond to your dominant thoughts and feelings. As you become more positive, optimistic and loving, you will naturally attract into your life more positive, optimistic and loving people.

By the Law of Sowing and Reaping you will reap exactly what you sow, and there is no area in which this is more true than in your relationships. You see it all around you, in all your interactions with others.

You get out of your marriage or your romance exactly what you put into it. The more of yourself that you put into a relationship, the more love, satisfaction and joy you will get out of it. Men and women are born incomplete, and need each other to become whole. They are born with complementary qualities and characteristics. Each one needs the other to fulfill his or her human destiny. Happy relationships go hand in hand with peace of mind, long life, health, happiness and abundance. Men and women with poor relationships, or no relationships at all, have more ill health and die younger than men and women who live happily together.

In fact, according to Ronald Adler and Neil Towne in their book *Looking Out, Looking In,* socially isolated people are two to three times as likely to die prematurely as those with strong social ties. Divorced men die from heart disease, cancer and strokes at double the rate of married men. The rate of all types of cancer is as much as five times higher for divorced men and women, compared to their single counterparts. If for no other reason than your desire to live a long and happy life, you should be very serious about building and maintaining excellent relationships with the most important people in your life.

WHERE IT BEGINS

Your self-esteem, how much you like and respect yourself, determines your personality and your level of happiness. High self-esteem leads to high performance and success in every area of life, while low self-esteem precedes and accompanies most failure and frustration.

The first part of self-esteem is the purely *emotional* component, the way you feel about yourself, separate and apart from anyone or anything else. The second part of your self-esteem is determined by your perceived level of *competence* in what you do. It is how well you feel you perform in the important areas of your life. This is called *performance-based self-esteem,* and it is an essential element of your personality.

When you feel that you are good at what you do, that you

perform well, you enjoy high self-esteem in that area. This feeling reinforces the other component of self-esteem, your sense of personal value. If you do well, you feel good; if you feel good, you do well. Each is dependent on the other.

Because your relationships are so central to your entire life, for you to enjoy sustained feelings of self-esteem, you must know in your heart that you are capable of entering into and maintaining a positive, healthy and constructive loving relationship with another person.

Feeling inferior or incompetent in your relationships undermines your self-esteem and self-confidence. Everything you do that enables you to get along better with the important people in your life improves your self-esteem. Effectiveness with others makes you feel more competent and complete and frees you to more readily become more effective in the other areas of your life.

There is a direct relationship between the *quality* of your relationships and your *level* of self-esteem and self-acceptance. You can only like yourself to the degree to which you fully accept yourself, and how much you like yourself is largely determined by how much you feel you are accepted by other people.

Most of us are raised with a form of *conditional* acceptance, and often rejection and disapproval from our parents. As adults, we seek the unconditional love and acceptance of others, and especially *one* special other, to compensate for what we feel we lacked as children. Our mental health depends on it.

SELF-ACCEPTANCE

You can never feel free to genuinely like yourself until you accept yourself completely, until you accept both your strengths *and* your weaknesses. And the key to *accepting yourself* is being accepted unconditionally by at least one other person whom you respect and admire, and even better, love. It is only when someone else accepts you, "warts and all," that you can relax and accept yourself as being a valuable and worthwhile person.

SELF-AWARENESS

For you to experience self-acceptance, you must first develop *self-awareness*. You need to understand *why* you think, feel and act the way you do. You need to be aware of the impact of the formative experiences of your life. You need to understand how and why you have become the person that you are today.

Only when you achieve a higher level of self-awareness can you move to a higher level of self-acceptance. You must to be more aware of who you really are before you can accept yourself. And it is only with a high level of self-acceptance that you can enjoy self-esteem—the key to a happy, healthy personality.

SELF-DISCLOSURE

Self-awareness, in turn, is based on *self-disclosure*. You only truly understand yourself to the degree to which you can disclose, or share yourself, with at least one other person. *Appropriate* self-disclosure means that you can tell someone else, whom you trust completely, exactly what you are thinking and feeling, with no fear of disapproval or rejection.

Psychotherapy is based on self-disclosure. Psychotherapists are successful to the degree to which they can get the patient to open up to them and tell them exactly what is causing them to be un-happy or ineffective.

One psychologist said recently, "If everyone learned to really listen to other people, 75 percent of the psychotherapists in the United States would be out of work by next Wednesday." To hon-estly disclose yourself to another person, you need to trust that other person. You need to know that the other person cares for you, and that he or she will not judge you or condemn you for something you have said or done in the past.

The great emotional problem of the twentieth century is guilt. Guilt arises from a feeling of worthlessness as the result of destruc-tive criticism and mistakes you feel you have made in the past. Most of us have done and said things we regret. We have hurt other people, and we are sorry about it. We can begin to free ourselves from these negative feelings by the act of telling someone else what we did or said. This form of catharsis, or cleansing, liberates us and allows us to get on with the rest of our lives. Repentance is not only good, but essential for the soul, for long-term happiness.

Honest self-disclosure is sometimes scary. It requires that you take a chance, that you make yourself vulnerable. But it is the basic precondition for mental health. When you disclose your thoughts and feelings openly and honestly to another person, you understand yourself better. You become more aware of who you really are. You see yourself and your life in a better perspective.

As you become more self-aware, you become more self-accepting. When you accept yourself unconditionally, you enjoy higher levels of self-esteem and self-regard. You feel better about yourself in everything you do. You liberate yourself from negative feelings that can hold you down and hold you back. With self-disclosure, you can get things off your chest and get on with your life.

INTIMACY AND GROWTH GO HAND IN HAND

One of the purposes of marriage and intimate relationships is to give you the opportunity to evolve and grow to your full capacity. In a fully trusting relationship, you feel free to tell the other person things you have done in the past and what you are thinking and feeling in the present. In sharing yourself honestly, you develop a deeper understanding of your own humanity. You become more tolerant, more accepting and more compassionate toward the human frailties of other people. You develop parts of your personality that would have lain dormant in the absence of a fully loving relationship.

Much of what we do in life we do either to get love or to compensate for the lack of love. Everyone needs to be loved and accepted unconditionally by at least one other person. It is only when your need for this form of emotional security has been satisfied that you feel free to turn your mind and heart to accomplishing what is possible for you in your external life. Love is like money: If you have an ample supply, you don't think about it very much. But if your supply is cut off for any period of time, you think about nothing else.

The cruelest punishment inflicted on prisoners is locking them away from all other human beings—putting them in solitary confinement. Depriving a person of human contact, of human interaction, is the worst thing that can be done to him or her.

Your highest aspiration should be to evolve and develop into the kind of person who attracts an ideal loving relationship into your life. This relationship makes it possible for you to enjoy the happiness and joy for which you were created.

Everything in the previous chapter on mastering human relationships is applicable to your loving relationships. In addition, there are many other things you can do, or stop doing, that can dramatically improve the way you get along with the important other person in your life. Let's start off with the six rules for success in relationships.

SIX RULES FOR SUCCESSFUL RELATIONSHIPS

The first rule is that *similarities attract*. You will always be the happiest and the most compatible with another person whose interests, tastes and values are similar to yours. The Law of Attraction states that you will be attracted to a person whose attitudes and beliefs are in harmony with your own.

The first area in which similarities are necessary in marriages and relationships is in attitudes toward money—how it is earned, how it is saved and how it is spent. The second area is attitudes regarding children—whether to have them, how many, and how to raise them. The third is attitudes toward sex. The fourth is religion, and the fifth is attitudes toward political and social issues. Attitudes toward people, social activities and how to spend leisure time are also important measures of compatibility. Similarities attract in spiritual areas as well, and this area can sometimes be more important than any other.

In each case, you will be most happy and most compatible with a person whose fundamental beliefs and values in these areas are most similar to your own. Most unhappiness and disagreements in marriages and relationships come down to fundamental disagreements about these basic issues of life.

The second rule for success in relationships is that *opposites attract*, but only in temperament. Nature always demands balance and harmony. And balance is most necessary in the temperaments of two people who have come together as one.

There is a simple test of compatibility you can apply to your intimate relationships. It is called "the conversation test." In a relationship in which you are temperamentally compatible with another person, there will be an easy ebb and flow of conversation. Each person will be able to talk as much as he or she needs to talk, and each person will have the opportunity to listen as much as he or she needs to listen.

This balance is very important. Each person has a certain amount of talking that he or she must do to feel healthy and whole. If people do not get the opportunity to do all of their talking with the person with whom they are involved, they will seek to fulfill their communication needs somewhere else. Almost all affairs in marriages begin as the result of a need to communicate more fully with another human being.

When people are temperamentally balanced, 90 percent of the time they spend together will be filled with easy conversation, going back and forth. The other 10 percent of the time will be filled with comfortable silences.

However, if one person needs to talk 70 percent of the time and listen only 20 percent of the time, and the other person also needs to talk 70 percent of the time and listen only 20 percent of the time, there will be a clash over what is called "air time." They will be continually struggling over who is going to get to talk the most, who is going to fulfill his or her needs at the expense of the other.

In this type of relationship, there will be one person who loves *more* and one person who loves *less*. Always, the person who loves more will bite his or her lip and give in to allow the person who loves less to do all the talking he or she wants to do. The person who loves less controls the relationship.

However, this is only a temporary solution. It inevitably leads to feelings of frustration and unhappiness on the part of the person who loves more, and who is not getting an opportunity to express himself or herself fully enough. Eventually these repressed feelings erupt in health problems or harmful behavior.

Another example of incompatibility is when both parties only need to talk 30 percent of the time and are comfortable listening 60 or 70 percent of the time. In this case, you would have 40 percent of the time the couple is together filled with uncomfortable silences. The two people would sit there with very little to say, feeling uncomfortable but not knowing how to break the silence. This, too, is an example of temperamental incompatibility.

The conversation test can be applied to your relationships with any of your friends, on any level, and of either sex. Your very best friends are those with whom you have easy conversations and easy silences. These are the ones with whom you are most compatible. But it is *most* important that you be conversationally compatible with your mate or your spouse if you want to be happy in your relationship.

The third rule for successful relationships is *total commitment* on the part of both people. Total commitment requires a heartfelt determination to make the relationship successful. If the two are compatible in their basic values and attitudes and are temperamentally balanced, it is much easier for them to make a lifelong commitment. A total commitment means that neither party ever considers or discusses the possibility of separating, breaking up or divorcing. Making a total commitment requires that you burn your physical and emotional bridges and refuse to consider any other option except making this relationship successful.

Many people avoid making a total commitment to a relationship, even a marriage, because they have been hurt in previous relationships. They feel that if they keep their options open, they will always have an emotional escape route. This lack of commitment, however, leads almost invariably to creating the exact situation that the individual fears. The relationship gradually deteriorates as one or both parties continue to hold back and to think of separation as the solution to the problems that inevitably arise between two people.

W. Scott Peck, in his book *The Road Less Traveled,* gives a beautiful definition of love. He says, *"Love is the total commitment to the full development of the potential of the other."* When you truly love another person, you want that person to fulfill his or her full potential, and to become everything that he or she is capable of becoming. If one or the other has the slightest reluctance or hesitation in creating or supporting every opportunity for his or her mate to grow and develop, what you have might be a relationship, but it is probably not real love.

A wonderful thing about human beings is that we are *free* emotionally only when we have given up all other options and committed ourselves whole-heartedly to one other person. It is only then that we are capable of developing the high-quality relationship that we need to complete our evolution as human beings.

The fourth rule for successful relationships is *liking*. It is more important and more satisfying to genuinely like your partner than to be in love. In a long-term relationship, people may fall in and out of love. The kind and intensity of emotion that each feels for the other will vary with the passing of time. But if the two people like and respect each other, the relationship can endure indefinitely.

When one person stops liking or respecting the other person, for any reason, the relationship is usually over. Many couples fall in love and then break up and never speak to each other again because they never took the time to fall in like, to learn to genuinely like and respect the other person as an individual rather than just as a romantic partner.

Marriages and relationships may not work out, but if they were initially based on liking and respect, the two parties can still communicate and interact on an adult level without the negative feelings that go with relationships that ended in which no real liking or respect ever existed.

THE BEST FRIEND TEST

An excellent way to tell if you are in the right relationship is "the best-friend test." In the ideal relationship, your mate will be your best friend. There will be no one in the world that you would rather be with, share with, talk to or spend time with than your spouse.

If for any reason you do not feel that your spouse or mate is your best friend, if you do not feel that you would rather be with him or her than anyone else, it is an indication that something is wrong in the relationship.

In every interview with couples who have been together for a long time, both the man and the woman describe the other as their *very best friend in the world.*

The starting point of a long-term romantic relationship is the feeling that you have *met* your best friend. One of the indications of this is the amount you laugh together. The amount of laughter in a relationship is a measure of the health of that relationship. When two people are ideally suited, they laugh a lot together, and at the same things. When two people are unsuited for any reason, they won't find much in common to laugh about. Their senses of humor will be different.

The fifth rule for successful relationships is that *similar self-concepts attract* and are most compatible. You will always be attracted to, and be most compatible with, a person who is just about as happy and as positive as you are.

The general tone of the relationship, the general level of optimism versus pessimism, is a good measure of the compatibility of self-concepts. Interestingly enough, people with *negative* self-concepts will be attracted to each other just as will people with *positive* self-concepts. They will marry, settle down and be quite content together for many years, if not for life. Their relationship will be based on the fact that they are both largely negative personalities. Similar self-concepts attract, whatever they are.

Give your mate a score on a scale of 1 to 100. Estimate what percentage of the time he or she is positive and optimistic versus what percentage of the time he or she is negative or pessimistic. Then give yourself the same test.

You will find that you are the most comfortable with a person who is pretty much as happy, or as unhappy, as you are. That's why it is said, "Birds of a feather flock together," and "Misery loves company."

If two people enter into a relationship and one of them is much happier than the other, there will be all kinds of conflict and unhappiness. Most relationships and marriages that break up do so as the result of self-concepts being out of balance.

In one study, researchers found that four out of five divorces in America are initiated by women who are "mad as hell and not going to take it anymore." It's amazing how many husbands and wives feel that they are being held back because of the negativity of their spouses. This is a serious problem in relationships in America today, and there is no simple solution for it.

The sixth rule for successful relationships is that there must be *good communications*. The primary reason for the success of marriages is that the two partners communicate well with each other. They are on the same wavelength. Each can sense what the other is feeling and thinking. They come to the same conclusions independently. They almost seem to "share a brain."

The primary reason for the failure of relationships is poor communication. The couple misunderstand each other and continually argue about large and small issues. Each is convinced that he or she is right and the other is wrong. They have a hard time with the idea that both viewpoints might be correct, rightly considered.

To build and maintain a high level of quality communications in a relationship, you require both a high *quantity* and a high *quality* of unbroken time with each other. Couples need to be alone together. They need to spend long stretches of time talking and listening in order to keep their communication channels clear. Whenever two people get so busy that they stop taking time to talk, you can be sure that there are troubles ahead.

Good communications require both speaking and listening skills, which you can learn. But *excellent* communications between a man and a woman also require an understanding of the major differences between them.

VIVE LA DIFFÉRENCE

Men and women are different in many ways and they have distinctly different communication styles. Generally, men are *direct* and women are *indirect*. Men are more focused on results and completion, or closure, than women. Women are more concerned about relationships and the process of communication than men. This can often lead to fundamental misunderstandings.

Take the case of a man and a woman who have been driving for two or three hours. As they go past a McDonald's, the woman says, "Honey, are you thirsty?"

The man, without looking around, simply says, "Nope," and continues driving. She bites her lip and feels hurt at his insensitivity. He is blithely unaware of what she was really asking, and he has no idea that she is now unhappy.

In her indirect way, she was saying, "I am thirsty; why don't we stop and get something to drink?" However, because of the way she phrased it, it went over his head completely. He missed the point.

Another example of this difference in communication styles is shopping. For a man, going shopping is a simple process with an expected result. He goes in, he purchases what he came for, and he leaves. Men in general don't like shopping; they feel uncomfortable doing it and they want to get it over with as quickly as possible. The ideal shopping trip for a man is dashing in and dashing out, leaving his car running in the parking lot.

For many women, however, shopping is a process, even a recreational activity. A woman does not necessarily even have to buy anything.

Shopping is a sensory experience for a woman, and when she is shopping with another person, it becomes a social experience as well. The conversation that takes place is as important as, if not more important than, what she buys. This is something that men have a hard time understanding.

Here is another example of this difference in communication styles. Men are oriented toward closure and completion. When a woman begins discussing a problem with him, he will almost immediately respond with what he considers to be a logical solution.

He will say, "Why don't you do this or try that?" He will then go back to reading his newspaper, or turn his attention to something else. He will honestly feel he has been helpful and has properly addressed the issue: her problem.

What he does not realize is that the woman is usually not asking for a solution, nor does she want his advice or his recommendations. What she wants is an opportunity to discuss the situation, to process the problem through a *dialogue* about it with the man in her life. She probably already knows what she is going to do, or not do. What she seeks is an opportunity to communicate, using this particular situation or problem as the basis for the conversation.

One of the things that men can do to improve their communications with the women in their lives is simply to refrain from giving advice unless it is clear that this is what she wants. Instead, listen attentively, pause, ask questions, feed back and paraphrase what she is saying to ensure you understand.

ASK HER ABOUT HER DAY

One of the best things a man can do when he comes home at night, or when they get together in the evening, is to ask her about her day.

Most men consider their workday to be the most fascinating experience since the dawn of civilization. However, when a man asks his mate about her day before he volunteers anything about his day, he is often amazed at how much *more* interesting her day was than his.

The first time a man asks the woman he cares about to tell him about her day, she will probably be shocked, and she may give a brief, dismissive answer. She won't really believe that he is really interested. She'll think he's just being nice. So he must persist. When she says, Well, I went to work and I had lunch with so-and-so and then I came home, he must ask her, like a detective, What did you do this morning? Where did you go for lunch? What did you do after that? What did you do this afternoon? How is everything going with that person at your work? and so on. If he pries a little bit into her day, he will find that it is often as interesting as anything he did.

An advantage of this approach is that he spends less time talking about his work after she has had a chance to talk about her day. Remember, it is not the content of the conversation that is important. It is the *process*. Expressing a genuine interest in your mate or spouse and then listening carefully to the other person when he or she speaks, deepens understanding and improves communications. It is only in this way that you can keep the relationship alive and growing.

THE KEY QUESTION

The most important question for you to ask and answer continually to maintain a successful relationship is, "What's important here?"

What's important is not winning the argument, or being right, but maintaining the quality of the relationship. What's important is that you continue to love and respect each other and live together in peace and harmony.

When you continually ask, "What's important here?" you see things more clearly and you will be guided to do and say what is most appropriate.

Practice the golden rule of relationships. Ask yourself, regularly, "What would it be like to be married to me?" Or "What would it be like if my mate treated me the way I treat him or her?"

If you do to your mate what you would like to see done to you, and if you refrain from doing or saying anything that you would not like your mate to do or say to you, you will be far more aware of the impact of your words and behavior.

Awareness is really the key. Life is the study of attention. If you pay attention to the small things in your relationship, the big things will take care of themselves.

SIX PROBLEMS IN RELATIONSHIPS, AND HOW TO SOLVE THEM

There are a thousand reasons why relationships don't work out, but you can probably boil them down to *six* major problem areas. These six problems lie at the root of most arguments, disagreements and divorces. All of them have to do with the self-esteem and self-image of one or both of the parties in the relationship.

The first major problem in relationships is *lack of commitment*. This is evident in the "go halfway" relationship or marriage so common today. Instead of full commitment, there is only partial or half commitment. One or the other says, "You go halfway and I'll go halfway." However, as soon as one party decides to go only 49 percent of the way, a split opens in the relationship. And this kind of split tends to grow wider rather than narrower. The parties dig in. One or the other then goes only 48 percent of the way, then 40 percent, then 30 percent and so on until he or she stops trying altogether.

You see an example of this when a couple gets married but each keeps a separate bank account. The household expenses are divided equally. Every dollar is counted as belonging to one or the other. They even lend each other money and keep accurate tallies of who owes what to whom. I saw one case in which household expenses were divided down to the penny, even including the cost of a postage stamp to mail the utility bill!

Two friends of mine, let's call them Mary and Joe, lived together for eleven years. They always talked about getting married,
but they never seemed to be able to make a decision. However,
from the time they moved in together, each person purchased and
paid for furniture and fixtures for the apartment separately from the
other. On the back of every item in their apartment was a little
sticker indicating who it belonged to. They never commingled their
funds or their property. At the end of eleven years, when they
decided to separate, they were able to divide all their possessions in
less than two hours. They had unconsciously been planning to go
their separate ways for eleven years by their very act of never fully
committing to the relationship.

Another example of partial commitment is a marriage contract
or a prenuptial agreement. These agreements make interesting reading. The first paragraph of one of these contracts states, "The two
parties, being very much in love and planning to live together
happily for all the days of their life, are hereby entering into this
agreement."

The rest of the prenuptial agreement details at great length how
the property will be split when they separate. They are, in effect,
planning the details of the separation even before they get into the
marriage.

When one party is not willing to commit totally to the relationship, this holding back triggers feelings of rejection and unworthiness in the other. It makes one person feel that he or she is not
good enough. He or she feels that this is the reason the other is not
willing to commit totally and unequivocally to him or her.

When Barbara and I got married, the minister showed us the
various marriage vows that we could take. We could choose our
own wording for the ceremony. As we went through the various
vows, I asked him, "Where are the words, 'Till death do us part'?"

The minister, a very fine man, explained that those words had
been deleted from most marriage ceremonies today. Most young
people did not want to have something so clear and unequivocal
put into their marriage vows. They wanted something that allowed
them more flexibility and more options.

I asked him if we could put it back in. He said that we could do
whatever we liked. So I insisted that the words "Till death do us
part" be part of our marriage ceremony. I felt that a wishy-washy
marriage vow such as one he showed us, "As long as we both shall

love," was the sort of marriage vow that suggested that they were probably not really serious about the long-term survival of their marriage.

The way to overcome a lack of commitment is to commit yourself completely to the relationship. Get into it with both feet. Never consider the possibility of the relationship failing. If, through no fault of your own, the relationship does not work out, at least it will not be because you were half-hearted about it.

The second major problem in relationships is *trying to change the other person* or expecting the other person to change. This is another subtle form of rejection. It is another way of saying, "You are not good enough for me the way you are."

Whenever you try to change another person you imply that he or she is unworthy, and you ignite feelings of anger and resentment.

The fact is that people do not change very much. As the comedian Flip Wilson said, "What you *sees* is what you *gets*." If the person you are considering marrying is not what you want to *get*, the time to do something about it is before you get married, not afterward.

The solution to the problem of trying to change the other, of trying to get the other person to lose weight, quit smoking, exercise, become more positive or anything else, is to simply accept the person as he or she is. If you cannot accept the behavior and the personality of the other person, that should tell you something. Acceptance is largely determined by compatibility. Acceptance is a good indicator of whether this is the right relationship for you. Nonacceptance before the marriage is vastly superior to having to deal with it afterward.

Sometimes, when you stop trying to change the other person and just accept him or her unconditionally, he or she will begin to change as a result of his or her own choice. Human beings can be perverse. Often they will persist in behavior that irritates you just because you are continually trying to get them to change. When you stop trying to change them, they will often change their behavior voluntarily.

The third major problem in relationships is *jealousy*. Jealousy is always experienced in the mind and heart of the person feeling the emotion. Shakespeare called jealousy the "green-eyed monster." It is a terrible negative emotion that arises from feelings of low self-esteem and personal inadequacy.

The person who feels jealous has doubts about his or her value as a person. He or she feels, "Nobody could ever really love me, being the kind of person I am."

This type of individual probably suffered from destructive criticism in childhood and negative experiences with the opposite sex as an adult. If a person never received the unconditional love of his or her parents or, even worse, if the parents rejected or disapproved of the child during the time he or she was growing up, when that person becomes an adult he or she will be very vulnerable to not being fully loved and accepted by others.

The antidote to jealousy is to realize that it has nothing to do with the other person. It has to do only with the low self-esteem of the person suffering from it. The way to get over jealousy is by working on self-esteem, by saying over and over, "I like myself, I like myself, I like myself."

When your self-esteem is high enough, when you like and respect yourself sufficiently, nothing that anyone else does or does not do will make you doubt your own personal value. You will be emotionally self-reliant, independent of the behavior of others for how you feel about yourself.

It is never a smart or clever thing to *deliberately* make another person jealous. Jealousy is a painful, destructive emotion, and it is not the sort of thing that one friend inflicts on another. Each of us needs to feel safe and secure in the relationship to which we give ourselves, and the deliberate provocation of jealousy shakes our security. Jealousy makes us feel miserable and unhappy.

The fourth major problem in relationships is *self-pity*. This occurs when you feel sorry for yourself for something that your partner has either done or not done to you or for you. Usually people who feel self-pity learned it from one of their parents who practiced self-pity as a method of interaction at home.

Often people indulge in self-pity—"Woe is me!"—when their partners are so busy or happy with work that they feel left out. The solution to self-pity is *not* to get your partner to do or stop doing something. The antidote is to get so busy with your own goals that you don't have time to feel sorry for yourself.

You are responsible for your own emotions. You are the cause of your own happiness or unhappiness. Nobody makes you feel anything. If you experience self-pity, it is because you *choose* to feel sorry for yourself. And you can choose another reaction if you want to. The basis of self-pity is the mistaken notion that someone else is responsible for making you happy.

Self-pity is a form of weakness and insincerity that stops you from becoming a completely fulfilled human being. If you are in a relationship in which the other person is feeling sorry for himself or herself, be as compassionate and as understanding as possible and then encourage him or her to get busy doing something that he or she enjoys.

The fifth major problem in relationships is *negative expectations*. These occur when you constantly expect the other person to do something to disappoint you. The fact is that your expectations tend to be fulfilled. If you expect good things to happen, you will seldom be disappointed. If you expect your partner to let you down, you will seldom be disappointed in that either.

The rule is to always *expect the best* of your partner. Perhaps the most wonderful words that one person can say to another are, "I love you, and I believe in you." Always tell him or her that you have complete confidence and faith in his or her ability to do anything that he or she puts his or her mind to.

It feels wonderful to go off to work in the morning knowing that the most important person in your life believes in you completely. And it is wonderful to come home at night to a person who has complete faith in your ability to succeed, no matter what the obstacles. Many of the most successful men and women who have ever lived owe their success to the unshakable positive expectations of their mate.

The sixth major problem in relationships is *incompatibility*. Incompatibility is a very sensitive subject, which many people do not even like to discuss. However, it is one of the most common problems that arise in relationships, and perhaps the most common reason why people are unhappy in their marriages.

Usually, when two people meet and fall in love, they are attracted to each other by things they have in common. However, as the years pass and they change, they often grow in different directions. They develop new interests, new tastes and new opinions. What was important to them when they first met no longer means as much, and it loses its power to bond the two together.

The most common time for incompatibility to occur in marriages seems to be between the ages of twenty-eight and thirty-two years. During their twenties, people grow and change at the most rapid rate of their adult lives. If a couple gets married during their early twenties, by the end of their twenties they may find that they have very little in common. They may find that they have become incompatible.

THE WARNING SIGNS

The first sign that a couple is no longer compatible is that the laughter goes out of their relationship. They don't joke together or find a lot of funny things in common.

The second sign is that the conversation dries up. They seem to have little to talk about. The home becomes a functional place where the couple just happens to live, rather than a place of shared warmth and harmony.

Each person preoccupies himself or herself with work or the children or something else. Each goes through the motions. Each puts on a good front for their neighbors and friends.

Many people who are unhappy in their marriages plunge into their work, working twelve and fourteen hours a day, so they do not have to go home. And the less time they spend with the other, the worse the relationship becomes. They have less and less in common.

If you find that the laughter and conversation are going out of your relationship, it's time to take action. If you feel that you and the other person have very little left in common, you should make every effort to rebuild the relationship. You should recognize that you have a serious, life-disrupting problem and sit down together and discuss it. You should make every effort to recreate what you once had.

Perhaps you need to take some time off and go on a trip. Perhaps you need to start taking an interest in each other's activities, or to develop new common interests. If you have invested several years and a good deal of emotion in building your relationship, and especially if there are children, you must do everything possible to save the situation.

HOW TO PUT THE LOVE BACK IN

One of the most powerful ways to put love back into a relationship is to realize that love is a verb: *Love* is an action word. "To love" requires that you do the things that a loving person would do if you wish to feel the emotion that a person in love would feel. You may be able to *act your way* back into loving the person you have fallen out of love with.

You learn to love another person by doing loving things with and for that person. Small attentions, little favors, kindnesses, gifts and other things that make the other person happy actually make you love the person more. When you stop doing these little things, you can begin to fall out of love. The emotional ties begin to unwind. The fires begin to die down.

The Greek word for this process of rekindling love through action is called *Praxis*. The Principle of Praxis states that you generate emotions in yourself by doing things consistent with those emotions over and over until they kindle into flames. You act your way into feeling, very much as we discussed in Chapter Three, The Master Program.

You can put the love back into your relationship by once more doing the things that you did during courtship. You can start to be more caring, more attentive, more understanding and more sympathetic. As you *act the part* of a loving spouse, you may find your feelings toward the other person beginning to change for the better. You can act your way back into love.

By thinking loving thoughts about the other and by talking to the other in a loving and courteous way, you can often rekindle the feelings that once brought you together. Look into the other person for the good qualities you once admired. Forgive and forget mistakes that the other person may have made. More than anything, acting your way back into love requires that you really want to stay with this person, that you really want to rebuild and preserve this relationship.

WHAT DO YOU DO IF IT CAN'T BE SAVED?

It may happen, as it often does, that the fire has gone out of your relationship completely. There is no longer any desire to make the emotional sacrifices that are necessary to save the relationship. The two parties have, in effect, become incompatible.

Incompatibility is the most common reason for the breakdown of any relationship. The average adult goes out with many members of the opposite sex to find even *one* with whom he or she is compatible. Why should it be so surprising that two people would evolve and develop into two dissimilar people? Why should it be so surprising that two people become incompatible?

Often you see couples sitting in restaurants eating quietly and not talking to each other. Or you will see people driving along together staring out into the traffic without conversing. These are indications that the couple has become incompatible.

BEGIN WITH ACCEPTANCE

The best thing to do when two people have become incompatible is simply to accept it. William James of Harvard said, "The first step in dealing with any difficulty is to be willing to have it so."

Much unhappiness and psychosomatic illness is caused by *denial*, refusing to face the fact that something is wrong in your relationship. Denial, or internal resistance, causes stress and tension. The unwillingness to deal with something so embarrassing and so threatening to one's self-esteem as a failed relationship is a major cause of illness, insomnia, headaches and expressions of negative emotion such as irritability, anger and depression. These are all symptoms of an underlying cause, which may be incompatibility in the relationship.

One of the most useful ways to deal with any difficulty in life is to ask yourself, "Is this a fact, or is this a problem?" If it's a *problem*, it is amenable to a solution. There is something you can do about it, and you can apply your intelligence to finding a way to resolve it.

However, if it is a *fact*, the smartest thing to do is to accept it. Facts are like the weather: There is nothing that you can do about them except to incorporate them into your world view and make provision for them. Many people cause themselves enormous amounts of unnecessary unhappiness by confusing the *fact* of incompatibility with the *problem* of incompatibility. When the fire goes out of a relationship, when the ashes go cold and incompatibility sets in, it is time for one or both parties to face the fact squarely and honestly and then do something about it.

The reason you enter into a relationship with another person is so that you can be *happier* inside the relationship than you would be outside of it. Many people enter into relationships in order to be happier and more fulfilled, and they instead find themselves unhappy and less fulfilled. Then they mistakenly cling to the relationship, forgetting the reason for entering it in the first place.

The reason that you choose to be with another person rather than to be alone is to make your life better, richer and more enjoyable. It is not to suffer and be miserable. An unhappy relationship robs you of your happiness and undermines your potential more surely than any other single factor.

Many people stay in bad relationships because they are afraid of *what others might say*. They are afraid of losing face with their parents, their friends and the people they work with. They force themselves to keep up appearances for the public while, behind closed doors, they are bitterly unhappy. They often feel trapped in a relationship that they cannot get out of without suffering intense embarrassment with the people they know.

The fact is that *no one else really cares* about your relationship as much as you do. In most cases, you will find that the people you thought would be the most distressed to learn of your failed marriage are not really concerned at all. Most people have so many problems of their own that they have very little time or energy to think about you and your problems. In fact most people spend the majority of their time, all day long, thinking about themselves. Even if you are very close to another person—a son, a daughter or a best friend—that other person really spends very little time thinking about you in the course of the day.

Your whole life could be falling apart, but to most other people, what they are going to have for lunch today is more important to them than your problems. Many people find that when they finally decide to leave an unhappy relationship, their decision has virtually *no effect at all* on the people around them. Others simply do not care. They may express a little sympathy and ask a few questions, mostly out of curiosity, but then they have to get home for dinner and get on with the rest of their lives, leaving you alone.

LET IT GO

The bottom line, based on my seminars and workshops with thousands of individuals and couples, is that the most foolish thing you can do is to stay in a bad relationship because you think that somehow it is going to hurt or upset someone else if you leave it.

The smartest thing you can do is to be perfectly selfish emotionally. If you are not happy and you cannot save the situation, then at least please yourself. Do what makes *you* happy. You can never make anyone else happy by being miserable yourself. Only happy people can make others happy. Never sacrifice yourself on the altar of someone else's happiness. You end up achieving neither your own happiness nor the happiness of the other person.

LOVE IS THE MOST IMPORTANT THING

The most important thing in life is love. The security and joy of a loving relationship is perhaps the most wonderful thing that a man and woman can experience.

You should do everything possible to build and maintain a loving relationship with another person, including listening, expressing gratitude and appreciation, treating the other person with kindness, courtesy, gentleness, patience and especially compassion. You should make every effort to build a loving relationship within which you can live indefinitely.

But if it doesn't work out, have the courage and character to accept that nothing in human life is either perfect or permanent. Have the honesty to accept that the kindest thing that you can do for someone else is to achieve your own happiness. If you face life as it is, and not as you wish it would be, you will be true to yourself and true to the most important people in your life.

ACTION EXERCISE

Since happy relationships are central to your self-esteem and happiness, make the decision to get your primary relationship in order. Resolve to sit down with the other person and ask him or her,

"What can we do more of, or less of, to make this a wonderful relationship?"

Change your order of priorities, of values, if necessary and make your relationship more important than anything else. Be willing to make sacrifices, changes, if necessary to ensure the quality and stability of your home and the emotional health of the person you care about more than anyone else.

A solid, supportive, totally loving relationship serves as the foundation upon which you can build a wonderful life. It is the true manifestation of the excellent person you are becoming. It is your key to health and happiness. Your relationship is a reflection of the person you really are and your assurance of a great future.

CHAPTER 11

Mastering the Art of Parenting

———

The most important and enduring relationship that you ever enter into begins when you bring a child into the world. Income, jobs, friendships, health and even marriages may come and go, but your role as a parent lasts as long as you live. The impact of your parenting can affect your child and your children's children for generations. Parenting is probably the most profound responsibility an adult can ever take on.

No one is born with the skills of successful parenting. We all begin as amateurs. Fortunately, you can learn a lot about how to be a good and effective parent by reading and seeking advice from friends, relatives, doctors and experts in the field. There are many fine books, magazines and articles containing advice and insights that can help you tremendously in being the kind of parent that you want to be.

WHAT IS THE TRUE ROLE OF PARENTING?

The most important single role of parenting is to love and nurture your children and to build in them feelings of high self-esteem and self-confidence. If you raise your children feeling terrific about themselves, if you bring them up full of eagerness to go out and take on the world, then you have fulfilled your responsibility in the highest possible sense. Conversely, if you give your child everything of a material nature but raise him or her lacking in self-confidence and self-esteem, you have failed in your primary role.

The average adult probably spends fifty years of his or her life getting over the first five. Abraham Maslow taught that we have two main types of needs that we strive to fulfill. These are the needs to fulfill our potential, our "being" needs, and the needs to compensate for our perceived deficiencies. The child raised without sufficient love tends to seek it all his or her life, rather than striving to realize his or her potential. Perhaps the kindest thing a parent can do is to give his or her child the love and emotional support the child needs to grow and thrive, creating a climate in which the child feels totally loved by the most important people in his or her life.

The growing child develops a healthy personality in direct proportion to the quality and quantity of love he or she receives. Just as a plant needs sunshine and rain, a child needs love and nurturing.

Parents want the very best for their children. They want to raise their children to be happy and healthy. Why is it then that so many children grow up feeling insufficiently loved? Why is it that parents somehow deprive their children of the love they require for healthy growth?

WHY PARENTS DON'T LOVE ENOUGH

There are two major reasons for the failure by parents to love their children enough. First, the parents do not love themselves. Parents with low self-esteem have great difficulty giving more love to their children than they feel for themselves.

The second reason that parents don't love their children enough is they often have the mistaken notion that their children exist to fulfill their expectations. A major cause of friction between parents and children is the parents' feeling or perception that the children are failing to "measure up" to what the parents expect them to be or do.

Many parents look upon their children as chattel, as a form of property. They feel their children are behaving properly only when they are doing and saying what their parents want them to. If the child's behavior differs from the parents' expectations, the mother or father responds with criticism. Without planning to, they withdraw their love and approval from the child. They step on their child's emotional lifeline. The child feels unloved and the foundation is laid for personality problems later in life. All negative or antisocial behavior is a cry for help, an attempt to escape the feelings of guilt, anger and resentment that begin with criticism early in life.

CHILDREN ARE NOT PROPERTY

The starting point of raising *super kids* is to realize that your children are not your property. Your children belong to themselves. They are a gift to you from high above, and a temporary gift at that.

I tell my children that they have been sent to me by God, and that my job is to love them and take care of them until they grow up. I treat them as if they are precious gifts loaned to me for only a short time. My job is not to make them conform to my expectations, but to encourage them to develop their own uniqueness and individuality.

Each child is unlike any other and comes into this world with his or her own agenda, with his or her own special talents, interests and abilities. What your child can and will become, no one can possibly know until much later. The child's job is not to conform to his or her parents' expectations, but to grow and flower and become everything he or she is capable of becoming.

Kahlil Gibran, in his wonderful book *The Prophet,* expresses this idea beautifully. He says, *"Your children are not your children. They are the sons and daughters of life's longing for itself. They come through you but not from you, and though they are with you, yet they belong not to you.*

"You may give them your love but not your thoughts, for they have their own thoughts. You may house their bodies but not their souls, for their souls dwell in the House of Tomorrow, which you cannot visit, not even in your dreams. You may strive to be like them, but seek not to make them like you. For life goes not backward nor tarries with yesterday. You are the bows from which your children, as living arrows, are sent forth."

CHILDREN ARE A PRECIOUS GIFT

When you look at your children as precious gifts that you can only enjoy for a short time, you see your role as a parent differently. When you celebrate and encourage the special nature and personality of your child, he or she grows like a flower in the sunshine. But if you try to get your child to be something he or she is not, your child's spirit will wither, and his or her potential for happiness and joy will shrivel like a leaf on a tree in autumn.

The Law of Correspondence states that your outer world of relationships will mirror your inner world of thought, and your true personality. What your children are and what they become will be very much a reflection of who you are as a person. Whenever you have a problem with your child, look into yourself and ask, "What is there in me that could be causing this situation?"

Most parents blame and criticize their children when their children do something that the parent doesn't like. However, superior parents look to themselves as the primary source of the child's behavior. They realize that the apple never falls far from the tree.

In their earlier years, children are almost totally reactive. Their behavior, good or bad, is very much a reaction to the way they are treated by their parents and the people around them. When the parent begins to accept responsibility for the child's behavior, real progress becomes possible in solving difficulties the child might be having.

LOVE MAKES THE DIFFERENCE

The most important consideration in raising super kids is the amount of love they receive. Children need love like flowers need water. You can never give a child too much love. A continuous flow of love and approval from the parent to the child is the child's lifeline to emotional and physical health. Almost all problems with children can be traced to the child's perception that he or she was not fully loved and accepted by one or both parents.

Lack of love, real or imagined, has serious consequences. Love deprivation can lead to physical or emotional illness, and even death. The damage caused by love withheld or curtailed can have a long-term, destructive effect on the personality of the child. Adults with emotional problems were invariably children whose parents didn't love them enough.

In the early part of this century, there was a theory of child-raising that held that the less contact a child had with adults in its early months, the healthier the child would be. It was felt that exposure to too many adults would expose the child to various infections.

Based on this theory, access to newborn children was severely restricted. Infants were touched as little as possible. Parents' visits were restricted. Aside from having their diapers changed and being given bottles, the children were left alone in their cribs as much as possible. But a terrible thing began to happen. Children being cared for in nurseries where they received very little contact refused nourishment. They became passive. They soon started to shrivel and some of them died.

This malady, "miasma," was also called the "failure to thrive" syndrome.

These children, deprived of love and touching in the first weeks and months after birth, actually lost all desire to live. They began to die at an alarming rate.

In one orphanage in New York State, forty-eight out of fifty babies died in a six-month period. Finally, the doctors and nurses realized that the children needed warmth and contact with an adult. When the nurses began holding the children, the "miasma" began to clear up and the children began to grow normally.

In a famous case reported in one of the psychological journals, a young boy, three years old, was left with a baby-sitter while his parents went out for dinner. Tragically, the parents were both killed in an automobile accident on the way home from the restaurant. The next thing the little boy knew, he was taken out of his home by the Social Services Department and put into a foster home. He never saw his loving parents again, and he was too young to understand what had happened.

He began to act up in the foster home. He wet the bed, he cried, he got into fights with other children and became a serious behavior problem. As a result, he was moved from foster home to foster home. And a remarkable thing happened. He stopped growing. For the next four years he had problems in home after home, and at the age of seven, he was still the same physical size that he had been at the age of three.

Then something wonderful happened. A loving couple met the boy in a foster home and applied to adopt him. They took him home and began to shower him with warmth and affection. They held him, talked to him, took him for walks and drowned him with love and unconditional acceptance. They hugged him and kissed him and held his hand.

Within a few weeks, the little boy started to grow again. In the next nine months, he grew a full four years' worth of height and weight and by the end of the first year with his new parents, he had reached the normal height and weight for his age. The powerful effect of love on children is amazing!

There are many examples of children who failed to thrive and grow physically as the result of love withheld. There are even more examples of children who fail to grow emotionally and mentally as the result of the love they needed for healthy growth being reduced or cut off when they were growing up.

These mental and emotional problems are manifested in behavioral disturbances, personality disorders, neurosis, psychosis and serious failures to cope as adults. Love deprivation is surely the most serious problem that a child can suffer during his or her formative years.

UNCONDITIONAL LOVE AND ACCEPTANCE

The key to raising super kids is to give them an unbroken flow of unconditional love and acceptance. Make it clear to your child that nothing he or she does could ever cause you to love him or her less than 100 percent. The most wonderful gift you can give your child is the absolute conviction that you love him or her completely, without reservation, no matter what he or she does and no matter what happens.

Whenever I have to discipline or correct one of my children, I always start by saying, "I love you very much, but you can't do this, or you have to stop behaving like that." I always make it very clear that I am unhappy with the behavior, not with the child. I have *trained* my children so that they understand this completely.

I used to say to my little girl, Christina, "How much does Daddy love you?" And she would stretch her hands out wide and say, "You love me *this* much." I would then say, "What about when I send you to your bedroom?" She would reply, "You still love me *this* much," with her arms open wide.

Then I would ask, "What about when I spank your hand or take away your toys and send you to your bedroom?"

She would then say, "'Daddy, you still love me *this* much," with her hands outstretched.

I would then ask her, with mock surprise, "How can this be?"

She would reply, "Daddy, no matter what I do, you *always* love me 100 percent."

Dr. Ross Campbell, in his book *How to Really Love Your Child,* says that your child is always asking you, one way or another, "Do you love me?" The only variable is how you answer.

Sometimes the child misbehaves as a way of checking on whether you really love him or her. The older and more mature children become, the more subtle they are about how they ask the question, "Do you love me?" However, the question is always the same. The excellent parent is one who always answers this question by telling the child, in every way possible, "Yes, I really love you."

HOW TO LET THEM KNOW

If you want to raise super kids, *tell them that you love them every single day*. You can never say "I love you" to a child too often. Even if your child pretends that he or she doesn't need to hear it, don't you believe it. Every time a child hears the words "I love you" from his or her parents, the child feels more secure and confident. His or her self-esteem increases. And the more they know you love them, the freer they are to love themselves.

There are three main ways for you to *tell* your children you love them regularly. First, tell your children that you love them with *eye contact*. Children have "emotional tanks," and they fill their "emotional tanks" by drinking in love from their parents through their eyes. Whenever you look at a child with loving eye contact, you make the child feel wonderful about himself or herself. From as early as six weeks of age, children are fascinated by looking into the eyes of someone who is smiling at them with warmth, love and affection.

Children who do not receive loving eye contact from their parents do not feel truly loved. They feel that something is wrong with them, and with their relationship with their parents. They feel insecure. They feel they have done something their parents don't like, and they don't know what it was.

In our society, sustained eye contact is usually accompanied by a criticism or a complaint. We fix our eyes on our children when we are angry with them, but we very seldom look intently at them just as an expression of love. Many children grow up feeling very uncomfortable with direct eye contact of any kind. They feel it is a hostile act and they look away to avoid it.

When people have just fallen in love, they sit and stare into each other's eyes for a long time. This is a way that one adult says to another, "I love you." You can try this with your children. You will be amazed at the impact that sustained, loving eye contact has when you give it to your children, especially if they have not experienced it for a while.

Second, you can tell your children you love them with *physical contact*. Hugging and kissing your children is the most wonderful way to convey to them, through touch, that you really love and value them. Virginia Satir, the family therapist, says that children require four hugs per day for survival, eight hugs per day for health and twelve hugs per day for growth. You just can't hug and kiss them too much when they're growing up.

Children who are not hugged and kissed by their parents eventually come to believe that they are not worthy of being hugged and kissed. They feel insecure. Their self-esteem suffers. Their personalities are affected. They react with destructive behavior.

Research shows that female children and male children are hugged about the same amount through the first year of life. After that, female children continue to receive the same amount of physical affection. But the amount of hugging that a boy receives drops off dramatically, to about 20 percent of that received by a girl by the age of five.

Some parents believe that if you give a boy too much affection, you will turn him into a "sissy." However, exactly the opposite is true. Boys who receive lots of hugging and physical contact from their parents grow up to be strong, masculine and self-confident. Boys who receive little or no physical contact from their parents can grow up feeling insecure, unloved and lacking in self-confidence.

There is a school of thought that holds that much of the extra aggressiveness boys show when they are growing up is related to this lack of hugging and physical contact, in comparison to that received by girls. Although this idea ignores the role of testosterone in making boys more rambunctious, you can still never hurt the physical, emotional or mental development of a boy by giving him too much physical warmth in his earlier years.

Third, and perhaps the most powerful way to tell a child that you really love him or her, is *focused attention*. Giving focused attention requires that you spend periods of unbroken time with your son or daughter. Children need to be with their parents. They need to talk to their parents, to relate to them, to be around them while they are growing up. They need this time like they need food for healthy growth.

The debate over "quality time" versus "quantity time" misses the point. The fact is that quality time is a *function* of quantity time. Quality time, those precious moments and experiences that you share with your child, comes as the result of spending large *quantities* of time with your child. And there's no substitute for it.

You cannot just say, "Well, let's have some quality time." You must be willing to invest a lot of time, perhaps many hours, if you want to enjoy the moments of "quality time" that are so important in the relationship between a parent and child.

There is probably no better way to build a high-quality relationship with your child than to schedule long unbroken periods of time with him or her. Your children need to communicate their thoughts and feelings to someone who is important to them, and you, as their parent, should be the most important person in their lives.

If their parents do not take the time to sit with them and listen, children will begin to spend more and more time with their peer groups. They will seek approval and acceptance from them, and be guided by their behavior and priorities.

The most positive influence you can exert in your teenager's life is to be the *primary* source of love, support and respect for your child. If your child does not receive this love and support from you, your ability to influence your child's behavior will begin to diminish rapidly. A gulf will grow between you. He or she will reject your advice, your values and your world view.

PRAISE AND ENCOURAGEMENT

Give your children continual praise and encouragement for the positive things they do, even small things. Praise and reinforce what you would like to see repeated. Praise them to build their self-esteem and self-confidence.

If your child comes home from school with grades ranging from A to D, compliment and praise your child on the good grades, and then encourage the child to do better in the areas where he or she is weak. Praise is like an elixir, or tonic, to the psychological health of your child. The child's personality is formed and developed by the love and praise he or she receives from you. When you praise and encourage your child for successes, you motivate him or her to achieve even greater successes so he or she can get even more praise and encouragement.

Praising raises your child's self-esteem and increases his or her self-respect. Praise improves your child's self-image. Praise causes your child to believe in himself or herself, and gives your child the confidence to try even bigger and better things.

VULNERABILITY

Never use *destructive criticism* on your children. They are extremely vulnerable to criticism of any kind from you. It tears them up inside. They may not react visibly, but inside they hurt terribly whenever they are criticized for any reason by the important adults in their lives.

Destructive criticism has done more to destroy more personalities than all the wars in history. Most of our adult personality problems were originally caused by destructive criticism from one or both of our parents. When we in turn criticize our child, he or she feels unloved, undeserving and insecure. Our child feels rotten inside. He or she feels discouraged and depressed.

Often parents criticize their children in an attempt to *increase* their effectiveness. However, destructive criticism actually lowers your child's estimate of his or her competence, his or her self-concept. As your child's self-concept diminishes, his or her level of effectiveness *decreases* commensurably. Criticism of any kind can cause your child's performance to deteriorate to the point where often he or she will avoid the activity altogether. Your child then gets worse, not better.

There is a wonderful little piece of advice by Dorothy Noltie which every parent should memorize. It is called "Children Learn What They Live," and it goes like this:

If a child lives with criticism,
He learns to condemn.
If a child lives with hostility,
He learns to fight.
If a child lives with ridicule,
He learns to be shy.
If a child lives with shame,
He learns to feel guilty.
If a child lives with tolerance,
He learns to be patient.
If a child lives with encouragement,
He learns confidence.
If a child lives with praise,
He learns to appreciate.
If a child lives with fairness,
He learns justice.
If a child lives with security,
He learns to have faith.
If a child lives with approval,
He learns to like himself.
If a child lives with acceptance and friendship,
He learns to find love in the world.

REMEMBER TO ASK YOURSELF WHAT'S IMPORTANT

Whenever you are faced with a challenging situation involving your child, you need, more than ever, to ask the question, *"What's important here?"* And the correct answer is always that raising your child with high self-esteem and self-confidence is your true aim and your real role. It is not to be *right*. It's not to get the child to conform to your expectations. It's to raise him or her happy, healthy and self-confident.

Listen to your intuition. After you have read all the books and taken all of the advice, the intuition of a loving parent is almost always superior to that of any other input. You will always know, deep inside, what is right for your child. And as long as your every decision and behavior is guided by love, you will always be doing the right thing.

WHAT CONDITIONS PRODUCE HIGH ACHIEVERS?

Dr. David McClelland of Harvard, author of *The Achieving Society*, did many years of research into parenting and how parenting styles affected achievement motivation in children. He found that there were two primary characteristics of the households that produced *high achievers*, defined as boys and girls who began to achieve noteworthy things in their teens and early twenties.

A DEMOCRATIC ENVIRONMENT

The first characteristic of both the household and the parenting style that produced high achievers was that it was *democratic*. The opinions of the children were solicited and respected. The children were encouraged to give their input on family decisions from an early age. They were asked what they thought and how they felt. Their input was carefully considered. The children's opinions weren't necessarily acted upon in every case. But the children's thoughts and ideas were valued. The whole family took time to discuss and agree upon matters together.

There are few things that make a child feel better than to be treated as an intelligent, thinking person by his or her parents. When you treat children as if they are important and intelligent, they will surprise you with how smart and insightful they really are.

Often around our dinner table, when I am wrestling with a problem at work, I will explain it in simple terms to Christina, who is twelve, and ask for her advice. She often comes up with remarkable insights. The old saying, "From the mouths of babes," turns out to be very true. Children can sometimes see situations with an objectivity and clarity their parents lack. When you ask for your child's advice in any situation, you may be surprised at the quality of the answer you get. But the most important thing is that you *ask*. This builds the child's self-esteem and sense of personal worth. Asking your child for his or her opinions or advice is a sign of how much you respect him or her, and it increases his or her self-respect.

POSITIVE EXPECTATIONS

The second characteristic of parents who raise high achievers is that of "positive expectations." High-achieving young people grow up in homes in which their parents are continually telling them how much they believe in them and how confident they are that they are going to do good work and accomplish great things with their lives.

When you say to your child, "You can do it," or "I believe in you," you encourage him or her to believe in himself or herself. You encourage your child to attempt more than he or she would in the absence of your words of encouragement. Children who grow up as the recipients of positive expectations always do better at everything they attempt.

Here's an important point. Positive expectations are not the same as demands. Many parents think that they are expressing positive expectations when in fact they are simply demanding that their children perform to a particular standard. A demand is always associated with *conditional love*, with the idea that if the child does not perform to expectations, the love and support of the parent will be withdrawn.

It is important to convey to your children that, no matter how well or poorly they do, you love them totally and unconditionally. If the child feels that your love will be withdrawn if he or she performs poorly, your child will be nervous and insecure. Even if your child does well, he or she will get no pleasure and no lasting satisfaction from his or her success.

HOMEWORK AND EDUCATION

Parents who raise high-achieving young people have specific attitudes toward homework. They are very clear about the importance of homework and of doing well in school. They insist that their children complete their school assignments on time. In every single study, the single most important factor accounting for high scholastic achievement is the parents' attitude toward learning and their involvement in the child's education.

One determinant of excellent schoolwork is where and when

the homework is done. In the homes that produced high achievers, the homework was done at the family dinner table before or after dinner, with the television off, and in the presence of the parents. The parents volunteered to help the children with their homework and to familiarize themselves with their children's assignments if necessary.

Low achievers, on the other hand, came from homes in which the parents sent the children to their rooms to do their homework, if they took any interest in the homework at all. When children are sent to their rooms to do their homework, the message they receive is that the homework, and therefore the schoolwork, is not important. Children who do not learn to complete their homework by the age of ten are very seldom able to do good schoolwork later in their academic careers.

If you want your children to do their best at school, you must get totally involved in every phase of their education. As I've said before, life is the study of attention. You always pay more attention to that which you most value. When you pay close attention to the schoolwork and school activities of your child, he or she places a far higher value and importance on those activities. If you ignore his or her homework and schoolwork, the child gets the message that they are unimportant and tends to ignore them as well.

BUILD THEIR SELF-ESTEEM

You can help build your child's self-esteem by teaching him or her to say, "I like myself," from an early age. I have them stand in front of the mirror and repeat, "I like myself, I like myself, I like myself." Children who learn to build and maintain their own levels of self-esteem have far better self-concepts than children who do not.

Children with high, positive self-concepts do well in school. They do not engage in vandalism or get into trouble. They don't do destructive things to their bodies. They are more capable of resisting the negative influences of their peer groups. They have stronger characters.

Children with high self-concepts, high self-esteem, are independent in their thinking. They are more likely to think for themselves, and to orient themselves toward success, achievement and personal fulfillment. They are more focused on realizing their potential than on compensating for their deficiencies.

When your child feels terrific about himself or herself, he or she develops better judgment about the things that are good for him or her in the long term. He or she develops the ability to delay gratification in the short term in order to enjoy greater rewards in the future.

SET A GOOD EXAMPLE

If you really want to raise happy, healthy, self-confident children you need to set a good example, to be a role model of the kind of person you want them to become.

Children learn largely by imitation during their formative years. They learn by watching you and listening to you and imitating your words and your behavior.

When you become a parent and set yourself up as a role model, you no longer have the luxury of doing and saying whatever you want. You have to be much more aware of your behavior and its likely impact on your children.

If you want your children to grow up with good health habits, you must set an example by eating the right foods and making the right foods available in your household. If you want your children to avoid drinking, smoking and other addictive habits, you need to set an example in your own behavior in these areas. If you want your children to spend more time reading, rather than watching television, you need to set an example by reading at every opportunity. If you want your children to develop patience, calmness, poise and self-control, you need to be a model of these qualities, even under the most trying of circumstances.

Children are always looking to their parents for cues on how to behave, and your being a good role model can have a greater influence than almost anything else you can possibly do in the lives of your children.

LOVE YOUR SPOUSE

Probably the kindest thing that a man can do for his children is to love their mother. And probably the kindest thing that a mother can do for her children is to love their father. Children learn about love by growing up in a household in which love is freely expressed and shared. They learn how to be loving adults by observing the love between their parents.

You may have been brought up by parents who were unaware of some of these things. They may have made many mistakes with you, especially the use of destructive criticism. They may have never given you the love and affection you required.

You're a creature of habit. Your natural tendency as a parent is to do the *same* things to your children that were done to you. You make the same mistakes. You do the same hurtful things and you feel badly about it. But *it's never too late*. If you have slipped into the habit of using destructive criticism on your son or daughter, there is something you can do right now to remedy the situation and rebuild your child's feeling of self-worth.

TAKING IT BACK

Sit down with your child, or children. Then, take a deep breath and *apologize* to them for all the destructive criticism, or physical punishment, that you have ever used on them. Tell them that you are sorry for everything you've ever said or done that hurt them or made them feel bad about themselves in any way.

One of the biggest complaints of children of all ages is that their parents never say "I'm sorry" or "I apologize" for mistakes they have made, or for hurtful things that they have said or done. Children are extremely sensitive to fairness and justice. They feel angry and hurt when they *perceive* that they have been treated unfairly or accused unjustly for any reason. If not resolved, this anger can last for years.

Your purpose in apologizing to your children is for you to *accept complete responsibility* for anything guilt producing that you have ever said or done. When you apologize, you demonstrate to your child that you are a human being. You are not perfect. You show him or her that you have the character and courage to admit that you were wrong.

Many parents refuse to apologize to their children because they fear that their children will not respect them. They feel that they have to project an image of infallibility or their children will take advantage of them. They are afraid that apologizing is a sign of weakness. Their egos are too fragile to even consider it.

However, exactly the opposite is true. When you apologize to your child, you increase his or her love and respect for you. You increase the likelihood that your child will cooperate with you in the future. When you don't apologize when you are wrong, you make the child angry and resentful. You lower your own value in his or her eyes.

When you apologize to your child, you remove the burden of guilt, negativity and unworthiness that has built up from destructive criticism in the past. By apologizing and admitting that you were at fault for your behavior, you set your child free. The results of the simple act of apologizing, of saying, "I'm sorry for what I did and said," can be immediate and amazing.

Many parents have seen their children transformed overnight by the simple exercise of sitting them down and saying, "I'm sorry for anything and everything that I have ever done or said that has hurt you in any way."

Children who have been unreachable, distant and estranged from their parents for months, or even years, have been reconciled with them almost immediately when the parent has had the courage and character to accept responsibility and to apologize.

Once you have apologized, promise never to use destructive criticism again. Give your children permission to remind you when you slip from time to time. From then on, whenever you forget your promise, whenever you say something in anger, immediately take it back and say, "I'm sorry."

Children are very resilient. They need and want their parents' love and respect so much that they will always forgive and forget. Once you have asked a child for forgiveness, and the child forgives you, the slate is clean. The child feels liberated, like a prisoner set free. And you are free as well.

When you apologize and say you are sorry to your children, you give them permission to admit that they also make mistakes. They don't have to invest enormous amounts of emotional energy covering up and defending themselves as most adults do. When you demonstrate that you have the courage and character to admit your mistakes, you set an example that builds courage and character in your children. They realize that they don't have to be perfect to be acceptable. They are valuable and worthwhile just as they are.

The most enduring relationship that you will ever have is with your children. This relationship will last for as long as you live. If you treat your children with love, patience and understanding, you will reap the rewards all the days of your life.

A QUICK SUMMARY

First, the primary role of parenting is to raise children with high self-esteem and self-confidence. This sets them up for happiness and achievement as adults.

Second, children need a continuous flow of unconditional love, approval and acceptance from their parents. This is their key requirement for healthy growth. If they don't get it, they seek it all their lives.

Third, tell your children you love them every day, in both words and actions. Give them loving eye contact, warm physical contact and focused attention. Spend lots of time with them, taking them on walks, to the movies, on trips and out on dates for lunch or dinner. Nothing tells your child more clearly how much you love him or her than your investing lots of your time in them.

Fourth, build a high-achieving environment for your children by getting involved with their education and their homework. Have positive expectations that they will do their very best. Tell them you believe in them. Value their opinions and encourage them to contribute their thoughts and feelings to the life of your family. Treat them with respect and they will respect themselves.

Fifth, remember that you are your child's primary role model. Your child, consciously and unconsciously, throughout his or her entire life, will strive to be like you, and will treat other people the way you treat him or her. If you treat your child with kindness, patience, love, respect and approval, your child will grow up to be a fully functioning, self-actualizing human being. You can't ask for much more than that, and you shouldn't be satisfied with anything less.

ACTION EXERCISE

Ask yourself what it would be like to *be your own child*. Put yourself in the position of your child or your children, and then evaluate yourself as a parent. What are your strengths and weaknesses? What do you do well and what do you do poorly? What are some of the things that you do that might be causing your children to grow up with lower self-esteem than you would like? What can you do, starting today, to be a better and more loving parent?

Go to your child and ask him or her if there is anything he or she feels you could do to be a better parent. Ask if there is anything you do that he or she doesn't like. Listen attentively to his or her answers and observations. Don't interrupt, explain or defend. Pause before replying. Question for clarification, by saying, "How do you mean?" or "For example?"

Paraphrase and feed it back in your own words. Finally, commit yourself to doing something, to acting on what he or she has told you. Words without actions are not credible.

You can become an outstanding parent by deciding to be one, and by practicing what you've learned in this chapter and in this book. This is perhaps the most important decision you ever make, and the one with the most wonderful payoff.

Mastery: The Power of Love

When I was a teenager, before I set out to see the world, I spent a good deal of time thinking about the meaning of life. "Why am I here? What is the purpose of life? What is the reason for existence? Who am I? Where did I come from? And where am I going?" I am sure everyone at some time has wondered about the reasons for his or her individual existence on this planet.

Even as a young man, I had come to the conclusion that *love* is the most important thing in the world. I traveled in more than eighty countries over a period of eight years, working at different jobs, learning different languages and getting into and out of different situations. All the while I still felt that love was the most important thing in the world.

I occasionally ask a person what he or she thinks is the most important thing in life. I believe that you can tell how emotionally mature a person is by his or her answer. In my judgment, the only correct answer is love. I have asked this question of leading business people, politicians, professionals and others from every walk of life, and I have found that even the most worldly and materialistic men or women will admit upon questioning that, in their heart, they believe love is more important than anything else.

In Chapter One, I defined success as a composite or blend of seven different ingredients. Each of these ingredients is affected by the amount of love that a person has within himself or herself and toward the rest of the world.

EVERYTHING DEPENDS UPON LOVE

You have *peace of mind* to the degree to which you love yourself and love others. You have high levels of *health and energy* to the degree to which you experience self-love, self-acceptance and the love and acceptance of others. You have *loving relationships* to the degree to which you love yourself and express your love toward others. In many cases, love is central to your level of *financial achievement* in life. Virtually all self-made millionaires are doing what they love to do. To the degree to which you love yourself and love what you are doing, you will set *high, challenging and worthwhile goals and ideals* to strive toward. Self-love and self-acceptance make it easier for you to gain greater *self-knowledge and self-understanding*. Finally, you achieve lasting fulfillment, *self-expression and self-actualization* in life to the exact degree to which you love and accept yourself and others unconditionally.

RELATING LOVE TO THE "LAWS"

You are a mental creature. Almost everything that happens to you happens as a result of the way you think. If you change or improve the quality of your thinking, you automatically change and improve the quality of your life. Several of the mental laws in this book relate to the importance of love and the development of a healthy personality. They are part of the achievement of worthwhile goals and aspirations.

The Law of Belief states that whatever you believe, with feeling, becomes your reality. If you love and respect yourself, and you believe yourself capable of accomplishing great things, you are almost certain to achieve far more than if you doubt yourself, or if you do not believe in your personal potential.

The Law of Expectations states that whatever you expect, with confidence, becomes a self-fulfilling prophecy. If you expect the best of yourself and others, which is the natural expression of a loving attitude, you will seldom be disappointed. You will acquire far more of the things you want if you confidently expect good things to happen to you, and you behave accordingly.

The Law of Attraction states that you invariably attract into your life people and circumstances in harmony with your dominant thoughts. When you think kind and loving thoughts about yourself and others, you attract kind and loving people to you. These people make your life a joy. They fill your life with happiness. They assure fulfillment in your work and satisfaction in your personal relationships.

The Law of Correspondence states that your outer world will be a reflection of your inner world. If you have a kind, gentle and loving nature, your outer world of relationships, health and material success will be marked by health, happiness and prosperity.

The Law of Concentration states that whatever you dwell upon grows. If you continually choose to think loving thoughts about yourself and others, you "grow" more loving relationships in every part of your life.

The Law of Substitution says that you can replace a negative thought with a positive thought. When you consciously select the content of your conscious mind, and keep your thoughts focused on love, patience, tolerance and forgiveness, you crowd out negative thoughts that disrupt your peace of mind, undermine your health and energy and harm your relationships.

Love teaches us the principle of nonresistance. The Bible says, "Judge not that ye be not judged," and, "Pray for those who spitefully use you." When you respond to anger and negativity with love and kindness, you not only preserve your own emotional integrity and maintain a positive mental attitude, but you also help the other person.

There is nothing that so surprises a person as to have someone whom they are mistreating respond to them with gentleness, courtesy and kindness. It frees him or her to stop the critical behavior and become a better person.

The Law of Superconscious Activity states that any thought, plan, goal or idea you can hold continuously in your conscious mind will be brought into reality by your superconscious mind. You can have a wonderful life, full of happy, loving relationships, characterized by health, energy and the experience of joy, by thinking continually about the things you really want in your life and keeping your mind off of the things you don't want.

LOVE IS THE ANSWER

Always, *love is the answer*. The one thing that you can never have too much of is love. You can never have too much love for yourself, and you can never give too much love to others. Lack of love, or love withheld, lies at the root of most personal and behavioral problems. Love is not only the answer, but it is the cure for most of life's problems.

THE GREAT ROBBER EMOTION

Whatever one's religious beliefs, it's hard to deny the universal truth of many of the biblical teachings. One of the most beautiful lines in the New Testament is "God is love and he that dwelleth in God, dwelleth in love and God in him."

It also says, "There is no fear in love, but perfect love casteth out fear."

These words are important to us because the great robber of human happiness is, and always has been, *fear* of some kind—fear of failure, fear of rejection, fear of criticism, fear of losing someone's love or respect, fear of ill health, fear of not measuring up to other people's expectations of us and a generalized fear of not being good enough.

The only way you can fulfill your potential as a human being is to gradually diminish the role that fear plays in your life and in your decisions. Your aim and your ideal must be to reach the point where you are not afraid of anything. When you eliminate fear you become completely self-confident, and your entire world opens up before you. And it is *love* that dissolves fear and eventually removes it from your life.

SELF-LOVE, THE BEGINNING

Self-esteem and self-respect are the foundation qualities of the truly healthy personality. Everything you do to raise your own self-esteem contributes to making you a happier human being. No matter how low your self-esteem is when you begin, you can ratchet it up one notch at a time, like jacking up a car, by doing some of the things we've talked about in this book.

You can speak to yourself positively all the time. You can visualize yourself as the very best person that you can possibly be. You can fill your mind with positive messages of hope and inspiration. You can associate with happy, optimistic, goal-oriented people. You can organize every part of your life to continually reinforce good feelings about yourself.

The more you like or love yourself, the more you will like and love other people. The amount of love and respect you have for others, and they for you, is in direct proportion to how much love you have for yourself.

The Law of Reversibility states that, just as feelings lead to actions, actions also lead to feelings. If you do and say the things that are consistent with loving yourself, it won't be long before you actually feel positive and loving toward yourself. If you do and say the things that are consistent with your desired results, the results will materialize around you. Love is the catalyst that activates the very best that is in you, and in the people and situations around you.

The only true measure of your beliefs is your actions. It is not what you *say*, or what you *wish* or *hope* that counts, but only what you actually *do*. It's actions, not words, that count. And there are several specific things you can do that combine to build within you the feelings of high self-esteem and self-regard that make everything else possible.

THE KEYS TO THE KINGDOM
OF PERSONAL ACHIEVEMENT

First, you can resolve to *accept yourself unconditionally,* no matter what you have done or not done in the past. You can stand back and appreciate your special qualities and attributes. You can emphasize your good points and ignore the areas in which you may not be as good as someone else. You can like and respect yourself exactly as you are rather than as you would like to be someday. The foundation of self-esteem is self-acceptance.

Second, you can build your self-esteem, and your sense of personal value, by *accepting complete responsibility* for your life and for the consequences of all your actions. When you become a self-reliant, self-responsible individual, you refuse to blame or criticize others, or make excuses for things in your life that you don't like. You work on those areas where you are unhappy rather than spending your creative energies dreaming up excuses or blaming your situation on others. An attitude of high self-responsibility is a fundamental part of high self-esteem, self-love and personal effectiveness. Each of these interacts on and reinforces the other.

Third, you can *set worthwhile goals for yourself.* The very act of setting a big goal for yourself raises your self-esteem. It improves your self-concept. Only a person who likes and believes in himself or herself will write down an exciting goal in the first place. And writing down the goal makes you like and believe in yourself even more. The very act of setting the goal is the starting point of becoming the kind of person you want to be. It is the demonstration of your attitude of self-responsibility. It is the key to taking control of your life and feeling terrific about yourself.

The fourth way to build self-esteem is to *take good care of yourself physically.* When you eat healthy, nutritious foods and get lots of sleep and regular exercise, you cannot help but feel better about yourself. The better you take care of yourself, the more self-respect and self-love you have. This feeling spreads into your relationships with others. When you treat yourself well, you treat others well.

Fifth, and perhaps the fastest way to boost your self-esteem, is simply to *repeat "I like myself, I like myself, I like myself"* over and over, fifty to one hundred times a day, until you implant this message deep in your subconscious mind. Eventually, your subconscious mind fully accepts this command as your operating instructions. Then you will notice the difference. Your body language, your attitude, your facial expressions and your tone of voice will all change for the better. You will feel more positive and enthusiastic about everything you do. You will be "programmed" to feel good about yourself.

THREE KINDS OF LOVE

The ancient Greeks divided love into three different categories. The first type of love they called *Eros.* This refers to self-love. Most people never get beyond this preoccupation with themselves and with their own feelings in the area of love. The primary reason for failure and unhappiness in life is low self-esteem. Because of their low self-esteem, most people become completely concerned with themselves and their own feelings to the exclusion of the feelings of others. They are *fixed* at the level of Eros. In extreme cases of neurosis and psychosis, they become unable to consider the feelings of others at all.

The second form of love is called *Filia*. This refers to the love of others. Once a person loves himself or herself, the natural tendency is to turn outward toward loving and caring for other people. This is the mark of the healthy, happy person.

Whenever you feel particularly good about yourself, you feel a greater sense of kindness, patience and friendship toward others, even strangers. Whenever you feel blessed in any way, you instinctively want to reach out to help others less fortunate. Self-love makes you generous and big-hearted in everything you do.

The third and highest form of love, according to the ancient Greeks, was *Charis,* from which we get our word *charismatic.* Charis refers to universal love, love for all mankind, and is the rarest type of love. Only a very few people ever rise to this level of personal development. Many of the greatest men and women who have ever lived, such as Jesus, Buddha and St. Francis of Assisi, were renowned for their amazing capacity to love so expansively. And these great lovers of mankind have had more positive impact on the history of mankind than all the kings and rulers who ever lived.

LOVE TRANSFORMS THE WORLD

Jesus of Nazareth is referred to as the "Apostle of love." The followers of Christianity consider Jesus to have been the perfect man, who expressed total and unconditional love for all people, even under the most trying and painful of circumstances. It is this model or ideal of perfect love that most people strive toward throughout their lives.

Prince Siddhartha, Gautama Buddha, who founded Buddhism in the sixth century B.C., continues to be an inspiration to millions because of his totally loving nature and his teachings for overcoming fear and attaining bliss.

St. Francis of Assisi is famous for expressing unbounded love, extending to the birds, the animals, the flowers and even the lowly worms and bugs. This standard of unconditional love for all living creatures has made St. Francis of Assisi a role model and a hero to millions of people down the generations.

Dr. Albert Schweitzer of Africa, whom I met and worked with in 1965, is recognized as perhaps the greatest humanitarian of the twentieth century. His overarching philosophy was called "reverence for life." He lived and practiced this philosophy for more than fifty years, ministering to the needs of the people of Central Africa. His example became an inspiration to millions throughout the world.

In our modern day, Mother Teresa of Calcutta has become perhaps the most respected person in the world. She has had a tremendous impact on the hearts and minds of millions of men and women because of her unconditional love toward the poor and dying in Calcutta, India. When she was once asked how it was that her Missionaries of Charity seemed so happy as they went about their tasks of providing solace to unfortunate people during their final hours, she replied by saying that each worker believes in the words of the Book of Matthew, "Inasmuch as you have done it to the least of these my brethren, you have done it unto me."

LOVE IS AN ACTIVE VERB

The word love is a verb, an active verb. Love is not just something that you *feel*; it is something that you *do*. In fact, because of the Law of Reversibility, whenever you engage in a loving behavior toward someone else, you deepen and intensify your feeling of love toward that person. The action of love and kindness generates the feeling of love and kindness.

Just as you can act yourself into love, you can act yourself *back* into love, even if you feel that the love you experienced earlier has diminished or gone.

The Greek word for this is "Praxis." Praxis means that it is the *practice* of the actions that accompany the emotion that actually creates the emotion itself.

You can act your way back into love by treating the other person exactly as you would if you were deeply in love with him or her. You can maintain the love in your relationship by treating the person as you did when you were courting him or her, or when you most intensely felt *in love*. If you continue to behave this way throughout the relationship, you will maintain the feelings of love that brought you together. But if a person forgets and starts to take the relationship for granted, if he or she stops doing the things that signify and demonstrate love, the feelings of love can begin to diminish, and problems may begin to arise.

THE KEY TO HAPPINESS

The happiest of all men and women are those who continually look for ways to show love, kindness and affection toward the people around them. Not only are they the most loved and respected by others, but they are also the healthiest and the most blessed of all human beings.

There is a wonderful poem by Leigh Hunt, called "Abou Ben Adhem":

> Abou Ben Adhem (may his tribe increase!)
> Awoke one night from a deep dream of peace,
> And saw within the moonlight in his room,
> Making it rich, and like a Lily in bloom,
> An Angel, writing in a Book of Gold;
> Exceeding peace had made Ben Adhem bold,
> And to the presence in the room he said,
> "What writest thou?" The vision raised his head
> And with a look made of all sweet accord,
> Answered, "The names of those who love the Lord."
> "And is mine one?" said Abou. "Nay, not so,"
> Replied the Angel. Abou then spoke more low,
> But surely still; and said, "I pray thee then,
> Write me as one that loves his fellow men."
> The Angel wrote and vanished. The next night
> It came again, with a great wakening light,
> And showed the names whom love of God has blessed,
> And, lo! Ben Adhem's name led all the rest.

SOWING AND REAPING

You can never have any more love for yourself than that which you *express* to other people. Love only grows by *sharing,* and the only way you can have any more love for yourself is by giving it away. The more you give away, the more you have.

By the same token, the less you express love, the less love you have for yourself. If you do not express love at all, you will turn inward on yourself and become angry, critical and unhappy.

The antidote to feelings of fear, doubt and low self-esteem is to get out and find someone else you can help, someone else you can express love toward. The best cure for unhappiness is to make someone else happy.

Most people have it the other way around. When they are feeling unhappy or unloved, they feel that the solution is for someone else to make them happy, for someone else to love them and solve their problems. However, love is something that you *do*. Love is expressed in positive and constructive behavior toward other people. If you practice expressing love, you will have no problem getting love back, and eventually filling your life with it. You control the amount of love you have in your life by how much of it you give away to others. Be generous!

Elizabeth Barrett Browning wrote one of the most beautiful poems on love ever put on paper. It has been one of my favorites for many years and it is called "How Do I Love Thee?"

> How do I love thee? Let me count the ways.
> I love thee to the depth and breadth and height
> My soul can reach, when feeling out of sight
> For the ends of Being and ideal Grace.
> I love thee to the level of everyday's
> Most quiet need, by sun and candle-light.
> I love thee freely, as men strive for Right;
> I love thee purely, as they turn from Praise.
> I love thee with the passion put to use
> In my old griefs, and with my childhood's faith.
> I love thee with a love I seemed to lose
> With my lost saints—I love thee with the breath,
> Smiles, tears, of all my life!—and, if God choose,
> I shall but love thee better after death.

Throughout the ages, the wisest men and women have come to the conclusion that nothing is more important than love. Since you are a self-responsible individual, it is up to you to improve the quality of your life by increasing and improving your expression of love and kindness to the people in your world.

NEGATIVITY IS THE ROADBLOCK

The greatest obstacles to the experience and expression of love are *negative emotions,* especially those of fear, anger, guilt and resentment. Almost everyone is still harboring negative feelings toward someone who has hurt them in the past. Many people carry around anger and resentment toward their parents for forty or fifty years, if not into their graves. It is quite common for people to still be angry and resentful toward someone in a previous relationship or marriage. Often an unsuccessful job, or a business venture that goes sour, will generate these negative emotions. If a person clings to these feelings, by dwelling upon them, he or she keeps them alive year after year, long after the incident has passed.

SET YOURSELF FREE

You can clear your mind and heart of the negativity you have built up over time with one decisive action: Issue a blanket pardon to everyone for everything that they have ever done to hurt you in any way.

The doorway that opens to a life of love and joy is forgiveness. Your ability to freely forgive other people, and to let the hurt go, is the true mark of integrity, courage, character and a fully developed personality.

Many people cling to their resentments because they feel that they have paid so dearly for them that they cannot possibly give them up. Sometimes people's entire lives are built around their past hurts and suffering. They have little else to talk about, and they dwell on their negative experiences continually.

Eventually, these people make themselves physically and mentally ill. Their repressed anger and negativity sooner or later erupt and spoil any new relationships that they try to build. They sabotage their own futures. And, in every case, there is only one solution and that is to forgive and let it go.

Forgiving another person is a perfectly *selfish* act. You do it so that you can be free. You forgive so that you can experience the happiness and joy for which you were created. And here is a little test: If you have truly forgiven another person, you can demonstrate it to yourself by doing the other person a favor, or sending the other person a gift. Only in this way can you prove to yourself, once and for all, that you are finally free of the negative emotions associated with that person. (Refer to "the letter" described in Chapter Five.)

If you find that you still cannot bring yourself to do a kindness for the other person, this should tell you something about your true feelings. This inability to forgive might be holding you back from loving yourself and other people. You might have your own foot on the brakes of your own future happiness.

THE GREATEST OF THESE

One of the most beautiful descriptions of love from the Bible is First Corinthians, Chapter Thirteen. We had this entire passage read at our wedding:

> Though I speak with the tongues of men and of angels, and have not love, I am become as sounding brass, or a tinkling cymbal.
>
> And though I have the gift of prophecy, and understand all mysteries, and all knowledge; and though I have all faith, so that I could remove mountains, and have not love, I am nothing.
>
> And though I bestow all my goods to feed the poor, and though I give my body to be burned, and have not love, it profiteth me nothing.
>
> Love suffereth long, and is kind; love envieth not; love vaunteth not itself, is not puffed up,
>
> Love does not behave itself unseemly, love seeketh not her own, love is not easily provoked, and love thinketh no evil;
>
> Love rejoiceth not in iniquity, but rejoiceth in the truth;
>
> Love beareth all things, believeth all things, hopeth all things, endureth all things.

Love never faileth; but whether there be prophecies, they shall fail; whether there be tongues, they shall cease; whether there be knowledge, it shall vanish away.

For we know in part, and we prophesy in part.

But when that which is perfect is come, then that which is in part shall be done away.

When I was a child, I spake as a child, I understood as a child, I thought as a child: but when I became a man, I put away childish things.

For now we see through a glass, darkly; but then face to face: now I know in part; but then shall I know even as also I am known.

And now abideth faith, hope, love, these three; but the greatest of these is love.

Many wise and intelligent men have written long explanations of the inner meanings of First Corinthians, Chapter Thirteen, but it is safe to say that what this passage tells us is that when we become totally loving human beings, we will understand all, forgive all, and experience true joy in every part of our lives.

THE TESTING TIME

One of the most important times to be loving is when you feel the least like loving. The time to draw on your reserves of patience, kindness and compassion is when you are the most displeased with another person. Obnoxious or unpleasant behavior is usually a cry for help and understanding. It is a way of expressing the frustration of not feeling truly loved and accepted. There is wisdom in the words, "A gentle answer turneth away wrath."

When you deal with a difficult person in a calm and loving way, you will often see a human miracle. You will often see his or her attitude and behavior change. You will often see a difficult person soften up and see his or her personality brighten. But, most important, when you act in a loving way, you maintain your own personal and emotional integrity. You feel good about yourself. You feel in charge of your inner and outer life.

A SIMPLE QUESTION FOR GUIDANCE

Some years ago, the best-selling book *In His Steps* was written about a small town in America where everyone began living the highest values they knew. Before saying or doing anything, each person in the town would ask himself or herself the question, "What would Jesus do?"

In other words, what would a person who was truly honest, truly kind, truly loving, truly patient, all-compassionate and all-wise do in this situation?

It was a wonderful story. After the initial problems of being misunderstood were surmounted, everyone in the town experienced greater peace and happiness. People and businesses were more prosperous. Misunderstandings were quickly cleared up. Throughout the entire town, there was a feeling of joy, happiness and peace.

CHANGE YOUR WORLD

You cannot change the world, but you can present the world with one improved person, *yourself.* You can go to work on yourself to make yourself into the kind of person you admire and respect. You can become a role model and set a standard for others. You can control and discipline yourself to resist acting or speaking in a negative way toward anyone for any reason. You can insist upon always doing things the loving way rather than the hurtful way.

You can use the *cognitive control method* to keep your mind calm and positive by thinking kind and loving thoughts about others. You can short-circuit your anger by thinking kindly about those who hurt you. By saying, "God bless him," or "God bless her," rather than thinking about how much he or she is exasperating you, you can neutralize your negative emotions, restore your calmness and increase your clarity of mind. You take another step on the pathway toward becoming an exceptional human being.

THE PURPOSE OF LIFE

"With all thy getting, get love." Everything you ever read about the meaning and purpose of life brings you back to the idea and the importance of love. Everything you do that makes you love and respect yourself makes you more capable of expressing love toward others. Every time you do or say anything kind or loving toward another person, you increase the amount of love you have for yourself. The action is reciprocal. One generates the other.

Every time you engage in a loving act, you make the world a better place in which to live. Each time you express love toward someone else, whether they seem to need it or not, you enrich and enhance the quality of his or her life. You simultaneously enrich and uplift the quality of your own. You put yourself on the side of the angels. You make your life a blessing to others and a wonderful experience for yourself.

One of the finest pieces of writing on love is "The Golden Gate" by Emmet Fox. It has been a source of inspiration for me for many years.

Love casts out fear.
It covers a multitude of sins.
It is absolutely invincible.
There is no difficulty that enough love will not conquer;
No disease that enough love will not heal;
No door that enough love will not open;
No gulf that enough love will not bridge;
No wall that enough love will not throw down;
No sin that enough love will not redeem.
It makes no difference how deeply seated may be the
     trouble,
How hopeless the outlook,
How muddled the tangle, how great the mistake.
A sufficient realization of love will dissolve it all.
If only you could love enough, you would be the happiest
     and the most powerful being in the world.

If you truly want to be successful and happy in everything you do, in every part of your life, you must learn and practice love on every occasion, at every opportunity. The expression of love and the actions of kindness must be as natural to you as breathing in and breathing out.

Some years ago I met a lovely woman, a grandmother, who told me a wonderful story. She said she had been raised in a home with truly loving parents, who had always taught her, and her brothers and sisters, how important it was to express and feel love for everyone, no matter how they behaved.

When her mother passed away, her brothers and sisters got together to divide their parents' possessions. This woman was married to a wealthy industrialist; she had no financial needs. In fact, there was only one thing that she wanted from her parents' home, and it was a plaque that had hung over the fireplace in the living room all the time she was growing up. Her parents would often point to the plaque when a problem arose with another person, and the advice on the plaque had guided her throughout her life. It said:

> Only one life, that soon is passed;
> Only what's done with love will last.

If you live your life guided by this powerful idea—the sum total wisdom of all the great lovers and thinkers of the ages—you will probably never make another mistake.

> Only one life, that soon is passed;
> Only what's done with love will last.

When you look back over the landscape of your life, you will find your most precious assets are the thoughts and memories of the people you've loved, and who've loved you.

Your biggest mistakes, your greatest regrets, are all associated with love—with not having loved enough, or having been loved enough.

Love is the beginning and the end. *Your purpose in life is to become a totally loving person.* Life is the study of attention. It is a matter of priorities, of choices. Your life is what you make it by the priorities you set and the things you choose to focus your attention upon. Your job is to live joyously, and this is only possible by filling your mind with thoughts of love, compassion and forgiveness.

> Only one life that soon is past;
> Only what's done with love will last.

This is the secret of the ages, the true foundation of all human greatness. It is the core value and the essential unifying principle of truly exceptional people. And the most wonderful thing about love is that you can fill your life with it by deciding to do so. The choice is yours. It always has been.

I wish you luck. I wish you success and happiness. And above all, I wish you *love*.

Brian Tracy / Speaker

•

Brian Tracy is one of the most popular professional speakers in the world. He addresses more than 100,000 men and women each year in private and public talks and seminars. His fast-moving, informative and entertaining seminars on personal success, sales, leadership and motivation draw capacity audiences across the country.

Brian speaks regularly for corporations, associations, annual meetings and conventions. He has addressed the executives and staff of hundreds of organizations large and small, carefully customizing each talk to the special needs of the audience. His clients include Ford Motor Company, Federal Express, Southwestern Bell, Northwest Mutual Life Insurance, IBM, Million Dollar Round Table, United Van Lines, Culligan, Baxtor-Travenol, Blue Cross/Blue Shield, Domino's Pizza, Arthur Anderson, Hewlett-Packard, and many others.

If you arc interested in having Brian speak for your organization, please phone 619-481-2977 and request a complete information kit, including an audio and video demo tape, biographical data and client list.

Brian Tracy International

•

Productivity & Profit Improvement Associates

Brian Tracy has produced more than 100 audio and video learning programs covering the entire spectrum of human and corporate performance. These programs, which have taken more than twenty years of research and experience to develop, are some of the most effective learning tools in the world.

Brian's multimedia training programs are used in companies and organizations large and small to improve managerial effectiveness, increase sales and empower individuals to achieve higher levels of performance. They have been translated into fourteen languages and are presented in thirty-one countries.

Each program is designed to ensure rapid learning and immediate results. Using a unique video-assisted format with Brian personally instructing each part of every program, combined with a special facilitation process including exercises, role plays, self-analysis techniques and audiotape reinforcement, each student emerges from the training at a whole new level of performance.

The training programs can each stand alone, or they can be combined into a training series presented over several months for maximum impact. Each program is content rich and designed to be custom tailored to the specific needs of the individual client.

The Phoenix Seminar on the Psychology of Achievement

This seminar/workshop, based on the principles taught in this book, is perhaps the most powerful exercise in personal and corporate transformation in the world today. This video-assisted, person-centered workshop empowers individuals to achieve at their maximum potential. They emerge with a greater sense of clarity, personal responsibility and commitment to themselves and the organization.

Participants become more positive, purposeful and self-directed. They learn to set goals, organize themselves for greater effectiveness and function as members of high-quality teams.

The Phoenix Seminar program consists of twenty-seven sessions with detailed workbooks, instructor's guide, exercises, and audiotape reinforcement for each person. It is fairly easy to present and very enjoyable to take. It can be given by certified in-house facilitators or by outside professionals.

Professional Selling Skills—The New Psychology of Selling

This is the world's best-selling audiocassette program on sales. Since it was upgraded and put into a video-based training format, it has been called "The most effective professional selling course ever developed."

The power of the course lies in its simplicity; it is stripped of theory and jargon, and based on twenty-five years of selling on the street. Participants, even experienced professionals and university graduates who've been selling for some time, are amazed at how well the ideas taught in this course help them to make more sales.

Individuals and corporations report immediate and sustained sales increases of 10 percent, 20 percent, and 30 percent per year after participating in this program. It has rapidly become the foundation training for many organizations. It is flexible, economic, and relatively easy to install.

The New Psychology of Selling includes thirty-five sessions with application exercises that allow the course materials to be tailored to the needs of the client company. Preprogram analysis includes a survey of the company's salespeople, sales managers, customers, products and services, and the competition. Based on this information, the course is organized around specific needs to solve specific performance problems.

The seminar is given over a three-day period in a classroom setting. It can be facilitated by certified in-house personnel or by outside professionals. Sales results are immediate, measurable and long lasting.

Advanced Selling Skills—The New Psychology of Selling II

This is the graduate program for the experienced professional who sells complex products or services in a rapidly changing, cost sensitive, highly competitive marketplace.

Advanced Selling Skills is a state-of-the-art, modern sales-training program that brings together the most helpful ideas and sales methodologies ever developed to assist salespeople with multicall, multidecisionmaker selling. It blends twenty years of research with a lifetime of practice to create a thoroughly practical, nontheoretical approach to selling in a tough, sophisticated market.

This is the perfect complement to Professional Selling Skills. It is a multimedia program with twenty-four sessions on video, accompanied by individual workbooks, application exercises and audiotape reinforcement. It can be conducted by certified in-house personnel or by outside professionals.

Strategic Planning for the Sales Professional

This unique program virtually ensures that each salesperson achieves his or her sales quota on schedule and on budget. The ten parts of this program are designed to take each person through a strategic planning process for the upcoming sales period. It shows them how to set clear goals and make detailed plans. It shows salespeople how to organize their daily, weekly, monthly activities to achieve dependable, predictable sales results.

This approach to planning exactly how sales goals are to be achieved is both powerful and effective. Salespeople emerge with greater clarity, purpose and personal determination and higher morale. Strategic Planning for the Sales Professional virtually guarantees a high return on the company's investment in sales training, marketing, advertising, promotion and product development.

The seminar is designed to be conducted over one or one-and-a-half days by in-house facilitators or outside instructors.

Superior Sales Management

This is the cement that holds all the sales efforts of the company together. It ensures that the company enjoys maximum sales results. According to McKinsey and Company, the job of the sales manager is the pivotal skill in the sales organization. Increasing the skill of the sales manager can do more to increase sales volume faster than any other change the company can make.

Superior Sales Management is the most complete, practical, powerful course on sales management ever developed. It turns average sales managers into excellent sales managers almost overnight, showing them how to improve sales results immediately.

Superior Sales Management covers twenty-four topics from recruitment, interviewing and selection to training, managing, motivating, delegating and disciplining.

This course is the key to building a world-class sales force that can outperform the competition in any market. It should be required for every sales manager at every level of experience. The results in the sales of the company are out of all proportion to the efforts of installing the program.

Superior Sales Management is designed to be facilitated over three days with video assistance, complete workbooks, application exercises and audiotape reinforcement. The course can be conducted by in-house instructors or outside professionals.

Time Management for Results

This program takes a total approach to teaching people a philosophy of time management that changes their attitudes toward time and time usage. It is a total approach to life management that brings about immediate increases in efficiency and effectiveness.

Participants learn how to set goals and priorities, eliminate time wasters, overcome procrastination and concentrate for maximum effectiveness.

Graduates of this course emerge more positive, more focused and with greater energy and commitment to getting the job done. They learn how to gain two extra hours per day of productive time, with lower stress and higher feelings of personal pride.

This multimedia program includes twelve sessions with audio, video and workbook accompaniment. It is easy to present and easy to participate in, and it can be conducted by either in-house or outside facilitators.

Achieving Personal and Corporate Excellence

This is an informative, skill-building, thought-provoking, one-day seminar on personal and corporate effectiveness that brings about immediate results.

Participants learn the twelve dimensions of personal performance and productivity. They learn about quality, service, ethics, teamwork and individual responsibility. They learn about accountability, communications, goals and priorities.

This course is the ideal foundation program for improving productivity, performance and morale in the organization. It gives everyone a common language and common denominators for resolving individual differences.

Achieving Personal and Corporate Excellence is a multimedia workshop designed to be conducted over one day. It consists of twelve sessions with workbooks and audiotape reinforcement. The course can be facilitated by in-house instructors or outside trainers.

Productivity & Profit Improvement Associates (PPIA)

This is Brian Tracy's national training and consulting arm, taking care of all sales, marketing and installation of Brian Tracy training programs.

PPIA's professional consultants and facilitators are trained and certified to install the training programs described above in companies of all sizes.

PPIA services include consulting, diagnostics, customizing of each program, facilitation and follow-up services to ensure retention and application.

PPIA offers train-the-trainer programs for each of the seminars and workshops described above. In-house personnel can be trained to customize any of these programs' internal presentation.

For information on PPIA programs and services, please phone 619-481-2977 (Fax 619-481-2445) or write to Productivity & Profit Improvement Associates, 462 Stevens Avenue, Suite 202, Solana Beach, CA 92075.

Maximum Achievement Materials

•

To continue your personal and professional development, you may want to acquire additional materials mentioned in this book. Here's how:

1. Catalogue of audio and video learning programs for continual reinforcement and skill development. Cost: no charge. Phone or write and we'll send you a copy.

2. Poem, "Don't Quit," 8″ x 11″, suitable for framing. Cost: no charge. Just phone or write.

3. Relaxation tape, 22 minutes (same one used in our seminars). Ten powerful affirmations with music, plus full script and detailed instructions for making your own tape with your own goals. Cost: $10.00, including postage and handling.

4. Goal-setting and achieving workbook 30 Day Action Planner, with complete step-by-step Masterplan for designing a blueprint of your ideal life, complete with special reinforcement exercises to "lock in" the goal-achieving process. Cost: $5.00 including shipping and postage. Phone or write.

5. Information on Brian Tracy seminars and workshops, corporate presentations, public appearances, and video-assisted training programs. Phone or write.

6. Live presentations of the Phoenix Seminar on the Psychology of Achievement in San Diego (4 days, Thur.–Sun.). Phone or write for details of dates, locations, accommodations and costs.

7. Correspondence: If you have any personal questions or observations, please write to me, and I'll respond personally.

I welcome your success stories and experiences applying these ideas to your life. Good luck!

Brian Tracy International
462 Stevens Avenue, Suite 202
Solana Beach, CA 92075
619-481-2977 (Fax: 619-481-2977)